HACKED

Feb 17

ALTERNATIVE CRIMINOLOGY SERIES

General Editor: Jeff Ferrell

Pissing on Demand: Workplace Drug Testing and the Rise of the Detox Industry
Ken Tunnell

Empire of Scrounge: Inside the Urban Underground of Dumpster Diving, Trash Picking, and Street Scavenging
Jeff Ferrell

Prison, Inc.: A Convict Exposes Life inside a Private Prison
by K.C. Carceral, edited by Thomas J. Bernard

The Terrorist Identity: Explaining the Terrorist Threat
Michael P. Arena and Bruce A. Arrigo

Terrorism as Crime: From Oklahoma City to Al-Qaeda and Beyond
Mark S. Hamm

Our Bodies, Our Crimes: The Policing of Women's Reproduction in America
Jeanne Flavin

Graffiti Lives: Beyond the Tag in New York's Urban Underground
Gregory J. Snyder

Crimes of Dissent: Civil Disobedience, Criminal Justice, and the Politics of Conscience
Jarret S. Lovell

The Culture of Punishment: Prison, Society, and Spectacle
Michelle Brown

Who You Claim: Performing Gang Identity in School and on the Streets
Robert Garot

5 Grams: Crack Cocaine, Rap Music, and the War on Drugs
Dimitri A. Bogazianos

Judging Addicts: Drug Courts and Coercion in the Justice System
Rebecca Tiger

Courting Kids: Inside an Experimental Youth Court
Carla J. Barrett

The Spectacular Few: Prisoner Radicalization and the Evolving Terrorist Threat
Mark S. Hamm

Comic Book Crime: Truth, Justice, and the American Way
Nickie D. Phillips and Staci Strobl

The Securitization of Society: Crime, Risk, and Social Order
Marc Schuilenburg

Covered in Ink: Tattoos, Women, and the Politics of the Body
Beverly Yuen Thompson

Narrative Criminology: Understanding Stories of Crime
Edited by Lois Presser and Sveinung Sandberg

Progressive Punishment: Job Loss, Jail Growth and the Neoliberal Logic of Carceral Expansion
Judah Schept

The Culture of Meth: Crime, Media, and the War on Drugs
Travis Linneman

Hacked: A Radical Approach to Hacker Culture and Crime
Kevin F. Steinmetz

Hacked

A Radical Approach to Hacker Culture and Crime

Kevin F. Steinmetz

NEW YORK UNIVERSITY PRESS

New York

NEW YORK UNIVERSITY PRESS
New York
www.nyupress.org

© 2016 by New York University
All rights reserved

References to Internet websites (URLs) were accurate at the time of writing. Neither the author nor New York University Press is responsible for URLs that may have expired or changed since the manuscript was prepared.

ISBN: 978-1-4798-6610-6 (hardback)
ISBN: 978-1-4798-6971-8 (paperback)

For Library of Congress Cataloging-in-Publication data, please contact the Library of Congress.

New York University Press books are printed on acid-free paper, and their binding materials are chosen for strength and durability. We strive to use environmentally responsible suppliers and materials to the greatest extent possible in publishing our books.

Manufactured in the United States of America

10 9 8 7 6 5 4 3 2 1

Also available as an ebook

For Pamela, who makes all things possible.

For the members of Union Hack. Thanks for the opportunity, the tutelage, and the good times.

CONTENTS

LIST OF FIGURES AND TABLES

FIGURE

TABLES

LIST OF ABBREVIATIONS

AI: artificial intelligence

ANPR: automatic number plate recognition

BASIC: Beginner's All-Purpose Symbolic Instruction Code

BBS: bulletin board system

CCC: Chaos Computer Club

DMCA: Digital Millennium Copyright Act

DRM: digital rights management

CFAA: Computer Fraud and Abuse Act

CP/M: Control Program for Microcomputers

CSI: Crime Scene Investigation

DARPA: Defense Advanced Research Projects Agency

DOS: disk operating system

EFF: Electronic Frontier Foundation

F/OSS: free and open-source software

FBI: Federal Bureau of Investigation

FISA: Foreign Intelligence Surveillance Act

FUBAR: fucked up beyond all recognition

GNU: GNU's Not Unix

HBCC: Homebrew Computer Club

IBM: International Business Machines

IRC: Internet relay chat

JSTOR: Journal Storage

MIT: Massachusetts Institute of Technology

MPAA: Motion Picture Association of America

NORAD: North American Aerospace Defense Command

NSA: National Security Agency

OECD: Organization for Economic Cooperation and Development

OS: operating system

PRISM: Planning Tool for Resource Integration, Synchronization, and Management

RGB: red, green, blue

RTFM: read the fucking manual

STEM: science, technology, engineering, and mathematics

TAP: Technical Assistance Program

TMRC: Tech Model Railroad Club

UNIX: Uniplexed Information and Computing System

USA PATRIOT: United and Strengthening America by Providing Appropriate Tools Required to Intercept and Obstruct Terrorism

VOIP: Voice over Internet Protocol

ACKNOWLEDGMENTS

This book emerged from a number of separate research projects spanning from my earliest days in graduate school to the first years of my professorial academic life. As a result, I am deeply indebted to many who have directly or indirectly shaped not only the development of my research but my trajectory as a burgeoning scholar. If the reader will indulge me, I would like to thank each of these people with the understanding that a few lines of text can do little to communicate the impact they have had. First, I have had the good fortune of having a number of mentors who have kindly directed me while tolerating or even indulging my (many) eccentricities. Thanks go to my mentors from Eastern Kentucky University (EKU), including Ken Tunnell, who taught me the meaning of academic integrity and the joys of writing. Thanks are also extended to Gary Potter, who helped challenge my perceptions of criminal justice policy and demonstrated the incendiary power of a well-timed joke. I also appreciate the efforts of Peter Kraska as he helped me develop a work ethic and a sense of rigor. In addition, I am indebted to Victor Kappeler who triggered my love of critical criminology and radical thought. It was Vic who initially encouraged me to write a book—a push I can never thank him enough for.

When I left EKU for Sam Houston State University to get my Ph.D., I was met with a dizzying culture shock. Fortunately, there were people there who helped protect me from myself while giving me the support and freedom to pursue my interests. Appreciation is given to Howard Henderson. He always had time to chat and his academic openness created some of my favorite moments of scholarly collaboration. He also helped teach me the value of (critically) thinking about the potential applications of research to the "real world." Dennis Longmire must also be thanked for his appreciation of philosophy and his thorough understanding of the value of human life. Last but certainly not least, I express my deepest appreciation to Jurg Gerber, who served as the chair of my doctoral dissertation and my co-author on various projects. He took me on as a student early and gave me the space to find myself as an academic. I'll also never be able to thank him enough for supporting me during the more turbulent times of my doctoral education—and for his sense of humor.

There have also been a number of friends over the years who have supported my research, provided their insights, or tolerated my long-winded and esoteric ramblings as I tried to make sense of my ideas. While a great many deserve my gratitude, I will focus on a select few for the purposes of brevity. First, I would like to thank my "EKU Crew" (who I sometimes refer to as my "Brain Trust" when I need to talk through something): Brian Schaefer, Edward Green, and Carl Root. Without these gentlemen, I may not have gone on to get my Ph.D. and, if I had, I certainly would not be as well-developed without them. In addition, they helped me hone my academic toolset over time, without which this book would not have manifested. I also need to thank my "SHSU Crew," including Melissa Petkovsek, Kimberly Chism, Maria Koeppel, Robin Jackson, Cody Gaines, Nancy Johnson, Jonathan Grubb, Leah McCoy (now Leah McCoy Grubb), Erin Castro, Matt Nobles, and Brenda Riley. Thanks for all of the good times. In particular, I want to express my gratitude to Melissa Petkovsek and Kimberly Chism, both of whom dealt with the brunt of my eccentricities and always indulged my need for a sounding board. I also admit that I deeply miss walking down the hall to pester them with my ideas (or, occasionally, a NERF gun).

My deepest appreciation is extended to the hackers of Union Hack (a pseudonym). Without them, this research would not have been possible. Even more, though, I greatly appreciate their humor, their insights, and their acceptance. They took me under their wing, so to speak, and showed me the ropes to an extent much further than any sort of social obligation required. Hackers are known for their fierce desire to learn—but Union Hack demonstrated a seldom-noticed willingness to teach as well. I cannot adequately express how much I appreciate that. I should also thank one particular member, Miles (pseudonym), for not posting the recording of me at DEF CON 21's Hacker Karaoke singing Aretha Franklin's "Natural Woman" to the Internet. I would also like to thank Rick (pseudonym) and his wife for letting me crash in their hotel when my flight out of Las Vegas was rescheduled.

The editorial staff at NYU Press also deserves recognition. I appreciate all of their effort in the editorial process as well as the opportunity to work with them. In particular, Ilene Kalish and Caelyn Cobb were instrumental in the process. I also would like to thank the editor of the Alternative Criminology series, Jeff Ferrell, who enthusiastically recruited me to submit the initial proposal for this book to the series (with some help from our mutual colleague, Mark Hamm). Despite his super-busy schedule, he has always taken time to help mentor young scholars as they attempt to navigate the murky waters of conferencing, publishing, and academe in general. I would also like to thank the anonymous book reviewers as well as Edward Green and Gary Potter who looked over prior drafts of select chapters.

Finally, I want to express my appreciation for the person who made all of this possible, my wife Pamela. When I decided that I wanted to be a professor instead of a cop, she wholly encouraged me and moved away from the only home she had ever known so I could pursue my dream. Her support allowed me to pursue my interests unfettered. She was often the first person to hear of any of my research-related ideas and I could always count on a frank assessment. She has never wavered in her support. As such, without her this book would not have been written.

Introduction

Toward a Radical Criminology of Hackers

In the expansive Rio Hotel and Casino in Las Vegas, I stood in line for around an hour and a half to pay for my badge for admittance into DEF CON 21, one of the largest hacker conventions in the world. The wad of cash in my hand felt heavier than it should have as I approached the badge vendor. DEF CON is an extravagant affair and attendees pay for it (though, from my own readings, the conference administrators work to keep the costs reduced). The line slowly trickled down the ramp into the hotel convention area where the badge booths were arranged. As I laid eyes on the convention, my jaw dropped. It was packed. Attendees were already moving hurriedly throughout the place, engaged in energetic conversations. Black t-shirts—a kind of hacker uniform—were everywhere. Las Vegas- and gambling-themed décor lined the walls and floors. Already, I could see a line forming at the DEF CON merchandise booth. Miles, a hacker I had gotten to know throughout my research, mentioned that if I wanted some of the "swag" or "loot" (the conference merchandise), I should go ahead and get in line, a potential three- to four-hour wait. Seemingly, everyone wanted to purchase merchandise to provide some evidence they were in attendance. Wait too long and the loot runs out.

After winding through the serpentine line of conference attendees waiting for admittance, I approached the badge vendors and (dearly) departed with almost $200. Stepping into the convention area, I felt that loss in the pit of my stomach. The con was huge and already bustling even though the badge line still wrapped around the interior of the enormous Rio hotel. I shuffled to the merchandise booth and scanned the prices. Merchandise was not extraordinarily pricey, but certainly not bargain-bin cheap either. I peered into my wallet to inspect my cash reserves—not wanting to spend too much. As a graduate student, finances were tight and I had to pay for this entire trip out of pocket. But I wanted a shirt; evidence of attendance.

My inner miser balked but I would later stand in line for two hours for this coveted piece of merchandise—a proud indicator of my attendance—while chatting up a fellow conventioneer about the state of camera technology and NSA surveillance (a popular item of discussion as the Edward Snowden leaks were still fresh). This process of indecision repeated itself later, when I finally broke down and purchased a set of lock picks.

Coming from what some would consider a working-class background, I am generally paranoid about money. As such, I am also sensitive to the spending habits of others. I began noticing that DEF CON attendees often carried around expensive equipment, and readily purchased gear or con merchandise from various vendors without a second thought. Coupled with the expense of Las Vegas itself, the price of the hotels, and travel expenses, DEF CON was certainly hard on bank accounts. While standing in the middle of the convention center, a custom DEF CON 21 floor decal beneath my already aching feet, I thought, "It would be difficult to participate in the hacker community if you were poor." While DEF CON provided just one example where I was confronted with the pressures of class circulating through hacking and technology, political economic factors surfaced and resurfaced time and time again throughout my research—a heartbeat under the floorboards of hacker culture. From the expense of such social affairs, the costs of equipment, the exposures to technology at an early age, the peer groups, the employment tendencies, and other factors that unfolded over the course of my research, it became apparent that socio-economic class—and the assortment of political economic factors that coincide—were vital to consider when examining hackers, their genesis, and their place in the world.

This excerpt is a narrative taken from my field notes and recollections about my time conducting ethnographic field research at DEF CON 21. I provided this vignette to both give the reader a sense of what it was like to attend the con and to introduce a key subject of this book: the political economy of hacking. Of course, the purpose is not—by any stretch of the imagination—to paint hackers as a spoiled group detached from material reality. Not all hackers are financially privileged and among those who are, some are fully aware of the advantage such privilege affords them. The importance of this narrative is to provide a glimpse into how *class* (and political economy more broadly) increasingly became a key variable of consideration in this analysis.

Many readers may find the link between economic factors and hacking to be unsurprising. The typical image of the hacker is an electronic thief curled over a computer double-fisting cans of Mountain Dew, stealing credit card numbers, and, if many portrayals are to be believed, wearing a ski mask in the privacy of their own home. Since theft is at the core of this image for many, it makes sense that money would be a central theme. As will be discussed in the pages to follow, however, this image of hacking is problematic at best, and outright ideological at worst. Hacking is more accurately defined as a broad technological subculture involving a range of cultural products and activities beyond technological crime. While, yes, it has been responsible for some illicit activities, hacking has also been instrumental in the development of many technologies often taken for granted—including the Internet itself. When this book presents the argument about the role of political economy in hacking, the reader should note that these effects are more pervasive than illicit economies alone. Intellectual property, media, labor, consumption, technology, and other factors related to capital and accumulation all play vital roles in the formation of the hacking community and its broader social context.

Take, for instance, a 1985 panel discussion at the Hackers Conference, a gathering of technological innovators and enthusiasts (Sterling 1992). This conversation featured major names in hacking at the time, including the likes of Bruce Webster, Richard Stallman, Bruce Baumgart, Richard Greenblatt, and Steve Wozniak, among others (Brand and Herron 1985). These hackers discussed what Steven Levy (1984) had identified as a "hacker ethic" in his *Hackers: Heroes of the Computer Revolution*. The conference also provided a forum to discuss software creation, intellectual property, business, and related issues. Hackers have historically played a major role in the computer and software industry, both as developers *and* entrepreneurs. Consider the following quotes taken from the panel (Brand and Herron 1985), which demonstrate, even in the 1980s, how pervasive political economic concerns were to hackers:

Some pirates copy software and they'll copy everything and put it in their collection, but if they find something that they do like and decide it's a good one, they'll go out and buy it because the producer deserves the money. (Steve Wozniak)

If you want to bring up the word "ethics"—I felt very uncomfortable last night with a couple of people who got up and talked about how they made their living stealing from the telephone company. I think it's one thing to be a high school kid wanting to show off that you're capable of making a phone call without paying for it, and it's something else to be an adult being in the career or encouraging people to be thieves. (Brian Harvey)

A perspective that hasn't been mentioned is that in times like the [Homebrew Computer Club], people had jobs. As Thomas Jefferson said, "I make war so that my grandchildren can study philosophy." The person who is studying philosophy is at the top of the food chain. The problem when the philosophers find they can sell philosophy is that suddenly it's the bottom of a food chain again. Only as long as it wasn't something that was commercially available could it have this pure aspect. (Ted Nelson)

It seems like there's a couple of interesting paradoxes that we're working here. That's why I'm especially interested in what Bob Wallace has done with PC-WRITE and what Andrew Fleugelman did before that with PC-TALK. On the one hand, information wants to be expensive, because it's so valuable. The right information in the right place just changes your life. On the other hand, information wants to be free, because the cost of getting it out is getting lower and lower all the time. So you have these two fighting against each other. (Steward Brand)

I think there is another kind of software piracy going on that's not discussed very much, and the villains are not high school kids who copy discs and break secret codes. They're executives in three-piece suits that work for large corporations and drive Mercedes. They make money off the results of research and education, and they don't kick very much back to support the next generation. (Henry Lieberman)

It's worse than that even, because at a university paid for by everyone in the country, an idea will be developed almost to the point where you can use it, but then the last bit of work will be done by some company and the company will get lots of money, and those of us who already paid for most of the work won't be able to use the results without paying again, and we won't be able to get the sources even though we paid for those sources to be written. (Richard Stallman)

Even among these top figures in hacking culture, issues of intellectual property, ownership, corporate exploitation, theft, and other economic concerns surfaced as vital problems confronting the hacking community. As such, to assume hackers are simply techno-vandals and thieves is horrifically myopic. Of course, it is easy to understand why such perspectives proliferate—they require little reflection about computer labor, industry, and criminality. Unlocking hacker culture, however, requires a deeper investigation that not only necessitates honest assessment, but also seeks to situate hackers within their historical and structural context. In this endeavor, attention to political economic factors is vital. While technology is often discussed as the primary interest of hackers, what they most intimately work with is actually *information*. This relationship places hackers at the precipice of political economic conflict. As Majid Yar (2008b, 196) describes, "Since the 1970s, western economies increasingly have moved away from their traditional dependence upon industrial production, and economic growth has come to depend upon the creation, exploitation, and consumption of information."

I have not been the only one to recognize the connection between hacking and the political economy. Previous academic works have tackled these dynamics primarily through a Marxist lens, observing how hacking is situated amid the conflicts and contradictions of capital accumulation. McKenzie Wark (2004), for example, uses Marx to discuss hackers as a kind of informational proletariat in an age where intellectual labor is increasingly controlled (by what Wark refers to as the *vectoral class*) and their fruits are increasingly proprietized. Similarly, Johan Söderberg (2002, 2008, 2013) writes about how hackers—with a specific focus on open-source software programmers—are situated within the dynamics of capitalism as a kind of intellectual laborer. Building from these analyses, this study presents a culmination of multiple research projects, including ethnographic field research and various content analyses, to describe hackers and the hacking community from a *radical criminological* perspective.

With roots in the theoretical and philosophical traditions of critical and conflict theories (e.g., Marxism and neo-Marxism), radical criminology presents a powerful arrangement of intellectual tools for understanding crime and crime control. Radical criminology has also provided disciplinary self-reflection, often describing how mainstream theoretical perspectives and scholars contribute to systems of oppression. Influenced by Marxism, early works in radical criminology sought to understand crime as a product of political economic structures (Bonger 1916). While the tradition originates in the early twentieth century, radical criminology exploded in the 1960s and 1970s with the radicalization of the academy amid this period's conflict and social change (Arrigo and Williams 2010). Criminological juggernauts of the time began to take seriously the idea of crime and crime control being linked intimately with class and conflict (Chambliss 1975; Quinney 1977; Spitzer 1975; Turk 1969). The push for a radical criminology at this time was also associated with members of the radical wing of UC Berkeley's School of Criminology (Stein 2014; Simon 2014). The school was closed in 1976 on the basis of real but relatively trivial issues, with the underlying impetus believed to have been driven by anti-leftist politics (Geis 1995). Perhaps this moment forecasted the neo-liberal and neo-conservative changes that were occurring and still yet to come within both crime control and university politics—trends that would imperil critical thought in the coming decades.

Despite such changes and setbacks, other criminologists have carried the torch of class conflict (see Linebaugh 2014; Lynch 1997, 2015; Lynch, Michalowski, and Groves 2006; Michalowski 1985; Pavlich 2001; Ross 1998; Simon 2014). Numerous journals now exist that regularly publish radical and related criminological analyses, including *Critical Criminology, Social Justice, Contemporary Justice Review, Crime Media Culture*, and *Radical Criminology*, to name a few. Radical criminology has also been a key influence in the development of other theoretical traditions of critical criminology, including New Left Realism (Lea and Young 1984), Peacemaking Criminology (Pepinsky and Quinney 1991), and Cultural Criminology (Ferrell, Hayward, and Young 2008).

Because of its sensitivity to class, conflict, and the relationship between individual and macro-structural contexts, radical criminology is an ideal theoretical tradition to guide an analysis of hackers. Most criminological scholarship has been content to neglect the role of class in its analyses despite the central importance of political economy in the shaping of crime, law, and criminal justice (Hagan 1992; Lynch 2015; Young 1981). As demonstrated throughout this book, class and other components of the political economy are instrumental in situating hacking as a late-modern subcultural phenomenon. Chapters 1, 2, and 3 discuss the ethnographic research that explores hackers and hacking culture, subsequently uncovering a number of findings which point to class and political economy as key factors to consider. These findings include hacking as (1) predominantly a middle-class affair, (2) a kind of labor, and (3) a development linked to a particular philosophic perspective described here as *technological liberalism*. Drawing from the tradition of radical criminology, these indicators are then used as a springboard for a Marxist analysis of hacking within the contradictions of capitalism, with particular emphasis on the processes that permit hackers to be subjected to mechanisms of social control. That said, other theoretical traditions in criminology serve to inform this analysis as well. Most notably is cultural criminology, which provides a toolkit to generate subcultural understandings that can be linked to broader structural dynamics. Since this examination specifically builds towards a political economic/Marxist analysis, however, I would argue that this study is best labeled under the umbrella of radical criminology. The following introduction will provide a brief overview of hacking from a historical and subcultural perspective, the various methodologies used throughout this book, and finally, a short synopsis of each chapter.

Hacking: A Brief Overview

For many, hacking is a term that invokes fear and confusion. In the public mind, hackers are simultaneously everywhere and nowhere—they lurk somewhere "out there" but possess real power to affect the lives of everyday people. In other words, hackers have achieved a mythological status in our society, heavily mired in social construction (see chapter 5) (Halbert 1997; Hollinger 1991; Skibell 2002; Wall 2007, 2012; Yar 2013). Believed to have incredible powers of technological manipulation, hackers are seen as contemporary equivalents to trickster figures of the past, such as Loki in Nordic mythology or the Greek Dolos. These perceptions have come a long way since the so-called golden age of hacking when hackers were largely viewed as "ardent (if quirky) programmers capable of brilliant, unorthodox feats of machine manipulation . . . [whose] dedication bordered on fanaticism and their living habits bordered on the unsavory" (Nissenbaum 2004, 196). Now, through the funhouse mirrors of media, political rhetoric, and the presentation (or misrepresentation) of statistics, hackers are often perceived as "young men whose pathological addiction to the internet leads to elaborate deceptions, obsessive quests for knowledge, and bold tournaments of sinister computer break-ins" (Coleman and Golub 2008, 256; see also Halbert 1997; Hollinger 1991; Skibell 2002; Wall 2012).

Over recent decades, hacking has become synonymous with technocrime to the point where the hacker has become the archetypal "cybercriminal" (Wall 2007, 46). While many hackers are extraordinary in their technological competence and many revel in pranks and tricks—and some engage in outright harmful criminal behavior—contemporary portrayals of hackers as nearly omnipotent techno-demigods that will one day bring the world to its knees are greatly exaggerated. Indeed, even the belief that all hacking involves technosecurity is a distortion. Hacking is an eclectic phenomenon with a storied history, encompassing a litany of activities such as programming, network administration, hardware hacking, and security, among others. In addition, while some hackers do pose threats to various entities and institutions, hackers have also been instrumental figures in the development of many technologies vital to contemporary life and commerce. In other words, hacking is not the exclusive domain of lone technological bandits surreptitiously plundering the digital landscape. Rather, hacking encompasses a broad technologically oriented subculture or community scattered across a wide arrangement of dispositions, orientations, and proclivities (Coleman 2010).

Hacking has expanded to become a worldwide phenomenon and, while exact figures are unknown, there are at least tens of thousands of people who currently identify as members of the hacking community. As hacking expands, so too does its corresponding academic literature. Studies have examined (1) various demographic and psychological characteristics of hackers, (2) subcultural features and dynamics of the hacking community, (3) virus/malware creation, computer intrusions, website defacements, and identity theft, and (4) potential explanations of hacking-related behaviors through criminological theory.[1]

While each of these bodies of literature is uniquely valuable in its own way, scholarship on the history of hacking provides some of the most useful insights into hacker culture. Hacking has enjoyed a famed history, despite only being in existence as a subculture for approximately sixty years. While not comprehensive, the following section should give the reader a sense of the origins and development of hacking through the years.

Hacker History

Origins of Hacking

As long as humans have been creatively involved with technology of any sort, hacker-like behaviors have existed. Examples of such tendencies occurred prior to any contemporary notion of hacking or hackers. In 1903, for instance, Guglielmo Marconi "was attempting to promote his patented radio system as a way to send confidential messages (even though total secrecy is impossible with broadcast media" (McLeod 2014, 4). During an initial demonstration, the device was set to receive a transmission from Marconi. Instead, another message "Rats. Rats. Rats," came through, followed by a series of obnoxious rhymes that mocked the inventor. Stage magician Nevil Maskelyn was to blame. He "gleefully explained to reporters that he was trying to expose the invention's fatal flaw" (McLeod 2014, 4). Such behavior might be described as hacking by some contemporary definitions. As such, placing a date on the origins of hacker-like tendencies and behaviors is difficult, if not impossible. Scholars generally agree, however, that the formation of hacking as a late modern technology-oriented subculture happened within the mid-twentieth century.

Hacking in this sense is believed to have originated in the 1950s and 1960s at the Massachusetts Institute of Technology (MIT) with the Tech Model Railroad Club (TMRC) (Levy 1984; Turkle 1984). As the name would suggest, the TMRC was initially composed of model railroad enthusiasts. These models, however, were more than toys that circled Christmas trees. They were intricate models driven by sophisticated electronic systems. For some enthusiasts, the electronic systems driving these trains became more interesting than the trains themselves. Discontent with the technical sophistication offered by model train systems, these early "hackers" were eventually drawn toward the most complicated technological systems available at the time: computers.

MIT students were the first to adopt the word "hack" as part of the subcultural argot (Levy 1984). The term was originally used to describe the elaborate pranks regularly conducted by MIT students, a tradition that continues to this day (Levy 1984; Peterson 2011). Among members of the TMRC, "hacks" also referred to quick-yet-effective solutions to a technical problem. The concept has evolved over time to take on a multitude of meanings (see chapter 2 for a full exploration of the meaning of hacking). Both *The New Hacker's Dictionary* and *The Jargon File*, an online resource for hacker argot, list nine separate definitions of the term (Raymond 1996; 2016). *The hack* has evolved into a chimeric concept, becoming associated with quick and messy fixes, sophisticated and elegant solutions, pranks, technological exploration, computer deviance, among other meanings. The term's meaning further fragmented and transformed through popular culture and public discourse (Wall 2012).

Early hacks developed by members of the TMRC included, for instance, the development of an early video game and some primordial advances in artificial intelligence. While creatively engaging computers, the TMRC exemplified subcultural and ethical characteristics that would come to define large segments of hacker culture in the decades to follow. Interested in technical systems and possessed by a desire for hands-on learning, these early hackers often found themselves at odds with university administrators who had an interest in using the machines for officially sanctioned "productive" activities and often secured the computers from potential harm that these hackers posed by tinkering with the monolithic machines—a tension that has repeated itself throughout hacker history. Indeed, the history of hacking is replete with examples of conflict between hackers and authority figures who restrict access to hardware and code.

Early institutional settings, primarily universities, were important in the genesis of hacking. Computers at the time were extraordinarily expensive and required tremendous amounts of space and maintenance to operate. For instance, the IBM 704 (which early MIT hackers described as the "Hulking Giant") was especially high maintenance. The machine "cost several million dollars, took up an entire room, needed constant attention from a cadre of professional machine operators, and required special air-conditioning so that the glowing vacuum tubes inside it would not heat up to data-destroying temperatures" (Levy 1984, 19). Universities also provided the curious-minded with greater degrees of freedom than found in other settings, like corporate offices. The confluence of institutional resources and intellectuality (though not entirely unrestricted) made universities like MIT, Harvard, Cornell, and Berkeley ideal places for early hacker culture to take root.

Hardware Hacking

With the advent of the microprocessor, computational technology expanded out of universities and corporations into the home, a trend that would only accelerate in the 1980s and 1990s (Levy 1984; Thomas 2002). As computers began to shrink in size, hackers found it easier to gain access to and manipulate computer hardware, marking a subgenre of hacking which would later become known as *hardware hacking* (Jordan 2008; Levy 1984). The interest in computer hardware was present among members of the TMRC, however, and, later, members of MIT's Artificial Intelligence Lab (Levy 1984). The enormous cost of these machines meant that university administrators were eager to protect university investments. In other words, tinkering with the internal mechanisms of the Hulking Giants was, to say the least, frowned upon. The *interest* in this hardware, however, remained evident, resulting in many hackers circumventing university rules and restrictions to get their hands on the computer hardware.

Hands-on approaches to computer hardware re-emerged with gusto in the mid-1970s to mid-1980s through groups like the Homebrew Computer Club (HBCC), which helped inspire one of the most influential figures in personal computing: Steve Wozniak (2006). Such hackers engage technology by "rewiring, re-soldering and simply cutting up and re-gluing the components of an existing pieces of hardware" (Jordan 2008, 121). These hackers "take the spirit of hacking into material relations, finding new and novel uses enabled by the soldering iron rather than the command line" (123).

As computer technology began to spread, so too did code. While many early computer aficionados would write their own programs, a demand existed for pre-designed software packages to help others take further advantage of these machines. The very nature of code, however, makes duplication relatively easy. Early hackers took to producing copies of software packages to share with each other. The willingness to share code brought hackers into conflict with those who distributed code as a commodity. One of the earliest recorded incidents of code-sharing among hackers being referred to as "piracy" and "theft" occurred when Bill Gates developed a Beginner's All-Purpose Symbolic Instruction Code (BASIC) interpreter for the Altair 8800. The interpreter was made available for presale among computer users but its release was continually delayed (Levy 1984). Eventually a member of the HBCC secured a leaked copy and produced duplicates for members of the club. Gates found out about these activities and penned an open letter condemning these copiers as pirates. Hackers were not so convinced, viewing the act as information sharing—marking a key point of tension between intellectual property owners and hackers that persists today (Levy 1984; Wark 2004). Since then, hackers have come together in the *warez* scene to *crack* software protections and share code among the community (Décary-Hétu, Morselli, and Leman-Langlois 2012).

Video Games and Software Development

As personal computing took off in the 1980s, so too did the demand for software packages, leading to the development of a swelling software industry. While early software was often developed for business use, the increase in personal use created a desire for computers to be used as entertainment devices. Video games thus became a booming industry in a relatively short period of time (Levy 1984). Faced with growing pressure from an increasingly competitive market, companies constantly sought to push the bounds of computer hardware to bring users the most sophisticated gaming experience possible. Because of the limited hardware capabilities of the time, this often required creating elegant and inventive ways to stretch computational resources. Hackers—experienced in finding creative ways to get the most out of computer hardware—thus became key figures in this new market. The demands of business, however, conflicted with the sensibilities of many hackers who were notorious for streaks of anti-authoritarianism and desires for personal autonomy. This meant that early hackers were simultaneously a bane and a boon for many business owners, and hackers who ascended the ranks often found it difficult to cope with such occupational demands (Levy 1984).

While instrumental in the proliferation of computer software, industry did not monopolize software development. Running parallel to the growth of proprietary software was a branch of code development that became intimately linked to hacking known as "free and open-source software" (F/OSS) (Coleman 2010, 2012, 2013; Coleman and Golub 2008; Jordan 2008; Thomas 2002; Söderberg 2002, 2008, 2013). Early hackers, like those at MIT, emphasized sharing code as both a practical and ethical consideration (Levy 1984). According to F/OSS hackers, code should be open to enable others to freely benefit from, change, and contribute to it. The developed programs are then said to be "free" in a dual sense—the software is to be provided to others free of charge and the code is made available for others to contribute to the project, incorporate into their own programs, and create their own derivations.

A particular piece of software emerged in the early 1990s that formed the backbone of the movement—Linux (Coleman 2013; Thomas 2002). Based off the UNIX (Uniplexed Information and Computing System) architecture, which was considered flexible and stable, Linux became the operating system (OS) of choice for F/OSS hackers over proprietary OSs such as Windows and Macintosh. Early hackers such as Richard Stallman—a prominent hacker who became enmeshed in hacker culture in the early 1970s while working at the Artificial Intelligence Lab at MIT (Levy 1984)—helped position Linux and F/OSS in opposition to for-profit software developers.

A schism formed in the F/OSS movement, however (Coleman 2013). Stallman and his acolytes held firm that all derivatives of their software—which had begun to be released under the GNU General Public License—should be free and open source as well.[2] Free and open-source software is therefore about "free speech." Code is considered analogous to speech and thus restrictions on the transmission and access to code are equivalent to restrictions on speech—which is considered categorically unethical. As such, Stallman's position was that all code should be free and any derivations of that code should also be free. This position is referred to as "free software."

The other side of the divide in the F/OSS movement is commonly referred to as "open source." Figures such as Linus Torvalds (known for starting Linux) advocate this position, which holds that the division between free and proprietary software does not need to be so rigid and that open-source software can be useful in the marketplace. In essence, there is room for proprietary ownership of code under this perspective, though open code is still viewed favorably because it is thought to generate better software through collaboration and transparency. Collectively, both sides of the schism are referred to as the free and open-source software movement but both have slightly different perspectives on the ethics of code. One eschews proprietary software licensing entirely while the other is open to derivative use of code in business.

The Phone Phreaks

Up to this point, hacker culture has been described as flourishing in spaces where computers were located. In the 1950s and 1960s, hacker culture was bound to universities and corporations predominantly. In the 1970s and 1980s, hacking expanded into the private sphere with the advent of personal computing. Other kinds of hackers, however, existed during the 1960s and 1970s who were not dependent on the spatial distribution of computers.[3] Perhaps the most famous of these were the *phone phreaks* (Pfaffenberger 1988; Taylor 1999; Turkle 1984).

Phreaks reveled in learning about (and manipulating) the inner operations of the massive telephony networks that developed in the U.S. and abroad. Functioning in many ways as early predecessors to contemporary network security hackers, phreakers frequently broke the law in their pursuit of knowledge, thrills, and respect. They frequently ran afoul of law enforcement as well as major telecommunications corporations like Bell (often referred to as "Ma Bell") who were frustrated at the ability of phreakers to perform various feats, like making free phone calls, through their wires. In addition, phreaking often involved what hackers refer to as "social engineering," or the manipulation of the human element of systems to gain access (Mitnick and Simon 2002). Phreakers would occasionally trick customer service agents, managers, technicians, and others for information necessary to access secure systems and information. This practice has endured throughout hacker culture. Even today, social engineering challenges are not uncommon at various hacker gatherings and events.

Perhaps the most famous phreaker emerged in the late 1960s: Captain Crunch (a.k.a. John Draper) (Pfaffenberger 1988). He derived his name from the breakfast cereal. As Sherry Turkle (1984, 225–226) explains, "In every box, there was a toy whistle, like the prize in Cracker Jacks. The whistle produced a 2600-cycle tone." This tone was the secret to making free phone calls across the largely analog phone systems of the time, which depended on audio frequencies to route calls and trigger various other functions within the system. In this particular case, "First, you dial a long-distance telephone number. Then you blow the Crunch whistle. This disconnected the dialed conversation but kept the trunk open without further toll charge. From that point on, any number of calls could be dialed free" (Turkle 1984, 226). Captain Crunch developed a reputation for mastery of the phone system which he supposedly demonstrated by making "the call around the world" (Turkle 1984). Sitting in a room with two separate telephones, he is said to have routed a phone call from one phone through various points across the world before making the second phone ring.

Phreakers also produced "boxes"—devices used to manipulate the phone system. Perhaps one of the most famous of these boxes was the "blue box" which allowed the user to route calls through the phone system. These boxes were typically used to make free calls. Captain Crunch was known to build such boxes (Levy 1984). Steve Jobs and Steve Wozniak began producing their own blue boxes after reading about Captain Crunch in a 1971 *Esquire* article (Levy 1984; Sterling 1992). Indeed, Steve Wozniak (or "Woz") himself was well respected as a hacker and phreaker himself with a penchant for pranks and jokes, like many of his contemporaries. For instance, "Woz once used his box to see if he could phone the Pope; he pretended he was Henry Kissinger, and almost reached His Eminence before someone at the Vatican caught on" (Levy 1984, 246). As demonstrated by Wozniak, hacking and phreaking are intimately linked—inseparable. The similarities and cross-membership between the two are hardly unsurprising, however. Both computers and telephone systems present interesting challenges and were ideal grounds for developing and demonstrating skill as well as conducting mischief. Woz would later become a member of the Homebrew Computer Club before fundamentally changing the nature of personal computing and co-founding the company Apple (Levy 1984; Pfaffenberger 1988).

Phreaking was an instrumental part of early hacker culture and its legacy still impacts contemporary network and security hacking. While the phone system has changed to make traditional phreaking techniques nigh impossible, phreaking is still practiced within certain sectors of the hacker community, particularly as telephony has come to rely so intensely on computerized VoIP (Voice over Internet Protocol) systems (Gold 2011). Perhaps the greatest legacy of phreaking is its effect on network hackers and the secrecy that permeates the hacker underground.

BBSs, Network Hacking, and the Eye of Sauron

The 1980s saw the creation of smartmodems, which allowed for computers to connect across telephone systems more easily than before. Combined with the growth of personal computers in the home, *bulletin board systems* (BBSs) emerged as central hubs for hacker culture (Sterling 1992). Hackers and other technologists would use smartmodems to dial into BBSs set up on another computer in different location. Acting as "informal bazaars where one could trade rare and sometimes-seedy information," BBSs were vital systems for cultivating hacker culture (Coleman 2013, 30). As Gabriella Coleman (2013, 30) explains, BBSs were "the basis for one of the first expansions of hacking through which hackers could interact autonomously, anonymously, and independently of official institutions." Here hackers could exchange messages, news, stories, exploits, and software. Some BBSs operated secretively—limiting the scope of membership through invite-only polices—while others were more open. These systems "often catered to more local audiences" because long distance phone calls were usually quite expensive at the time (31). Because of this locality, participants in BBSs would sometimes schedule meetings where they could engage in face-to-face interactions. Despite popular assumptions, many hackers thrive on physical as well as digital interaction (Coleman 2010).

Smartmodems, however, were not just used to connect to BBSs. Like phone phreaks, many hackers delighted in using these devices to search through telephone networks for other computers they could infiltrate and explore (Thomas 2002). Part of the fun was simply *finding* these servers as they constituted interesting and thrilling places to explore, much like stumbling across an unknown cave in the middle of the woods. In this early practice, it was often easy to penetrate these servers as their only protection was "security through obscurity"—confidence that no one could get on the system without knowing which number to dial. Knowledge of such computers discovered on the telephone networks spread through word of mouth and lists maintained on BBSs, including numbers that dialed into government and corporate servers. Another method for figuring out a computer's corresponding telephone number were war dialers—named after the 1983 movie *WarGames* (Thomas 2002). These programs would dial random phone numbers and record those that connected to computers on the other end (Thomas 2002). Hackers could then share the results of their explorations on BBSs, much like current urban explorers often share the results of their "meat space" (as some hackers would call it) explorations in online forums and blogs (Garrett 2013).

In the early 1990s, BBSs were replaced by *the Internet*, which dramatically expanded the communicative capabilities of hackers and technological laypersons alike. "If the BBS felt like a small, cramped, and overpriced studio," Coleman (2013, 32) explains, "the Internet was more like an outlandishly spacious penthouse apartment with many luxurious features." These technological developments provided hackers with numerous spaces to communicate and operate across a range of hacking activities.

Not everyone connected to these networks appreciated hackers' antics. Like J. R. R. Tolkien's Eye of Sauron, the gaze of law enforcement and corporate interests turned toward hackers and other potential threats to network security. Immense commercial and governmental interests became tied to the future of connective technology. Many politicians and the general public were also growing wary—even fearful—of hackers, an anxiety which increased drastically following the release of *WarGames* (Skibell 2002). As a result, network security exploded, transforming almost overnight into a booming computer security industry and an immense government surveillance regime that culminated in programs like the National Security Agency's Planning Tool for Resource Integration, Synchronization, and Management (PRISM) system (Yar 2008b).

While law enforcement was initially absent in the digital realm, many hackers will point to one U.S. Secret Service operation in 1990 as a watershed moment for hacking and its relationship to law enforcement: Operation Sundevil (Halbert 1997). While other stings and arrests proliferated in the late 1980s, Sundevil was perhaps the most discussed and noteworthy of these early operations (Sterling 1992). Involved was a nationwide effort led by the U.S. Secret Service in conjunction with other agencies culminating in only three arrests and the execution of twenty seven search warrants. A litany of computers, parts, storage media, notebooks, and even proprietary telephone system manuals were also seized. As with most social control interventions, this had an effect on the hacker community: "Fear of establishment clampdowns has thus acted as a cultural binding agent for those on the margins of mainstream computing. On an official level, it has led to the formation of such representative bodies as the Electronic Frontier Foundation (EFF), whilst further underground, the antipathy caused by the perceived over-reaction of various agencies to computer underground activity has led to increased feelings of 'them against us' and more secrecy" (Taylor 1999, 29).

The early 1990s saw the death of BBSs, an event "hackers would not let slip away without due commemoration and celebration" (Coleman 2013, 31). DEF CON was organized by The Dark Tangent (a.k.a. Jeff Moss) in 1993 as a relatively small gathering of hackers to socialize following the closure of many BBSs (DEF CON 2016). Intended to be a one-time event, DEF CON has become one of the largest hacking conventions in the world (there are many hacker conventions, and DEF CON was not even the first with both SummerCon and HoHoCon preceding it).[4] While the stereotype of hackers as chronic loners exists, the history of hacking is marked by the emergence and passing of various forms of *social* interactions, many of which involve physical, face-to-face interactions including many hacker meetings and conventions (Coleman 2010, 2013).

Cryptography and the Rise of Security Hacking

In the 1980s, the ease of transmission—and interception—of electronic communications created a demand for publically available encryption protocols (Levy 2001). Prior to this era, access to encryption was limited. The NSA (National Security Agency) was "concerned about the spread of high standards of encryption and sought to restrict their distribution" (Jordan 2008, 119). Accessing information and developing intelligence would become drastically more difficult for them if everyone could freely encrypt data (Levy 2001). Indeed, private businesses were seldom allowed to develop and employ encryption without the consent of the NSA and, when permitted, would frequently be required to include backdoors for the agency.

Various supporters of what became known as the public key cryptography movement pushed for encryption algorithms the public could use (Levy 2001). These advocates penned various political essays and sometimes identified themselves as *cypherpunks* or *crypto anarchists* (discussed further in chapter 3) (Levy 1984; Jordan 2008). Cryptography helped provide many hackers with the tools necessary to circumvent increasing controls placed on networks, particularly by the state (Levy 2001). Of course, such efforts also brought these hackers into conflict with the U.S. government, notably the NSA, who feared the expansion of cryptography among the general public. While this type of hacking perhaps reached its peak in the 1990s (Jordan 2008), the tradition of cryptographic programming still persists within the community around projects like The Onion Router (TOR) and Pretty Good Privacy (PGP).

Since hacking and technology have developed in tandem over the years, it is unsurprising that the proliferation of networked computer systems coincided with the expansion of yet another subgenre of hacking—one which has become the primary object of fear and fascination in the public mind—*security hacking*. An interest in security has always been present, to one degree or another, in hacker culture. The hackers of the TMRC were known for devising methods to bypass early password protection systems on the Hulking Giant computers. They also used lock picks to access computers and code that had been stored away from them. Phone phreaking encouraged manipulation of telecommunications networks. BBSs and the Internet permitted the creation of repositories to store and share a wide assortment of data including tools and instructions on how to circumvent security protocols. Combined with the influence of cryptography, it is no wonder that many hackers became fascinated with security systems. As one hacker remarked in an interview, "The reason for such an interest in hacking networks and security is because those are where the most interesting problems are."

Over time, participants in this genre of hacking have come to be divided into subtypes, often along moral or ethical lines. The labels "white hat" and "black hat"—which draw from Western cinema tropes where the protagonists wore white cowboy hats while the villains donned black headwear—are perhaps the most often used. These labels are used to denote the difference between hackers who seek security vulnerabilities to learn or improve computer security from those who would use such skills to harmfully exploit vulnerabilities, often for personal gain, prestige, recognition, or excitement, among other motivations (Taylor 1999; Thomas 2002; Turgeman-Goldschmidt 2011). The distinction has also been described as "hackers" versus "crackers," though the latter originates from hackers who specifically worked to break copy-protection mechanisms on software. In addition, another genre of hacking can be categorized under the security label "lock-picking enthusiasts." Since the early days of hacking at the Massachusetts Institute of Technology—when hackers would often find ways to infiltrate offices where code sheets had been stored away from them—lock-picking has been a lively, if academically underappreciated, component of the hacker community.

Increased law enforcement pressure, the proliferation of computer networks, the rise of security hacking, and other factors culminated in what some have described as the *hacker underground* (Coleman and Golub 2008; Thomas 2002). While difficult to define, hackers in the underground generally possess a contempt for institutional regulation of technology and a penchant for illicit technological activity, notably computer security, malware, and cracking. Though not all technocriminals come from the hacker underground, many in the hacker underground engage in crime. In addition, the computer underground does not necessarily operate as a discrete component of the hacker community. Instead, its borders are permeable and hackers may drift in and out of the underground over their life course.

Like the punk scene of the 1970s and 1980s, "zines" were popular methods for circulating sub- or counter-cultural knowledge among hackers. One of the most instrumental zines that emerged for the hacker underground was *Phrack*, a portmanteau of "hack" and "phreak" (Thomas 2002). *Phrack* began in 1985 as the result of two hackers, Knight Lightning and Taran King, who were interested in creating a resource for the computer underground available through their bulletin board, the Metal Shop AE (Sterling 1992; Thomas 2002). *Phrack* embraced the "information wants to be free" maxim and reveled in what some consider dangerous knowledge. Articles on topics ranging from "how to open pad locks" to "how to make various explosives" were featured within its pages. "To most people outside the hacking world," Paul Taylor (1999, 58) explains, "the promulgation of such information would seem, at best, of dubious value, and, at worst, extremely irresponsible." In true hacker fashion, the publication of such material did not manifest through crime sprees or terrorist attacks but, rather, through an intense desire for hidden knowledge (Sterling 1992). *Phrack* also served as a guide to the culture of the hacker underground, often presenting a "who's who of computer hacking" (Thomas 2002, 226). In 2005, publication of *Phrack* was "officially" cancelled on its sixty-third issue, though five issues have been intermittently published over the years since then with the last released in 2012.

Transgression, Humor, and Political Activism

In the late 1980s hackers and other technologists began using their skills for political activism (Coleman 2014; Jordan and Taylor 2004; McKenzie 1999; Meikle 2002; Taylor 2005; Van Laer and Van Aelst 2010).[5] Though many hackers claim to eschew politics, the history of hacking is mired in conflicts with authority to some degree or another. Thus hacker culture possesses a political edge. Some hackers, however, embrace political activism—a trend that has recently captured headlines with groups like Anonymous, LulzSec, RedHack, milw0rm, and others. Chapters 3 and 4 discuss hacker politics in greater detail.

One particular influence worth discussing is the role of the countercultural hippie anarchist youth organization of 1960s and 1970s called the Youth International Party, or the Yippies (Coleman and Golub 2008; Sterling 1992; Thomas 2002). The Yippies were known for often humorous and trickster-like protests and media manipulations. For instance, Abbie Hoffman, a co-founder of the Party, recalls when the Yippies went inside the New York Stock Exchange in 1966 and threw $200 from the visitor's gallery to the Exchange floor (McLeod 2014). Many traders stopped what they were doing and dived for the money, providing a very real demonstration of the greed of Wall Street. The Yippies also nominated a pig named "Pigasus" for President of the United States in 1968 as a transgressive protest against American politics at the time (McLeod 2014; Thomas 2002). This kind of publically confrontational, satirical, and humorous form of protest would reemerge over time again and again in hacker culture.

The Yippies also made other contributions to hacker culture, perhaps explaining the endurance of their legacy. The political pranksters published a newsletter called the *Party Line*, which was taken over by two Yippie hackers named "Al Bell" and "Tom Edison" and rebranded as *TAP* (the *Technical Assistance Program*) (Sterling 1992; Thomas 2002). While the publication started as an overtly political newsletter, *TAP* began to focus more on the "technical aspects of telephony" in addition to lock-picking, machine manipulation, and other decidedly hackery topics under the stewardship of Bell and Edison (Thomas 2002, 16). Thus *TAP* served as both a political and technical publication for phreaks and hackers alike.

Publication of *TAP* ended in 1983 after Edison "had his computer stolen and his apartment set on fire" (Thomas 2002, 116). Other hacker publications, however, replaced *TAP*, including *2600: The Hacker Quarterly*, a zine directly influenced by the political and technical sensibilities of the Yippies and *TAP* (Sterling 1992). Deriving its name from the 2600 Hz signal used by phreakers to manipulate the phone systems, *2600* began publication in 1984 and has become one of the most prominent hacker zines in the world. In the tradition of *TAP*, *2600* was politically engaged, particularly in issues surrounding technology, free speech, privacy, and corporate and government power (Thomas 2002). Even the founder and editor's pseudonym evinces the political nature of the publication—Emmanuel Goldstein, the quasi-antagonist of George Orwell's *1984*. The first issue of *2600* was "a three- or four-page printed pamphlet that talked about the tyranny of the phone company and the political responsibility people had to be aware of its power" (116). *2600* has also organized ten politically sensitive hacker conventions starting in 1994 with HOPE (Hackers on Planet Earth), with the most recent in 2014 called HOPE X.

In 1996, Omega, a member of the Cult of the Dead Cow (a prominent hacker group founded in 1984), coined the term "hacktivism" to describe the use of hacking for political protest.[6] Others avoid "hacktivism," instead adopting terms like *electronic civil disobedience* to distance technological protest from the negative connotations associated with hacking (Meikle 2002). Both security hacking and hacktivism, therefore, emerged in the latter years of the twentieth century as prominent and visible faces of the hacking community. While not all those who engage in electronic forms of dissent are hackers *per se*, many key hacktivism figures and groups are drawn from the ranks of the hacker community (Jordan and Taylor 2004).

Perhaps the earliest hack performed for political protest was in 1989 with the creation of the WANK (Worms Against Nuclear Killers) worm (Iozzio 2008). Worms are pieces of software that replicate and spread from computer to computer, often with the objective of depriving access, reducing or halting bandwidth, damaging data, or resulting in other consequences. The WANK worm, designed by still-unidentified hackers, targeted certain NASA offices and ran a banner "across system computers as part of a protest to stop the launch of the plutonium-fueled, Jupiter-bound Galileo probe" (Iozzio 2008). Since this time, numerous hacker groups and tech savvy protestors have used technology as a means for social change.

While many hacktivist tactics have involved the subterfuge, sabotage, and other digital guerilla tactics, some hackers have also organized to advocate for political change *within* governmental systems. For instance, the German Chaos Computer Club (CCC), founded in 1981, has emerged as Europe's largest hacker group (Jordan and Taylor 2004). The Club is officially registered as a not-for-profit association and, over the years, has acted in the form of a political lobbying group. Through governmental lobbying, publication, public speaking, and other tactics, the CCC "advocates more transparency in government, communication as a human right, and free access to MTIs [media technologies and infrastructures] for everyone" (Kubitschko 2015, 391).

Hacktivism currently is a contested topic circulating in the media. Much of the attention toward hackers and hacktivism has been aimed at the political resistance of hacker groups such as Anonymous, a loosely knit collective of hackers and activists. Anonymous emerged from 4chan, a prominent online community that became (in)famous for offensive, wild, and often humorous antics, most notably its "random" section called "/b/" (Coleman 2014; Olson 2012).[7] Such antics are often described as "trolling," a type of behavior that is said to be done for the "lulz," a "spirited but often malevolent brand of humor entymologically derived from lol" (Coleman 2014, 4). Considering the connection between hacking and trickster/prankster behavior since the early MIT days and the influence of political protest groups like the Yippies, it is unsurprising that hackers and other Internet denizens would be attracted to "lulz"-inducing activities like trolling (Levy 1984; Peterson 2011; Thomas 2002). This dark sense of transgressive and in-your-face humor has greatly informed Anonymous. Beginning with "Project Chanology" in 2008, a "lulzy" protest of the Church of Scientology for its surreptitious and abusive practices, Anonymous has evolved as a dynamic and fragmented collective of Internet protesters.[8] Groups like LulzSec and AntiSec emerged from Anonymous, engaging in high-profile security and network hacks such as the exfiltration of email and credit card information from the security company Stratfor. The often flamboyant and confrontationally humorous ways in which Anonymous conducted its protests has contributed to the relative success of various protests movements, such as Occupy Wall Street (Coleman 2014). In addition, Anonymous and other hacker groups were also involved in the controversies surrounding the online whistleblowing group WikiLeaks in the early 2010s (Coleman 2014; Leigh and Harding 2012; Steinmetz 2012). Such methods have also helped galvanize the stigma associated with hackers, and the public image of the hacker now wears a Guy Fawkes mask.[9]

Currently, hacking is a global phenomenon with hackers occupying a wide assortment of positions throughout society. Many have risen into prominent ranks in business, with some becoming technological moguls themselves like Steve Wozniak. Some have become respected members of government agencies. For instance, Mudge (a.k.a. Peiter Zatko) was a prominent member of the hacker group Lopht and was instrumental in the exposure of multiple security vulnerabilities including the buffer overflow (Thomas 2002).[10] In 2010, he worked for the Defense Advanced Research Projects Agency (DARPA) of the Department of Defense as a program manager (Mills 2010). Some hackers have been more covert and illicit, engaging in various forms of criminal activity. In other words, hacking involves an extraordinarily diverse community occupying multiple technological and social domains, including security,

F/OSS programming, hardware hacking, network administration, and hacktivism, among others.

Throughout its history, hacking has enjoyed many splits, twists, and turns. While this is an undoubtedly incomplete historical account of hacking (such an endeavor would be worthy of its own book!), the point is to give the reader some understanding of the development of hacking as a phenomenon and to also hint at some of its complexities. Indeed, the previously described history of hacking may be best thought of as a Western or American chronology. While undoubtedly interconnected, the historical circumstances of hacking in other societies are currently understudied and poorly understood. To further develop the reader's familiarity with hacker culture that emerges from this (confessedly) predominantly Western history, this review now turns to various descriptions of a cultural spirit or ethos that is said to permeate much of hacker culture, often referred to as *the hacker ethic*.

The Hacker Ethic

Throughout the history of hacking, various authors have attempted to explain a common cultural spirit—a certain *je ne sais quoi*—that runs through the hacker community. Though taking on different interpretations, one of the most common framings of this spirit has been through a "hacker ethic." Hacker culture has evolved over time, to be sure, but there are characteristics that seem to persist (Coleman 2013). Thus, discussions of the "hacker ethic" and similar cultural values may provide the reader with a more comprehensible understanding of hacker culture in the general sense. Coleman (2012, 2013), however, warns against reifying the idea of an overarching and consistent ethos guiding the hacker subculture. She argues that the subculture contains a great deal of diversity, which may not be adequately represented by one encompassing idea of the hacker ethic. Much like any narratological framing of an issue, certain details may be omitted, overgeneralized, or overemphasized. Thus discussions of the hacker ethic may not reveal the full depth of difference within the hacker community. The reader should therefore mind Coleman's warning as this overview unfolds. That said, these descriptions (discussed further in chapter 4, and to a lesser extent, chapter 3) are extraordinarily useful for situating hacking within a broader social structural context. In addition, this book will offer nuance to many of these discussions of the hacker ethic throughout.

Steven Levy (1984), author of the foundational hacker history *Hackers: Heroes of the Computer Revolution*, coined the term "the hacker ethic." Stemming from his interviews with numerous members of the TMRC, HBCC, and others, Levy articulates six core values that underpin this ethic, which, for some, has become the primary gospel of describing hacker culture—or, at the very least, the "golden age" of hacking. The first value is defined as follows: "Access to computers—and anything which might teach you something about the way the world works—should be unlimited and total. Always yield to the Hands-On Imperative!" (40). While not a complete categorical imperative for all hackers, many believe that *access* to technology is a fundamental value and even a right that should be afforded to all. The ability to work directly with technology allows both the hacker and the technology to operate fully—neither can function optimally without the other. This value also indicates a desire to actively engage technology and data, a trait Levy that labels the *hands-on imperative*. Rather than passively consume technology and media, hackers instead choose to study and tinker with systems. This tendency can lead to creating new or improved systems as well as an ability to manipulate them. This component of the hacker ethic has parallels with other do-it-yourself subcultures present among many punks and anarchist groups (Ferrell 2001).

The second value of the hacker ethic described by Levy (1984, 40) is related to the first: "All information should be free." A common and related proclamation made by many hackers is that *information wants to be free*—a saying first articulated by Steward Brand in the aforementioned panel discussion among various hackers in the 1980s following the publication of Steven Levy's (1984) *Hackers* (Brand and Herron 1985). As renowned hacker Richard Stallman (2002, 43) asserts, this is not "free" in the sense of "free beer" but free as in "free speech." This belief can sometimes get hackers into trouble. For example, some hackers believe computer security is an aberration because it restricts access to data (Hollinger 1991). They hold that the "real 'criminals' in the world of computers are the private corporations, institutions, and governmental agencies who wish to deny access [to] or charge fees for the use of this wealth of information" (Hollinger 1991, 9). As such, some hackers seek to illegally break open computer security measures merely as acts of defiance. In fact, merit within the community adhering to the hacker ethic is achieved by breaking these locks (Skibell 2002). Of course, the belief that all information should be free also underpins decidedly non-criminal forms of hacking, like free and open-source software development.

"Mistrust authority—promote decentralization" comprises the third value of Levy's (1984, 41) hacker ethic. For many hackers, authority figures are those who seek to limit access to computers and to control the flow of information. For the early MIT hackers, that authority came in the form of university administrators who would limit time and access to the Hulking Giant and other institutional computers. Such restrictions are notably easier if power and control are centralized. Much like the logic underpinning the construction of the Internet, decentralized systems allow resources, like information, to route around any obstructions. Centralized systems, on the other hand, are much more difficult to circumvent. To prevent restrictions on access to computers, code, and other forms of information, hackers often favor decentralized systems. This predilection can be observed in various file sharing protocols, like BitTorrent, or even anonymity-preserving software like The Onion Router. Decentralized systems are harder to shut down.

According to Levy (1984, 43), the fourth component of the hacker ethic is: "Hackers should be judged by their hacking, not bogus criteria such as degrees, age, race, or position." Generally, hackers do value skill and style as the greater measures of a person. Levy's arguments here, however, reveal some of the romanticism that runs through his writing. Much like with almost any other social collective, hackers are not immune to issues of social stratification or inequality (these issues will be discussed in greater detail in chapter 1). That said, hackers generally do at least *try* to strive for meritocratic forms of social organization.

The fifth and sixth values of Levy's (1984, 43, 45) hacker ethic are related: "You can create art and beauty on a computer" and "Computers can change your life for the better." From this perspective, hackers believe that computers are more than overblown calculators useful for business and accounting. Rather, computers themselves are wondrous machines capable of creative production. Computers can produce music, pictures, and other works of art. Additionally, computers invite a particular cultural aesthetic on their own. These machines were also believed to be able to ascend humanity through the powers of computation and automation: "Everyone could gain something by the use of thinking computers in an intellectually automated world" (48).

Breaking away from Levy's (1984) characterization, Richard Barbrook and Andy Cameron (2001) describe a pervasive ethos among hackers and Silicon Valley technologists which they term the *Californian Ideology*. According to the authors, the Californian Ideology "promiscuously combines the free-wheeling spirit of the hippies and the entrepreneurial zeal of the yuppies. This amalgamation of opposites has been achieved through a profound faith in the emancipatory potential of the new information technologies" (Barbrook and Cameron 2001, 364). Emerging from the leftist politics of the 1960s, subscribers to the Californian Ideology rejected the hippie idea that a return to nature was necessary for social progress. Instead, this ideology embraced a sense of technological utopianism—*better living through technology*. For Barbrook and Cameron, this sense of technological determinism melded with a "libertarian individualism" to become the "hybrid orthodoxy of the information age" (366). In much the same spirit as this book, these authors saw dire implications for this ideology in the replication of capitalist systems of oppression. The libertarian sensibilities and technological utopianism of the Californian left and hackers privileges a capitalist development of technology with little criticism of capital accumulation. Chapter 3 explores these implications, and others, in greater detail.

Bryan Warnick (2004) adopts a different perspective than previous authors, viewing hacking as unified through a particular perception of physical and social reality. Drawing from the linguistic theory of George Lakoff and Mark Johnson (1980), he argues that such an ontology is structured by a particular metaphor: *the world is a computer*. This metaphor falls under the category of *ontological metaphors*, which are "metaphors that express non-substances as substances" (Warnick 2004, 267). The non-substance in this case is technology—the computer. The *world as a computer* metaphor allows for hackers (and others who adopt this metaphor) to perceive the world as being open and intricately connected. Everything has a logical function and place. We can understand the hacker ethic through the metaphor because it states that, "(1) a computer system functions best under circumstance X; (2)

the world is a computer system; [and] (3) therefore, the world functions best under circumstance X" (274).

Many qualities of the so-called hacker ethic can be understood as arising from this metaphor that structures perceptions of reality. For instance, the emphasis on individualism among hackers can be understood as arising from this metaphor. The computer "opens a new space—a space without physical rules or boundaries, ready to be shaped by the individual imagination. It is a realm where omnipotence is possible. The absolutism of power in this new space creates a radical individualism" (Warnick 2004, 273). Similarly, hackers greatly value freedom and openness, particularly in regards to personal autonomy and the availability of information. This appreciation can be said to stem from "the experience of networked environments where each individual part contributes to the proper workings of the functioning whole. Since nodes of a system cannot afford to be 'secretive,' each part must contribute and share what it can for the good of the system, and so also should the human being in society" (273–274).

Even hackers' appreciation of privacy may find roots in the *world as computer* metaphor because it "mirrors the experience of anonymity in computer worlds" (Warnick 2004, 274). Thus, those conditions under which a computer operates best are seen as the circumstances optimal of all other systems, including social life, politics, economics, etc. For example, any restrictions on the flow of information—a condition necessary for optimal computing—particularly in politics or business, may be seen as inefficient at best or outright morally repugnant at worst.

Other authors have described the hacker ethic more generally as a "work ethic . . . [that is] gaining ground in our network society" (Himanen 2001, 7). These authors draw from the work of Max Weber to juxtapose the hacker ethic against the Protestant ethic (Brown 2008; Himanen 2001; Kirkpatrick 2002). According to Weber, the Protestant ethic involved a strict separation between one's labor time and recreation. Work was for work and leisure was for a scant period of downtime. Further, this ethic mandated that one's time would be best spent productively at all times, delaying pleasure through leisure until the afterlife. The hacker ethic implodes this dichotomy between labor and leisure. In an increasingly globalized, high-technology, late modern society, this traditional divide has become untenable, particularly among white-collar and related intellectual laborers. Increasingly, one's labor time is supposed to become increasingly pleasurable while one's leisure becomes more productive. For example, it is no longer enough to passively listen to music or watch movies in contemporary society, particularly among youth tech culture and hackers. Instead, one should build on these creative works through remixes or mash-ups (Brown 2008; Lessig 2008). Cultural works—music, movies, and books—are no longer only generated by professionals (labor) to be consumed by the masses (leisure). Rather, individuals can simultaneously engage in both production and consumption together. In addition, under the Protestant ethic, work was not viewed as a source of satisfaction in and of itself. Rather, work was valued for the potential wealth it generated—a signal of Godliness and likely outcome in the afterlife. Thus work was more a means to an end. In opposition to this, the hacker ethic states that *work should be a source of pleasure in and of itself* (Himanen 2001). This Weberian approach to the hacker ethic will be revisited later in chapter 4.

According to Gabriella Coleman and Alex Golub (2008), hackers cannot be understood through binary logics of "good/bad," "criminal/non-criminal," or "hero/villain." Instead, hacker culture presents an assortment of moral and ethical dispositions. For these authors, the hacker ethic does not exist as one unifying ethos, but as a fragmented morality underpinned by liberalism. Thus hacker alignments are split into three "moral expressions," which the authors identify as *crypto-freedom*, *free and open-source software (F/OSS)*, and *the hacker underground*. In *crypto-freedom*, some hackers seek methods to protect their data—in this case through encryption—against unwanted intrusion, particularly from the government as a way to protect free speech and privacy. This expression coincided with the rise of public key cryptography and so-called cypherpunks.

Under the *free and open-source software* expression of liberalism in the hacking subculture, we find the reassertion that information wants to be free (Coleman and Golub 2008). Free and open-source software involves communities of programmers coming together to collaboratively develop software. The free exchange and open access of code is necessary for such an endeavor to work. In F/OSS there is a subtle distinction between free software and open-source software, the latter of which permits investment and business support. "While the political and economic ideology of free and open-source software (F/OSS) focuses on liberal values of freedom and efficiency," Coleman and Golub (2008, 262–263) explain, these hackers also revel in "the service of creating useful knowledge, the hallmark of Jeffersonian liberal science, combined with a romantic drive for self-creative expression and self-cultivation typical of Millian notions of liberty" (citations omitted).

The final moral expression of liberalism in the hacker subculture discussed by Coleman and Golub (2008) is *the hacker underground*. It is here we find hackers actively transgressing and defying major government agencies and corporate powers through technological and social manipulation. Hackers' identities are subsumed in secrecy, which "differs from the social organization of F/OSS projects that pride themselves in upholding structures of accessibility and transparency" (Coleman and Golub 2008, 265). Here, liberalism is radicalized to the point of challenge and confrontation with those in power in the desperate struggle to break away from control.

A Methodological Review

Chapters 1, 2, and 3 serve as a foundation for the radical criminological approach taken in this book. These chapters are grounded in research that is ethnographic in the sense that it rests "on the peculiar practice of representing the social reality of others through the analysis of one's own experience in the world of these others" (Van Maanen [1988] 2011, xiii). The first two sources of data used throughout were part of a larger ethnographic field research project involving semi-structured interviews and participant observation.[11] This approach permits an inductive understanding of people's lived experiences within the nexus of culture, social structure, politics, and material conditions. As Howard Becker (1966, vi–vii) states, "To understand why someone behaves as he does, you must understand how it looked to him, what he thought he had to contend with, what alternatives he saw open to him; you can only understand the effects of opportunity structures, delinquent subcultures, social norms, and other commonly invoked explanations of behavior by seeing them from the actor's point of view." Ethnography, therefore, not only allows for the painting of a subcultural portrait, bound by the confines of the frame, but such approaches also allow for groups to be situated within their broader social context—if the ethnographer is willing to look for these connections. Additionally, ethnography permits an appreciation for the human dimension of social life. Rather than view actors as subservient to socialization and enculturation, ethnographic methods are open to the dialectic between structure and agency as "the product of collective human praxis" (Willis 1977, 4).

During the course of the field research, the researcher began attending public meetings for a hacker group called Union Hack (a pseudonym) in June 2012. In this study, overt participant observation was used and was chosen for ethical as well as pragmatic reasons (Bulmer 1982). Hackers are often intelligent with access to resources. Deceit may therefore unravel quickly. Approximately 137 hours and 20 minutes were spent in the field. Field exposure ranged anywhere from 40 minutes to 17 hours at a time.

The group met regularly at a local restaurant and would often adjourn afterward to bars and occasionally a local "hackerspace," a physical and cultural space setup for hackers to work on various projects both collectively and in isolation. Meetings had been occurring with some degree of regularity for years. Many members came and went over the years but a core of people endured, serving as lynchpins for the group and transmitters of the cultural milieu for newcomers. Recurring characters throughout these pages, Rick, Harvey, and Susan are three such members who served as cultural epicenters for Union Hack.[12] Some members maintained friendships outside of the group, while others only interacted within the context of monthly meetings. Most gravitated toward Union Hack because of its open and welcoming disposition and its promise of engaging discussion, an often-welcome release from whatever troubles peppered their lives. Meetings frequently continued far past the restaurant closing times into nearby bars and other locations where conversations would continue. Union Hack provided a kind of safe space for socializing in a world that sometimes does not make it easy for the geeky, nerdy, and tech-savvy to find welcoming environments for face-to-face interaction. Outside of such settings, conversations would often continue over emails or IRC (Internet relay chat). Many members would also make a yearly pilgrimage to DEF CON, a social gathering that members of Union Hack encouraged me to participate. The event, while fun and exciting, was bittersweet as it marked the end of the formal data collection process in this analysis, which ended in August 2013.

In addition to participant observation data, sixteen in-depth semi-structured interviews were conducted with fourteen members of the group or their close affiliates. Informed consent was gathered and a pseudonym was assigned to each participant to protect confidentiality. Interviews ranged from 58 minutes to 5 hours and 4 minutes. With the exception of two, all interviews were audio-recorded and fully transcribed using the parroting method. Refer to the appendix for tables describing interview date and length of interviews (table A.1) and time spent in the field (table A.2).[13]

The third source of data includes ethnographic content analysis data (Altheide 1987), which are primarily used in chapters 2 and 3 in conjunction with the previously described observational and interview data. This content analysis data was pulled from *2600: The Hacker Quarterly*, one of the "first significant hacker publications" (Thomas 2005, 604). Created by Emmanuel Goldstein (pseudonym of Eric Corley) in 1984, this "zine" features articles written by hackers in addition to short stories, book reviews, and editorials.[14] Considering its wide distribution and immense readership, *2600* is an ideal source of supplementary data for the ethnographic field research. Because the ethnographic data are more localized, inclusion of a broader data source—while not as deep—may provide additional context enriching the overall analysis. Such data are valuable because ethnographic content analysis is used "to document and understand the communication of meaning, as well as to verify theoretical relationships" (Altheide 1987, 68), a venture with which the current analysis is concerned.

The sample for this study was drawn from forty-one issues of *2600*, ranging from the Spring 2002 issue to Spring 2012. This time period was selected because the Spring 2002 issue was published shortly after the events of 9/11, which shaped the United States' security policy (Cole and Lobel 2007). This period has greatly affected hackers (and continues to) through an increase in scrutiny and developments in the area of information security. The time frame from the sample runs to Spring 2012, the most recent issue at the time of data gathering, providing an eleven-year period for analysis. Items included from the zine for analy-

TABLE I.1. Content Analysis Sample Descriptive Statistics

Items	Full Sample	Chapter 2 Subsample	Chapter 3 Subsample
# of Items	893	193	239
Articles	839	163	197
Editorials	41	29	35
Reviews	2	0	1
Short Stories	8	1	6
# of Authors	611*	143	152

* Some authors included here may be duplicates with slight variations on names like kaige and kaigeX. Omitting duplicates brings the number to 608.

sis include articles, editorials, book reviews, and short stories. Letters to the editor were excluded, as time constraints during data collection would not permit their inclusion. In total, over 839 articles, 41 editorials, 8 short stories, and 2 reviews (collectively referred to as *items*) comprised the sampling frame.

To generate the subsample for analysis, purposive sampling was used to find all relevant items within the full sample (all forty-one issues). For the analysis in chapter 2, each item was examined for any discussions concerning the nature of hacking and hackers. The items were also screened for the analysis of hackers' perspectives on the state (featured in chapter 3). Once relevant items were identified, they were flagged and logged in an electronic dataset. Notes were taken briefly describing the content of the item to provide context for later analysis. Then, each item was analyzed for passages that were directly relevant to research questions under investigation. These passages were lifted from the zine and preserved in the electronic dataset. This process resulted in the creation of two subsamples for analysis (table I.1). The subsample in chapter 2 consists of 163 articles, 29 editorials, and 1 short story, by 143 different authors. For chapter 3, the subsample is composed of 239 total items with 197 articles, 35 editorials, 6 short stories, and 1 book review.

The aforementioned data constitute the more "formal" data gathering process underpinning the earlier sections of this book. This description, however, does not include other communications, explorations of hacker cultural products, scholarly writings, and historical documents that have informed this work. In total, this book serves as the culmination of at least five years of research, study, reflection, and exploration of hacker culture and related issues.

Analytic Approach: Grounded Theory

The coding approach adopted for the current study is *grounded theory* (Charmaz 2002, 2006; Clarke 2005; Glaser and Strauss 1967). Grounded theory has a long history of application in ethnographic field research and in qualitative interviews more generally (Clark 2005; Charmaz 2006). Grounded theory methods of analysis "consist of flexible strategies for focusing and expediting qualitative data collection and analysis" and "provide a set of inductive steps that successively lead the researcher from studying concrete realities to rendering a conceptual understanding of them" (Charmaz 2002, 675).

Grounded theory gets its name from the idea that theory should be *grounded* in data and research (Glaser and Strauss 1967). The approach was developed in response to the dominant belief that theory would be first composed and then data would be found to test it. Rather, Barney Glaser and Anselm Strauss (1967, 1) raised the point that it is just as important to consider "how the discovery of theory from data— systematically obtained and analyzed in social research—can be furthered." Kathy Charmaz (2002, 677) adds to the discussion when she states that "data and theorizing are intertwined. Obtaining rich data provides a solid foundation for developing robust theories."

The coding procedure adopted here includes three stages of analysis. In the first stage of coding, all of the data (interview, participant observation, and content analysis) were scanned for passages relevant to the research questions under investigation. Each of these passages was given a short description describing the nature of the discussion in the greater context of the data. The objective in this stage was to plainly state what the author is conveying in matters pertinent to the relevant research question. In the second stage, each passage was examined again alongside the results of the first wave. At this stage, passages and descriptions were distilled down into short words or phrases that attempted to capture the essence of what the author was conveying. The goal of this wave was to find words or phrases that best summarized the meaning given by the authors to allow broader comparisons to be made between portrayals. In the third stage, the data and the results of the previous stages were analyzed for common themes permeating the data. As such, the process is iterative and pyramid-like, proceeding inductively from a broad swath of data to fewer and fewer themes and categories. The results of this process are detailed in each subsequent chapter in the various tables enumerating the dominant themes presented.

Chapter Overview

The first section of this book, chapters 1 through 3, begins humbly by exploring more immediate personal and subcultural dynamics among the hackers and hacker cultural products studied. Chapters 4 and 5 subsequently build from the foundation laid by these earlier chapters to draw broader connections between hackers and social structural forces, particularly political economic factors. Chapter 1 begins by exploring demographic characteristics and developmental factors in the lives of hackers. While multiple conclusions are extracted, based on this study and verified by others (such as Bachmann 2010; Holt 2009, 2010a; Schell, Dodge, and Moutsatsos 2002; Schell and Holt 2010; Schell and Melnychuk 2010; Taylor 1999), it appears that the typical hacker is racially white, masculine-gendered, and, perhaps most important for the overarching theme of this study, *decidedly middle class*. Indeed, various indicators explored throughout the lives of hackers point toward a middle-class upbringing and lifestyle for many hackers. Though it is not determinative, *class matters* for participation in hacker culture.

Having established that hacking is linked to class, chapter 2 presents the results of an analysis seeking the subcultural essence of hacking—and answers to the questions, "What does it mean to hack?" and "What is a hacker?" The results indicate that hacking is a phenomenon much more complex than mere computer intrusions and technological trickery. Indeed, the analysis reveals that hacking is best thought of as a kind of late-modern transgressive craft and subsequently summarizes the essence of hacking into a single word: *craft(y)*. Finding that hacking is a kind of craft also means that hacking is, at its core, a form of labor—and that labor is a defining cultural feature.

With hacking described as both a phenomenon tied to class *and* comprising a form of labor, the analysis in chapter 3 focuses on hacker perspectives on the state. Such an examination is useful because it not only generates insights into hacker perceptions of authority but it also reveals philosophical underpinnings running through the hacker community. In particular, the results support the assertions of Coleman and Golub (2008) that the philosophy of liberalism saturates hacker culture. Refining such insights, this analysis describes a hacker philosophy based on liberalism but shaped by work with technology and rife with a sense of technological utopianism. This philosophical perspective is described as *technological liberalism.*

With a foundation now linking hacking to class, labor, and technological liberalism, chapter 4 builds from the insights of previous chapters to advance a political economic understanding of hacking from a Marxist perspective. In this chapter, hacking is analyzed for its workings in the contradictions of capitalism. This analysis builds toward describing how hackers have become simultaneously a boon and a bane for this mode of production. In this manner, hackers are a key source of labor and intellectual property for capitalists but also present a threat to their ability to accumulate in an age where the economic system is increasingly dependent on intellectual property and digital networks. Chapter 5 then turns toward discussing the ideological processes by which hackers are constructed as a problem population, thus permitting the implementation of formal social control. In particular, three ideological formations are discussed as instrumental in legitimating legislative, law enforcement, and corporate control of hackers. This includes the construction of hackers as dangerous criminals, the reification of intellectual property, and the portrayal of technological infrastructures as standing on the edge of ruin. These processes, as contended here, allow capitalism to gain from hackers, their labor and cultural products, while also permitting mechanisms of suppression against the segments of the hacking community deemed threatening to capital accumulation.

The various analyses presented in this book are designed for both students and academics alike who wish to gain a comprehensive social, structural, and cultural understanding of hacking. Any issues dealing with subcultures, technology, deviance, and control in society are likely to be complex and this book does not shy away from such intricacies. Should readers persevere, they will be rewarded with a conceptual and theoretical basis to inform their own understandings of hacking, technology, and society more generally. Only by directly confronting and struggling with these confluences can we grow as engaged thinkers on human action, technology, and political economy. Let's begin.

PART I

Setting the Stage

1

The Front End of Hacking

To provide a holistic account of hacking, one should start from the beginning, so to speak. This analysis therefore begins by examining factors associated with growing up as a hacker (see also Bachmann 2010; Holt 2009, 2010a; Schell, Dodge, and Moutsatsos 2002; Schell and Holt 2010).[1] Subsequent chapters will pull readers upward through levels of analysis, building towards a broad political economic, or structural, discussion of hacking.

Two areas of hackers as individuals are explored through semi-structured interview data with insights from ethnographic participant observation (see the book's introduction). The first includes demographic characteristics including age, race, gender, perceived social class, and occupation. Developmental factors that potentially influential in participants' maturation as hackers are then discussed. These factors involve educational experiences, perceived influences and levels of support provided by parents, as well as first exposures to technology, the concept of hacking, and the hacking community. As argued here, these factors are potentially significant catalysts toward becoming a hacker. Though other elements are explored, this analysis concludes that hacking is a heavily class-based phenomenon, with most hackers being culled from the ranks of the middle class. Tables 1.1 and 1.2 provide summaries for many of the background characteristics and developmental factors discussed in this study.

Demographic Characteristics

The analysis of hacker backgrounds begins with a description of general demographic characteristics: age, family status (marital status, children), self-perceptions of social class, occupation, and educational background. While the primary contribution of this chapter is to consider hacking as a middle-class phenomenon, this section includes expanded

TABLE 1.1. Demographic and Background Characteristics*

Name	Age	Race/ Ethnicity	Gender	Education	Occupation/Field	Marital Status	Has Children
Aidan	27	White	Male	Associate's	Field technician	Married	No
Danny	23	White	Male	In college	Computer security**	Single	No
Gilbert	24	White	Male	Bachelor's	System administrator	Single	No
Harvey	41	White	Male	Bachelor's	Independent IT consultant	Married	No
Jensen	61	White	Male	Bachelor's	Technician/contractor	Married	—
John	30	White	Male	Some college	Web hosting manager	Married	No
Keith	27	White	Male	In college	Technician	Single	No
Miles	37	White	Male	Some college	Security research scientist	Single	No
Pete	35	White	Male	Honorary doctorate (otherwise, no advanced degrees)	Computer security researcher	Divorced	Yes
Raj	37	Indian	Male	Master's	Software development (customer-facing)	Single	No
Rick	50	White	Male	Bachelor's	Software engineer	Married	Yes
Roger	27	White	Male	In college	Retail	Single	No
Russell	~30	White	Male	Bachelor's	IT technician	Married	Yes
Susan	~37	White	Female	Bachelor's	IT management	Divorced?	Yes

* Some participants were vague or unwilling to be specific on certain demographic characteristics. Thus, approximations are presented for some (designated by '~'). In addition, some participants did not volunteer certain information. In these instances, the entry is left blank.
** As this participant is currently in school working towards a career goal, the occupation listed here is aspirational. Other participants in school, however, are currently employed in areas related to technology.

TABLE 1.2. Demographic and Background Characteristics (cont.)*

Name	Socio-Economic Class Growing Up	Father's Occupation	Mother's Occupation	First Exposure to Computers or Similar Technology (Age or period)	First Exposure to Idea of Hacking (Age or period)	First Exposure to Hacker Community (Age or period)
Aidan	Middle	Automotive mechanic	Respiratory therapist	~5–7	~12–14	~13
Danny	Middle	Engineer (Ph.D.)	Jeweler	~10–11	Seventh grade	~Seventh grade
Gilbert	Middle	Food scientist	Teacher	Elementary school	Before junior high	College
Harvey	Middle	"The professions"	Homemaker	~6	Before age 14	Early 1980s
Jensen	Middle	CPA	Portrait artist	Grade school	During college	1970s (with phone phreaking)
John	Middle	Stay-at-home parent	Lab technician	~5–6	Ninth grade	Twelfth grade
Keith	Middle	Computer programmer	Stay-at-home parent	~6–7	End of elementary school	~24
Miles	Upper-Middle	Middle-management	Stay-at-home parent	~Kindergarten	~12–16	Late 1980s
Pete	Middle	Marine	Stay-at-home parent/book retail	~6–8	Childhood	~16–17
Raj	Upper-Middle	Medical doctor	Beautician	~12	~7	~26
Rick	Upper-Middle	Engineer	—	Elementary school	High school	High school
Roger	Middle	Software engineer	Office sales	~8	Teenage years	Teenage years
Russell	Middle	Automotive mechanic	Mortgage company employee	~9–10	~12–14	21
Susan	Lower-Middle to Middle	Computer engineer	Homemaker	~4–5	Unsure	College

* Some participants were vague or unwilling to be specific on certain demographic characteristics. Thus, approximations are presented for some (designated by '~'). In addition, some participants did not volunteer certain information. In these instances, the entry is left blank.

discussions of the race and gender disparities found within Union Hack and the hacker community more generally. Class is not the only form of social stratification and such flagrant disproportionalities in race and gender worthy of at least a momentary discussion in their own right. While the frequencies provided are based on the interview data, observational study of DEF CON 21 participants also supports the general demographic distribution in this sample. These findings also parallel previous research on the age, race, gender, marital status, and education of hackers (Bachmann 2010; Schell, Dodge, and Moutsatsos 2002; Schell and Holt 2010; Taylor 1999).

Age

The age of participants in this study ranged from 23 to 61 years old with an approximate average of 34.71 and a median of 32.5 (some participants only gave approximate ages). As evidenced here, the members of Union Hack come from a wide arrangement of generations—perhaps a relatively unique feature of a group subjected to criminological inquiry. The oldest subject interviewed was Jensen. With grey hair, an easy demeanor, and an intensely deep knowledge of hacker history and technological lore, he grew up in a time before computers, becoming acquainted with technology through radio and audio equipment. Danny was the youngest participant interviewed. At age twenty-three, he was a spirited and anarchistic hacker who was born in an age overrun with computer technology (the Internet was almost always a part of his life). Though Danny was the most junior of the hackers interviewed, that is not to say there are not younger hackers. As will be discussed, many hackers get involved in technology early in life. Many children and teenagers were observed participating in hacker culture during the course of the field research. Some of the older participants even brought their children to enculturate them into the hacker community. For ethical considerations, these minors were not interviewed.

As previously argued, not all hackers conform to the stereotypical image of the computer vandal. Those who have engaged in illegal activities or otherwise got themselves into trouble did so when they were much younger, typically during adolescent years through early twenties (see Yar 2005). Such results are unsurprising, however, as this is consistent with prior research on the age-crime curve (Gottfredson and Hirschi 1990). Self-identification with the hacker community also does not seem to correlate with level of involvement in criminal activity. In other words, self-identification as a hacker does not appear to hinge on previous or current involvement in computer crime. For those hackers who do engage in criminal activity later in the life course, there appears to be variation in frequency and duration of offending, with some drifting in and out of illicit activity over time.

Family Status

Hackers are often stereotyped as anti-social loners, spending hours in front of a computer monitor in lieu of human interaction. Ignoring that such a stereotype is rendered problematic by the presence of the hacker community (and evident in the volume of loquacious and sociable individuals I met over the course of the research), this perception is further eroded by the presence of marital and familial ties, like parenting, present among the interviewees and further noted in observations. Just like most other groups, hackers as social creatures who may seek affection, intimacy, camaraderie, and even familial bonding (Coleman 2010, 2013). In this study, five of the interview participants were married at the time of research with two being either divorced or separated from long-term relationships. Of the unmarried or never married, four are under the age of 30—an age group where being unmarried is more likely generally. Additionally, four of the interviewees had children. One of the interview participants, in fact, was the son of an older participant.

Socio-Economic Status

In a finding that will be revisited again towards the end of this chapter (and will reemerge in part 2 of this book), all of the interview participants in this study perceived themselves as members of the middle class or some variant thereof in this study. Of course, most persons—regardless of their actual socio-economic position in society—tend to regard themselves as middle class. It would make sense, however, that hackers tend to be of the middle class because of the relative privilege such economic positioning affords. In addition, the following two subsections concerning occupation and educational attainment are associated with such class positioning. Even among hackers who engage in illicit activity, middle-class stationing is apparent. Consistent with research on juvenile delinquency, white-collar crime, drug use, and other areas of criminological inqury, criminality is not the exclusive purview of the poor.

Occupation

At the time of research, ten interviewees were employed in legitimate technology sector occupations including systems administration, programming, and technician work. One participant was in school (otherwise unemployed) and working towards a job in computer security at the time of study. Two participants, while their jobs did not involve technical work directly, were employed in management and customer relations in technology industries. One participant held a non-technical retail job. In general, though, the participants held occupations compatible with their interests in technology and hacking. If they did not, then they at least professed a desire to work in such an area. While not an absolute, hackers have a tendency to gravitate toward white-collar jobs. Though only gleaned through observation, it appeared that younger hackers, however, much like their non-hacker peers, are still likely to work in menial or service sector jobs when employed. Such are the disadvantages of youth in the contemporary job market.

Educational Attainment

Unlike many populations characterized as criminal or deviant, the hackers in this study were relatively educated. All of the interviewees had acquired some form of higher education with the exception of one who subsequently was awarded with an honorary doctorate. At the time of the study, two persons had attended some college, three were enrolled in college, one had attained an Associate's degree, six had Bachelor's degrees, and one had a Master's degree. These results are mirrored in the demographics research conducted by Michael Bachmann (2010) and Bernadette Schell, John Dodge, and Steve Moutsatsos (2002). The disproportionately high attainment of higher education degrees may be, at least partially, a result of economic privilege (see Reay et al. 2001). While many of the participants had some form of higher education, participation in these institutions is not necessary for inclusion in the hacker community. As Raj, one of the participants, explained, "The good thing about programming is that some of the best programmers I know don't have a college degree. Some of the best *hackers* out there don't have a college degree." Regardless, there appears to be a connection between education attainment and participation in hacker culture.

Race

As noted in other studies, this examination similarly found a tremendous racial representation gap among hackers (Bachmann 2010; Schell, Dodge, and Moutsatsos 2002; Schell and Melnychuk 2010; Söderberg 2008; Taylor 1999). Thirteen interviewees were white with one person being of Indian (non-Native American) descent. The conclusion drawn here is that the majority of members of the hacker community appear to be white. Similarly, observations made during field research seem to support such conclusions. Of course, the distribution presented here also belies some of the diversity present in the community. While observational data seem to confirm a white majority, it is not exclusively so. For instance, at the various Union Hack meetings, there were at least two African American men who would intermittently attend along with a regular attendee of Iranian descent. An Asian American woman also attended three meetings during the time of my research. At DEF CON 21, numerous members of other racial/ethnic backgrounds could be found scattered throughout the convention. Regardless, the conclusion that the majority of the hacking community is white is hard to avoid.

When pressed, some of the participants discussed why there may be such underrepresentation of people of color in the community. Some admitted to giving it relatively little thought. "Union Hack as a group, I'm not sure why," Aidan stated. "Yeah, I honestly have no idea. I never really thought about it." Harvey, drawing from works like Richard Herrnstein and Charles Murray's (1996) *The Bell Curve*, states that it may be down to differences "in how people are wired." He elaborates by stating, "One thing is that if you are . . . if your roots are developed in a cold place where there is nothing to do but abstraction, you are going to be more geared toward it. And probably better at it. I am familiar with the IQ test differentials. I am familiar with . . . *The Bell Curve*, Murray, Jensen, and all that. . . . I think those things, we should not shy away from them but we should be very careful about how we approach them." In other words, Harvey offers potential biological/biosocial explanations for representational differences, though he does offer a note of caution about such accounts.

Raj explained the disparity as a result of a "numbers game" potentially related to structures of opportunity. "I think it's just a numbers game, man. It's a numbers game or . . . you know, what ethnic subgroups are actually pursuing higher education? I mean, you have a group of twenty black, twenty Hispanic, twenty Asian kids . . . eighteen of the Asian ones are going to go to college, five of the blacks, and probably five of the Hispanics. And from them its . . . Okay, well, four are going to major in computer science and they got a good one out of the other bunch here . . . But it's . . . It comes down to a numbers game." Research on differential structural opportunities seems to support Raj's position to some degree, however, particularly insights from racial/ethnic underrepresentation in STEM (science, technology, engineering, and math). While the gap is closing, there is a prominent underrepresentation of minorities, particularly African Americans and Hispanics, in these areas (National Science Foundation 2013). Reasons for this underrepresentation "are complex and exist at several levels (individual, family, the educational system, the workplace, and in society at large)" (Burke and Mattis 2007, x–xi). In other words, various environmental, institutional, or structural barriers exist to obstruct racial minority participation—similar obstacles may exist for membership in the hacker community. In addition, racial differences may also be linked to class divisions. The history of race in the West has been built on political economy and intimately linked to class structures (Gans 2005). The marriage of race and class has also contributed to the differential availability of opportunities between racial groups and the poor generally, particularly in regard to opportunities for upward mobility (Wilson 1987). The connections between class and hacking may therefore involve broader social forces which marginalize many non-Whites, similar to those which may preclude proportional minority representation in STEM fields.

Gender

Much like the large disparity present between whites and other racial/ethnic groups, a similar gender gap is also present.[2] Thirteen out of 14 of the interviewees in the study were men. In observations of the hacking community, a gender disparity and a kind of technological masculinity is evident (Jordan and Taylor; Tanczer 2015; Taylor 1999; Turkle 1984; Yar 2005). That said, women do exist in the community and improvements in representation seem to be emerging over time (Kubitschko 2015). When asked about this gender gap, much like with race, many of the participants stated that they either did not know or had not thought about the issue. When explanations were offered, there were certain commonalities. For instance, some cited intrinsic differences between men and women as the cause, some of which were rooted in biology. "There's just different wiring," according to Harvey. Others situate these differences in early childhood development and socialization. Miles describes such a perspective by stating, "Women aren't—from a very young age—encouraged to do the things that would cause them to develop an interest in science and technology."

The cultural milieu of the hacker community and other STEM-related areas are also said to potentially push women away from participation. One such dynamic is a potential "creep" factor that some hackers may possess toward some women. "There is also an unfortunate culture which tends to view women in a very weird and creepy way," Harvey explains, "because there aren't many women known, it's like, 'oh, wow, female creature!' And then, you know, she gets . . . she can never escape being a woman." He goes on to explain that part of this may be a result of sexual objectification "the fact that the instant they walk into the room everybody wants to touch their breasts." At the root of such issues, Keith comments, is that there is a tendency toward a culture of masculinity and vulgarity among many hackers. Jensen claims that the competitive (masculine) drive in many hackers may also dissuade women from participation as well. When these factors, and others, are aggregated together, there are therefore a number of "barriers to entry" in place (Keith). In other words, as Miles states, the result is that "it's a stacked deck" against women. While these explanations are not a comprehensive, they at least reveal some diversity in perspectives toward gender representation in the hacker community.

One of the younger members of Union Hack, Roger, indicated that there may be a generational difference and that gender issues may be waning, "I feel like from a perspective where I haven't gotten to see maybe what the older generation has seen." He explains:

> I'm pretty used to women or females in my groups taking the same interests. Most of the girls in my group of friends are . . . we love to say "we love pretty women" because most of them are pretty attractive. And have the same interests. As gamers they can hold their own and talk at the same level forever about any topic we can think of. Games, psychological issues, political issues, philosophical issues. More video games, game industry. I'm extremely used to women holding their own. So, I don't even see a different aspect at all. But I do recognize that there is still is broadly overall not as many.

Perhaps there is reason for optimism in this regard—perhaps the gender barrier is, if not dissipating, at least becoming more permeable. That said, current events involving certain pockets of tech and video game culture indicate that tension still exists. For example, recent vitriol toward prominent "geek" or "nerd" women in the area of gaming has become startlingly evident given such controversies like the so-called Gamergate fiasco. The women targeted by Gamergaters spoke out against sexism and discrimination within gaming culture and the video game industry. As a result, some were met with insults, harassment, and even threats. Media critic Anita Sarkeesian received assault, rape, and death threats from men within gamer/tech culture for speaking out against sexism.[3] While there may be hope for gender equality, there is still work to be done—tech/hacker culture not excluded.

Further insights on the gender gap can be harvested from prior research in hacker culture. Taylor (1999), for instance, offers three possible explanations for this disparity. One is *societal factors*, such as gender roles, which tend to favor technical development as a masculine endeavor. Another is that the *masculine* (and sometimes misogynist) *environment* of hacker culture may deter women from participating. Men within hacker culture have ways of enacting masculinity—of "doing" gender (West and Zimmerman 1987). Such performativity and aesthetics create a cultural milieu sometimes steeped in a technological masculinity, which may be off-putting to many women. The final reason

Taylor (1999) gives specifically involves the *masculine language* used by men in the hacker community and STEM areas. Hacker exchanges are often steeped in technical jargon and an argot that can be male-centric. As a result of these factors identified by Taylor, women may be steered away from participation in hacker culture.

Additionally, the latter two dimensions that Taylor (1999) discusses parallel Turkle's (1984) exploration of hacking involving a culture of *computational masculinity*, dominated by young men. Such a culture is said to be concerned with technological and relational control. Similarly, Jordan and Taylor (2004, 117) summarize the issue in the following terms, "While it would be misleading to brand all hackers sexist, there is no denying the competitive, masculine nature of the hacking community." The result is a kind of "locker room" culture that "may discourage women from involvement in hacker circles and activities in spite of any genuine interests they might have" (Yar 2005, 394). Participant observation indicates that presence and acceptance of women may have changed (at least slightly) in the hacker community since these previous studies (Jordan and Taylor 2004; Taylor 1999; Turkle 1984; Yar 2005). A general culture of technological or computational masculinity, however, appears to persist.

Developmental Factors

The previously described demographic characteristics are vital for understanding the origins of hackers—they provide a snapshot of identity and stratification. These are not the only elements, however, that brew a hacker. Collectively, our lives are shaped by important players and liminal moments. Participants were hence asked about certain influences and events that may have influenced their trajectory as hackers. These include parental relationship dynamics, formal education experiences, and initial introductions to technology, the concept of hacking, and the hacker community. Each is discussed here in turn.

Parental Support and Influence

Parents. They brought us into this world (and, as my mother was fond of reminding my brother and I when we wore on her last nerve, they can take us out of it). They also help mold us into the people we become.[4] While some lessons can be directly administered, others can be more indirect and subtle. Parents can model behaviors, values, beliefs, attitudes, and other traits to the observant eyes of a child. As such, this study briefly explores how hackers may have been impacted by parentage. First, a description of a potential relationship between parents' occupations and the occupational pursuits of the participants is provided. Perceived levels of parental *support* for their interests in technology or hacking are then given. Support, however, concerns a more direct relationship between parental actions/vocalizations and hacker interests (e.g., "don't do that," "you're doing great," "try it like this"). Support therefore involves active efforts on behalf of parents to instruct and model proper personhood. Parents, however, may act in ways which otherwise influence hackers-in-development—those passive moments when a child indirectly learns through subtle messages not packaged as lessons, but instructive all the same. A mother fixing household appliances instead of buying new ones may teach a kid to value ingenuity and hands-on repair. A father spending his spare time tinkering in the garage indicates to a child that working with one's hands can be enjoyable and satisfying in and of itself. In this vein, this study also explores participants' descriptions of perceived parental *influence* as well.

PARENTS' OCCUPATIONS

First, there seems to be a relationship between their parents' occupations and the interests held by the participants. Twelve out of fourteen of the interviewees had at least one parent with some sort of technically oriented job with an equal proportion possessing some sort of white-collar job. The jobs held by their parents often involve some sort of hands-on or scientific orientation.

The jobs held by participants' parents seem to have a relationship with the participants' own interests and occupations. For example, Aidan adores robotics and hardware hacking. His father worked as an automotive mechanic and also performed machine repair. Similarly, Russell's father was a Harrier jet mechanic in the U.S. Marines. Russell describes himself as a "builder," interested in working hands-on with hardware and such—having done some of this in his previous job working in the Navy. In the area of software, Keith and Roger both had fathers who were involved in computer programming—a domain both of them share interests in as well. While the relationship between an interviewee's parents' occupations and their own interests are not perfectly associated, there seems to be a link for some.

PERCEIVED PARENTAL SUPPORT

The perceived levels of support parents' provided for technological development were also explored in this study. Here, eight interviewees asserted that their parents were overtly supportive of their interests in learning and technology. Roger, whose father was also a member of Union Hack and included in this study, explained, "I got into computers at a young age thanks to parents pushing me into it." For these participants, their parents actively supported their involvement in computers and related endeavors.

Five participants described their parents as not explicitly supporting their interests *but also not discouraging them either*—a sort of support by omission. These parents were viewed positively as they implicitly supported their efforts to learn about technology and hacking by not interfering or simply tolerating the behavior. Keith describes how his parents' reaction to him disassembling a computer when he was around ten years old, "I don't think that he [his father] was really that surprised. I think that his reaction was more of just the generic face palm kind of thing. My mother was much more angry about it. But I think they kind of realized it wasn't necessarily a bad thing. They . . . you know, that kind of curiosity that early would likely pay off later." When I probed further, asking if they were supportive of his behavior as long as it was not destructive, he replied, "Sort of . . . They were . . . They didn't discourage it actively. They put up with it." For Keith, the only behaviors related to computers and hacking that his parents did not support were his unhealthy sleeping and activity habits: "Anytime that I didn't have school the next morning I was on the computer 'til four or five or sometimes six or seven in the morning. And they had the understandable parental reaction of, 'that's probably not healthy.'"

In a similar way, Pete described how his parents encouraged him to learn, even if they did not necessarily understand what he was learning:

They've always . . . like, my mom has always encouraged my intelligence . . . And so she's always encouraged my music and the outlets of focus and helped me get structure. And she never really said, "don't be involved in computers." And I think she understood . . . she may not have understood what it is but I think she allowed for it to flourish. And my dad . . . you know, I used to ask a lot of questions when I was young. And my parents would do their best at answering them. So, I think, yeah . . . I think both of them really tried to encourage the constant effort of learning. And, you know, that's how I am. I live to learn. I live to improve.

In this context, Pete's parents were supportive of his efforts to learn. They may not have been overtly supportive of his interest in computers due to their own lack of understanding but they implicitly supported the behavior by providing an environment that "allowed for it to flourish."

Some parents provided both explicit and implicit support during technological development. For instance, Gilbert explained, "At first, my dad taught me how to use the computer. We had our first computer . . . Yeah, he taught me how to run commands from DOS [disk operating systems] and how to run things." When I prodded further about how his parents supported his involvement in computers, he elaborated: "I think to some extent it was just letting me explore without . . . They didn't try to stop me in any way . . . 'He's interested in this, let him do it.'" In this case, his father helped to push him into exploring computers but then stepped back and allowed for Gilbert's own interest and curiosity to take over.

Contrary to the previously described experiences, one interviewee, Miles, asserted that his parents were unsupportive of his efforts to learn outside the classroom. As he stated, "There were some complicating issues involving my family where I was . . . I didn't have . . . assistance from my parents and . . . In dealing with those things. And I was told, you know, basically everything was my fault so . . . But . . . I didn't really have a particularly social, supportive family." He further elaborated on his parents' perceptions of him being involved with computers, "They didn't understand it. . . . I think that they saw it as a word processor . . . and not something . . . not something to learn about in and of itself." In this manner, Miles claims his interests in computers occurred in *spite* of the parental support (or lack thereof) he received.

Finally, one interviewee, Harvey discussed how his parents, while initially not disapproving, became more unsupportive after he got in trouble for hacking. He describes his parents as specializing in staying unaware of most things at that point. And I don't think it was because they actually knew what was going on. But they sort of figured I was just doing stuff . . . But . . . yeah, I don't think they really noticed until they got calls from people who are interested in law enforcement. And then . . . They started to take notice and think things were bad. But I mean, you know, at that point I had been phreaking for a while and I knew how to wire up an external phone line and how to hide a modem, and all sorts of things. There was not much a parent could do.

Later, he elaborated further by stating, "I would say at the end of it, my parents really wanted me to stop playing with the computer."

PERCEIVED PARENTAL INFLUENCE

Beyond supporting participants' development as hackers—either through direct encouragement or providing an environment where they were free to pursue their interests—parents can also *influence* the proclivities of burgeoning hackers in other ways. Such influence is buried in the implicit activities which children are particularly adept at observing. Even though eight interviewees described their parents as explicitly supportive of their development, ten indicated that their parents were influential. John described learning to appreciate problem-solving and tinkering through his father: "My dad, you know, has all the time . . . putting kids through private school . . . is a pretty big financial drain on a single income family. And . . . so, my dad worked on a lot of things just to keep things going. And . . . he had . . . a pretty good approach to problem-solving. So, a lot of solving problems and kind of . . . Mac-Guyvering things came from him." In essence, according to John, his father influenced his appreciation of problem-solving and repairing. Russell describes his father, an auto-mechanic, having a similar influence, "I mean, I definitely tend to be more of a builder so . . . I mean, I think my father's influence in that of just fixing and learning how things work . . . Are really . . . really helped influence me."

Previously, Miles stated that his parents provided him with little to no support for his interests in learning and hacking. Despite this absence of support, he admits that his parents still had an influence: "My father was, you know, a reasonably intelligent guy and he had a lot of interests . . . You know, hunting, fishing, woodworking . . . you know, he could fix the lawnmower or he could . . . He could do shit. So, from when I was really very, very little, you know, I always had, you know, like, a little hammer and some nails and, you know, I could always make stuff." Miles' parents were said to influence his interests in security-related issues because his mother "was kind of afraid of everything" which supposedly encouraged a distorted fear of the world around him. In addition, his curiosity about security was said to be triggered by his parents because they "would always be in my shit." Those parental experiences allegedly triggered an interest in constructing and deconstructing security systems through hacking. Miles, then, despite having an unsupportive family environment, still claims to have been shaped by the context his parents provided.

Parental influence, however, may not involve a clean transfer. There is the possibility that parents' interests may negatively influence developing hackers away from technology. At an early age, Susan describes being exposed to computers and instruction in programming. As she left for college, however, the exposure to computers temporarily drove her away from working with them. When asked if her parents influenced her interests, she stated:

> Actually had the opposite effect. That's why my undergraduate degree is in psychology. So, I just had a lot of exposure to computers. All growing up they [computers] were all very easy and, for me, it was a normal part of life. And I think if you look at computer people, you see that they aren't very social and they are a little bit nerdy. And kind of like the way I rebelled against that was to pick up something that was very socially oriented . . . I mean neuroscience not so much . . . I chose psychology and then I picked something within psychology that was a little bit more challenging.

In this scenario, Susan describes how her parents, particularly her father, influenced her interests in computers and her skills as a programmer. The problem was that this influence eventually drove her away. Now, while she is still relatively skilled, she chooses to focus on a lot of the social components of the hacker community.

Only two of the interviewees asserted that their parents did not have an influence on their interests in hacking and computers. Aidan summarizes this absence when asked about the influence his parents' may have had: "Not at all, really. Neither one of them are very technically savvy. Pretty much nobody in my family was really very technically savvy. So, I mean, the personal computer thing wasn't . . . I pretty much did all of that on my own. And it was, pretty much getting everything myself. There wasn't really interest in it in my family." Raj described his parents' influence a similar manner, "Yeah, that was all me. They weren't pushing me to . . . to learn about it [computers] one way or the other." In both cases, the interviewees asserted that their parents had no or little influence on their interests in technology and hacking.

School Experiences

As children grow older, the number of people and institutions in their lives proliferates. Though parents may disproportionately care for many children at an early age, another institution becomes a central point of contact: schools. To explore the role of formal education in their development, participants were asked about their experiences with these institutions, both in grade school and higher education. In grade school, the interviewees reported a wide range of disparate experiences. Public schools were largely associated with negative experiences such as anti-educational peer climate. When asked about why he loathed public school so much, Roger stated, "It was inefficient. You'd get crowded in with a whole bunch of kids . . . Teachers are way overworked . . . You hated being there every moment because no one wants to be there and you are putting a whole bunch of people who really hate being there with a whole bunch of people that don't know or care to learn . . . It was horrible."

"Busy work"—assignments given to keep a student busy rather than intellectually engaged—was also cited as a problem. As Keith explained, "Essentially they gave you a large packet of work . . . The packets were largely worksheets and fill-in-the-blank problems and things like that that were just essentially 'look through the book for this keyword and fill it in.' There was nothing engaging at all about it so I didn't bother." In these educational settings, particularly in public schools, some of the interviewees reported feeling unengaged with the material—a lack of challenge was present. Jensen described a sense of apathy towards grade school because it was too easy which supposedly induced him to be an "underachiever" with "high IQ versus low performance."

Other interviewees reported more positive experiences in education. These tended to involve private schools of different sorts. These schools were thought to be more focused and more engaging. John describes his experience in a Catholic high school:

> There is definitely a different atmosphere in terms of what you're responsible for and not being held to a lot of standards that are . . . And I . . . Having a bit more focused expectation on the kids, you know . . . saying, "John, you are responsible for these few things. Either you do it or you don't do it. And that determines whether you succeed," [and that] lends itself to a better education. And the smaller class sizes. You know your teachers. And in this case we grew up with the same kids from kindergarten and, at that point, in high school with the same four sets of kids for four years too.

In this explanation, John describes a sense of satisfaction with his education having a more customized approach to learning with smaller classes and familiarity in his cohort. Roger also compares his seemingly dismal public school experience with that of private school:

> That was actually a fantastic experience. I was learning at a much quicker pace. Classes were smaller and more intimate. In my grade level there was about eight or nine of us. Sometimes there were a few classes that mashed up with a few people of lower grade levels so they would run up to like 13 or 15. And it was still pretty big. Teachers were very knowledgeable and we were learning . . . we were learning at a much more rapid rate. We were learning ahead of grade levels. I was passing classes with 90s. There was no homework. It was very . . . It was very efficient and very useful.

School was thus more enjoyable because of the more efficient learning structures and the absence of what Keith identified as "busy work." Overall, the education experience was considered better when the environment was perceived as engaging, challenging, and efficient.

For some of the interviewees, their experiences in higher education were also problematic. The alleged uselessness of some courses was rejected by Rick:

By that time I was already way smarter about computers than almost anybody else that was in school because very few people actually had computers. But I had literally two years full-time experience messing with computers and other hacker groups and other things. And so when I went back I went, "okay, now, now that I know what to do with them and there is somebody that's going to actually teach me how to deal with them." That was, like, awesome. So, when you go to college—you've been to college [gesturing towards me]—you go and they tell you, "okay, you're a freshman. Well, everybody has to take English and History and Political Science and all of these other crappy-ass classes that nobody wants to take. Everybody has to take them." And so I did that like my first year and suffered through a bunch of classes but I had a computer class and I aced it and was like, "this is awesome!" But you can only take one and I'm like, "what? That's kind of fucked."

In this experience, Rick expresses frustration with being forced to take classes in which he was uninterested. In this sense, learning *generally* is not necessarily the objective. Rather, the desire is to learning about a specific topic of interest. Overall, the interviewees expressed appreciation for school when the environment endorsed challenging, engaged learning over topics of interest. Indeed, participants with these experiences reported the highest GPAs—A averages being more likely. School experiences seemed to be viewed negatively if the learning was overly simplistic, unengaging, unchallenging, or perceived as irrelevant, which were subsequently reflected in more reported C-average grade performances.

Introductions to Technology, Hacking, and the Hacker Community

Though often passed by with little pomp and circumstance, there are moments in our lives which help define our life course, even if we sometimes cannot fully grasp their gravity at the time. This analysis attempts to chart some of these milestones that occur in the hacker upbringing—events that *must* occur at some point for a person to become a member of the hacker community. Examined are participants' introductions to (1) computers or related electronics, (2) the idea of hacking, and (3) the broader hacker community. As argued here, each of these represents a pivotal moment in bringing a person close and closer to subcultural embeddedness. This analysis attempts to document these events and at what point they occurred during the life course. Of note, since the interviewees were asked to recall time period of exposure, dates and ages often lack specificity. The results are still useful because they provide a temporal approximation.

INTRODUCTION TO TECHNOLOGY

The ages in which the interviewees reported first experiencing technology (mechanical or computer) were generally around pre-adolescence, ranging from approximately four to twelve years old. For many, these machines were viewed with a sense of wonder and curiosity. Perhaps this age is vital for hackers as few other age groups are capable of such immediate and visceral fascination as children—and few are capable of doing so in a way that cements such interest for life. This section will briefly provide snapshots of the hacker recollections before providing insight into their common elements.

For many of these participants (n = 10) first exposure occurred at home. Aidan describes his first experience when his father picked up a TI (Texas Instruments) machine that "took cartridges similar to Atari cartridges. It had the gold fingers on it and . . . you had to do everything manually through the keyboard. It plugged into a RGB [red, green, blue] video port on your TV so you could load it up on the TV and you had to basically manually do everything on there. You couldn't save but it was very similar to Atari and had all kinds of stuff. I can't remember a lot but you could pretty much do anything on that." For Keith:

> I was probably six or seven . . . somewhere in that general vicinity when I first was using a computer on my own. I remember being amazed when my father brought home his first laptop. It was one of the old ones that . . . brand DOS. It had the hinge in the middle of the computer where the screen was only, you know, half the depth of the computer. I know that when I was probably eight or nine we got our first upgrade for that computer, where I think his job actually furnished a new computer for us. I wound up taking the old one apart [laughs] and getting into a rather large amount of trouble for doing so.

For these hackers exposed at home, computers were things that embedded themselves into the private sphere. They were lugged into the home and became permanent fixtures—objects of wonder nestled atop familiar desks or connected to recognizable devices like televisions and phones, transforming them into something else entirely.

Others came to technology through peers. Harvey describes his first exposure occurring around the age of 6 through some friends in his neighborhood, "I knew a number of people who had Apple II's . . . and, before that, there were things like Kaypro's and a number of those older CP/M [Control Program for Microcomputers] machines because we were in a neighborhood with a lot of engineers." In this case, friendships (and their parents' occupations) facilitated his introduction to computing technology. Computers, in this manner, were immediately set up as social devices. Sure, they could be worked on in isolation, but they also were a way to connect to with others, even in their immediate social sphere.

Sometimes first exposures can be from an institutional setting, like schools. Miles describes his first run-in with computers in kindergarten: "By a series of coincidences combined with [the] social strata of my classmates . . . we had probably the first computer lab in the city. And we started out with crap like MasterType and MathBlaster on the original Apple II, I think, even before the 2e and 2+ came out." Rick, on the other hand, describes his first exposure with computers involving going to his father's place of employment and watching a massive computer at work: "So, he brought me down there to watch with this punch card thing to put it in the things. They [the programmers] gave it to the monkeys behind the glass [the computer engineers] who ran it and we sat and waited . . . At the time it was a form of early daisy wheel printer, but it, you know, was this spinning disk with all the letters on the outside and it went 'bahp, bahp, bahp, bahp, bahp, bahp, bahp' [printer sounds] and I watched that for an hour and thought it was the coolest thing ever."

In a business setting, children are seldom encouraged to tinker with technology—particularly because computers during this time were extraordinarily expensive. As such, Rick differentiates between his initial contact with computers and his first *hands-on* experience, which occurred at school: "But my first experience *using* a computer was actually in elementary school where they actually brought teletype terminal and clunked it down in the middle of the classroom. It was the, I guess it must've been fifth grade, it was the special day for people to come in and tell you about stuff when you are going to grow up and kind of things, and somebody came in to tell us about this computer. So, we played *Adventure* on the Teletype. The Crowley and Woods original" (emphasis added). *Adventure*, or *Colossal Cave Adventure*, was a text-based adventure game produced in the 1970s. Even in these school environments, kids could crowd around these black-screened relics and engross themselves in an interactive narrative. It is not hard to imagine the allure for kids, particularly those already interested in technology.

Indeed, video games seemed to play a key role in some of the participants' initiations to computing (see Holt 2010a). Rick described playing *Adventure* on the Teletype. Miles's first experiences involved educational games. Right after his exposure to the Texas Instruments machine, Aidan counts using the old Atari 2600, a gaming console, among some of his earliest experiences. John recounts his first exposure involving his father's Commodore 64 and the game *Haunted Hill*. While Harvey was never a big gamer, he communicates the importance that video games hold in triggering interest for a number of hackers, "I think video games got us, a lot of us, into it because that was how you started learning to write your own code and how to de-protect it." Many games incorporate various copy-protection methods. Early introductions into hacking activities, for some, emerged from learning circumvention techniques for these measures (see Downing 2011).

As previously stated, most of the early exposures to computing technology occurred at an early age for the participants—pre-adolescence—similar to the findings of Holt (2010a). In addition, these recollections were given with a sense of nostalgia. Even the most seemingly insignificant details are recounted with a smile and a glint in the eyes. For children, these are machines of mysticism and wonder. They are almost magical. They are not just means to an end—for kids these objects are fascinating in and of themselves. Kids are seldom satisfied with surface appearances. They want to dig deeper. They ask probing questions, go venturing off looking for caves to explore, and, in some cases, crack open computer hardware to see what makes them tick. Perhaps this nostalgia stems from memories formed when the world was still a place that was largely unknown—but potentially magical and ready for exploration. To develop as a hacker, it may be important to harness childhood fascination, parental support, and surplus time at an early age to foster the competencies necessary to be a successful hacker later in life.

My own experiences with technology make it easy to understand this allure and subsequent nostalgia. My first exposure to computing occurred with the old Nintendo Entertainment System video game console. I remember running my fingers along the golden prongs within the cartridges with a kind of reverence. I can still recall the feeling of the boxy controller in my hands as I scooted across the floor to negate the glare from our living room window across our 19 inch tube television. My brother and I would take turns passing the controller back and forth as we tried to get past the second level of Mega Man 2. These kinds of experiences and memories build an enduring interest and adoration—a potential propulsion for future interests in computing technology.

INTRODUCTION TO HACKING

For most of the interview participants (n = 8), exposure to the idea of hacking came after their introduction to computers. For three of the participants, the experiences with computers and hacking as a concept were so close together temporally that charting a clean timeline is difficult. One participant was unfortunately uncertain of when they first came across the term "hacker." Of those who did recollect, however, eight occurred around adolescence (approximately twelve to sixteen years old), four were pre-adolescent (younger than twelve years old), and one (older) hacker was post-adolescent and in college.

Additionally, eight interviewees were able to remember *how* they came across the term (the others were uncertain). For some, their introduction to hacking—as a formal concept—emerged from their social connections (n = 3). For instance, Harvey was scripting war dialers as a kid: "But anyway, we were writing this little war dialer to dial all night long and return numbers . . . interesting numbers to us. And I remember being told that was hacking." Importantly, Harvey was engaging in hacker-like behaviors *before* exposure to the idea of hacking. Most of the other interviewees were similarly involved in hackery behaviors and patterns before they came across hacking as a more formal concept.

Some participants came across the idea of hackers through media (n = 4). Russell describes hearing the term while seeing the movie on a date: "I've always been interested in how things worked but I remember seeing . . . seeing the cheesy movie Hackers in the theater . . . It was one of my first dates. And I remember going to see that and I was like, 'I never thought of making machines do something that they weren't supposed to do.' And I do remember that it was kind of pivotal like, 'there is a hacker subculture. There is, like, a subculture called hackers that are all about computers.' And I was like, 'I got to look more into that.' And so that is kind of my . . . the movie Hackers actually had an influence on me [laughs]." In this scenario, like Harvey, Russell was already doing a lot of things some would consider to be in the realm of hacking. He began to associate with the term and becoming interested in pursuing the hacker culture as a result of his exposure to a movie.

For some, the 1983 movie *WarGames* was their first exposure, a not uncommon experience among hackers of that generation. As Coleman (2012, 105–106) explains, "Apparently the movie appeals to a slew of nerdy types across Europe, Latin America, and the United States, leading them to incessantly demand from their parents a PC [personal computer] and modem, which once they got, commanded their attention while they were logged on for hours on [BBSs]." As such, it seems that media constructions simultaneously arose from the hacking community as well as engendered further growth and popularity of hacking recursively.

Unlike the previously discussed cases, Danny described first coming across the hacker community through exploration on the Internet: "I've been poking around in them [computers] since I was maybe ten or eleven but I didn't really find out what I was doing, or even really what 'hacking' was, until about seventh grade. That was when I started reading the Happy Hacker website by Carolyn Meyer. I learned later about some infighting that had been going on between her and some other people, and that served as my introduction to hacker drama. After that, I eventually moved on to textfiles.com and from there to *Phrack*, *2600*, and HackThisSite, and from there to where I'm at now." (HappyHacker. net is a website specifically dedicated to providing a safe place for fledgling hackers to build their skills).

INTRODUCTION TO THE HACKER COMMUNITY

For almost all of the interviewees, exposure to the hacker community came after their first experiences with computers or introductions to the idea of hacking. The majority of these interviewees came across the community around adolescence (n = 8). The remainder were exposed around college or sometime in their mid-20s (n = 6). In other words, interest in hacking seems to pull people toward the hacker community. While some of the hackers developed peer associations that helped get them interested in hacking, their own drive seems to work recursively with social relationships to pull them deeper down the rabbit hole of hacker subculture.

Six of the interviewees were introduced to the hacker community through electronic means such as BBSs and online forums. Miles describes his first exposure through BBSs: "I think that was about the time I got my first modem and started dialing into BBSs. And at that point, now I had . . . people, you know, somewhat that I could communicate with. And that's actually, you know, where I met some of my best friends." His experience with groups which met physically came later. As BBSs became less common and the World Wide Web became prominent, more hackers found the community through the Internet in venues like online discussion boards. As Aidan elaborates in response to being asked about his first exposure to the hacking community: "The hacking community . . . was online forums. It was after the BBS days. There wasn't . . . BBSs weren't a big thing but it was starting to get more geared towards forum based stuff so . . . I was involved in several of those." In these cases, the subjects were already familiar with the idea of hacking but became involved in the hacker community through electronic means. An overt physical hacker community was not readily apparent and, as such, using telecommunications to connect to others with similar interests were used. For Danny, it should be noted that his first exposure to the idea of hacking—which occurred online—was also his first exposure to the hacking community. Unlike the others, his first exposure to the community occurred in tandem with exposure to the idea of hacking.

Face-to-face hacker groups, however, served as the introduction to the community for eight of the participants, one of which was Union Hack specifically. Susan describes being taken to her first Union Hack meeting in college—where she ironically majored in psychology/neuroscience to break away from computers: "I think it was probably . . . It probably wasn't until college when someone brought me to a Union Hack meeting . . . It was a bunch of people hanging out in [location omitted] talking about the . . . I mean, a lot of it was nostalgia and stuff people had done on BBSs and that was kind of my coming up to speed with it. Just people talking about different things they did. I think as I started going to more and more meetings there were actually people who are very active." Gilbert described his first experience with a hacker group in similar terms, "I guess I would say my first serious involvement with what I consider the hacker community would be. . . . Wouldn't be until college when I joined a [programming group]. So that was in-person." John had his first exposure through a subcultural zine which then led him to a Union Hack group meeting. In all of these cases, the authors were introduced to a face-to-face group after they were already (1) personally interested (or at least skilled) in computers and (2) exposed to the idea of hacking.

Conclusion: Hacking as a Middle-Class Phenomenon

The results presented in this chapter serve to qualitatively situate hackers in a demographic and developmental context. Such an analysis is worthwhile because hackers do not emerge from the *ether*, ready to code or crack. Hackers, like everyone else, have personal histories that propel them through their life course. In exploring these factors, it was uncovered that—according to the interview data—ages ranged from twenty-three to sixty-one with an average in the mid-thirties. Generally, the participants were white, perceptibly middle-class males employed legitimately in technological occupations. In terms of education, the majority of the participants had degrees beyond high school diplomas or were working towards such degrees. Notable demographic imbalances exist as well and were briefly discussed, notably those concerning race/ethnicity and gender gaps.

Beyond demographic characteristics of hackers, this study also examined developmental factors that may have helped influence interviewees' participation in hacking. The results of the school experiences data show that hackers seem to fare better in educational environments that challenge and promote specialized learning in areas of their interest. Additionally, efficiency seemed to be valued in education—work that did not directly contribute to learning (i.e., "busy work") was frowned upon. While hackers generally tended to express a preference for private schools over public, this is a result of the particular educational environment these schools were seen to provide rather than any particular aversion to government-sponsored education generally.

Parents were also explored as a potential influential factor in development as hackers. Participants' parents overall seemed to hold technological occupations, which indicates that parents may share or transmit proclivities towards technology. At the very least, such occupational preferences may have demonstrated to participants that work with technology was a viable life choice. Parents' occupations also further solidify the connection between hackers and middle-class status; most parents held traditional middle-class occupations that provided the funds to afford computer technology.

Additionally, the participants' accounts of parental support and influence point to an environment that, for most, fostered the interest and autonomy to engage technology made available to them. Generally parents appeared to support the participants' engagement with technology or, at minimum, did not obstruct their engagement. Even if support was not provided, many hackers reported parents at least influencing their interests and development in various ways. Overall, while measuring the magnitude of any sort of effect parents may have had on participants, there seems to be a relationship that, for most, nurtured their development and interests.

Finally, participants were asked about periods in which they were first exposed to computing (or related) technology, the idea of hacking, and the hacker community. The hackers in this study reported initiations into technology at an early age, usually pre-adolescence. The participants' introduction to the idea of hacking usually followed after exposure to technology during adolescence. Introductions to the hacking community predominantly happened later in adolescence or after. These results indicate that, generally speaking, there seems to be a temporal ordering for exposure and development that begins at an early age. Interest in technology comes first and then a person drifts towards hacking as a behavioral and cultural outlet towards adolescence. Once the hacker subscribes to the notion of hacking, participation in the community seems to follow. That said, some seem to associate with other hackers before self-identification as one occurs (which seems to happen in tandem with exposure to the idea of hacking).

Of primary concern for the overall project advanced in this work is that many of these factors uncovered through this analysis indicate that hacking is a heavily *class-based* phenomenon. Their self-identification as middle class, school experiences, parental occupations, peer relationships, and other factors all point to this conclusion. The sample for this study, however, is relatively small. The astute reader may begin asking about the generalizability of such a claim that hacking is a largely middle-class phenomenon. Fortunately, this study is not the first to make such an observation, at least among hackers in the West. Johan Söderberg (2008, 28) states that "[a] quick glance is all it takes to confirm that the social base of the hacker movement is heavily skewed towards *middle-class* males living in the West" (emphasis added). For Douglas Thomas (2002, xiii), "the typical hacker is a white, suburban, *middle-class* boy, most likely in high school" (emphasis mine). Alan McConchie (2015, 881) similarly concludes that "hackers are overwhelmingly male, white, and from *privileged economic positions*." Even science fiction author and futurist Bruce Sterling (1992, 59) acknowledges that hackers "often come from fairly well-to-do middle-class backgrounds."

Practically speaking, it would make sense that hackers would come from middle- or upper-class socio-economic backgrounds, if only based on the raw cost of the high technology necessary to become involved as a hacker, particularly at an early age. While the cost of technology is declining over time, access to computer hardware—notably during the period most of these participants were children or adolescents—is often costly and out of reach for many without some sort of surplus finances. For example, some of the participants in their late thirties and older grew up in a period where few households had access to computers compared to today. The Apple II was one of the first personal computers some of the older participants had access to. This computer, one of the first to gain even a modicum of popularity, was approximately $1,200 (for a bare-bones model) in 1977. According to the Bureau of Labor Statistics inflation calculator, a $1,200 computer in 1977 would cost approximately $4,600 today. This estimate does not account for the cost of any additional hardware, software, or any other devices necessary for learning. In short, there seems to be a cost barrier to entry for hacking.

Indeed, the relative ease with which the middle and upper classes can overcome such cost barriers may also help explain why hackers are often exposed to high technology so early in life. Remember, for ten of the participants, their first exposures to technology were at home. Even though computers are getting more affordable over time, having a computer was still a luxury even up to fifteen years ago (and still is for many). Being able to afford computers is more likely to occur for those in the middle and upper classes. There may be some truth to the notion that, to become a reasonably competent hacker, economic privilege helps. While not required, there is an advantage in having enough resources to begin working with computers at an early age. In addition, recall that many of the home environments described by the participants—from parental occupations to support and influences towards technological development—seem to indicate that much of their development was situated in a seemingly middle-class family context. As such, beyond such financial privilege that may have been afforded, middle-class environments are often more conducive for educational stimulation, which may also impact an individual's trajectory towards hacking.

Additionally, racial/ethnic disparities seen in the hacker community may also be linked to class as persons from minority backgrounds are much more likely—through various historical, cultural, social, and economic forces—to be disadvantaged economically. As such, class may also help to explain the lack of presence of racial/ethnic minorities, though other forces of structural disadvantage may also be at work as well.

The educational experiences and backgrounds of the hackers also point towards middle-class existence. If we were to look only at educational attainment, a link can be seen between participants' largely middle-class upbringing and developmental context and their likelihood of obtaining higher education degrees. After all, the likelihood of obtaining a college degree increases as one moves up to socio-economic ladder (see Reay et al. 2001). Going to college can be hard enough. It is difficult to deny that persons from relatively impoverished backgrounds would face additional barriers as college can be an expensive experience, more so now than in previous decades. As such, persons from middle-class backgrounds are in a relatively privileged position, which can go a long way towards supporting someone through college (though, such advantages may be dwindling as social inequality and the stagnation of the middle class persists)—not to mention the more tacit social advantages that such upbringing may yield towards higher education. Other research on hackers and hacker culture has similarly found that hackers are generally above average in education levels, with many having "at least a community college education" (Schell and Holt 2010, 201; see also Turgeman-Goldschmidt 2011). Indeed, Bachmann's (2010) demographic study of hackers found that 89.5 percent of the hackers in his sample had at least *some* college, 65.3 percent had at least a college degree, and 27.4 percent had post-graduate degrees, education attainment rates far above average.

Indeed, evidence exists that supports the notion that hackers become middle class during their lives if they did not begin there in childhood. Among the hackers in Union Hack, the majority were gainfully employed as white-collar workers in the tech sector at the time of the research. Research by Schell, Dodge, and Moutsatsos (2002, 111) found that hackers approaching thirty years of age or older were likely to be "gainfully employed" with a mean salary of $56,081 (see also Schell and Holt 2010). Similarly, Orly Turgeman-Goldschmidt (2011, 35) reported "above average" income levels for the hackers examined in her sample.

All of this is not to say that persons coming from more disadvantaged backgrounds are wholly excluded from the hacker community. There are certainly members who circumvent these barriers and find ways to access technology. In fact, the origins of the hacker community at MIT involved instances of early hackers finding ways to access the enormously expensive computers available at the time (Levy 1984). Additionally, some hackers are known to scrounge or dumpster dive to acquire computer parts. Regardless, the argument presented here is that because (1) it is *easier* for a person from a middle-class background to access technology, and (2) middle-class upbringings may yield social advantages conducive for interest in—and development of skill toward—technology, hacking appears to be a predominantly middle-class phenomenon, at least in the United States.

To summarize, while multiple factors were explored in this chapter that may influence a hacker's development, many of them seem to indicate that hacking is largely a middle-class affair. Such a simple conclusion has profound implications. Recognizing a class-based disparity in the hacker community opens up the analysis for further inquiry in the broader forces that shape the political economic landscape, which creates the conditions for the individual development of hackers as described here. As contended in chapter 4, Marxist and radical criminological thought helps synthesize the findings in this chapter and others into a broader context. Before delving into the broader political economics of hacking, however, this study now moves to the next level of analysis—subcultural. In doing this, the question "what is a hacker?" is explored, yielding a result that only further indicates political economic issues surrounding hacking.

2

Craft(y)ness

By examining personal demographic and historical characteristics of hackers, chapter 1 establishes a link between hacking and class. This chapter progresses forward through levels of analysis—from individual to group and subcultural dynamics.[1] In particular, this chapter addresses the seemingly straightforward—yet crucial—question: "What *is* a hacker exactly?" For many in the public, hacking is synonymous with technocrime and other forms of technological malfeasance, an image shaped through social construction, predominantly through the media (Halbert 1997; Hollinger 1991; Skibell 2002; Taylor 1999; Wall 2012; Yar 2013). When pressed further to describe what is involved in hacking and who becomes a hacker, certainty gives way to confusion, and most people struggle to explain hacking beyond computers and a symbolic connection to criminality. They might even use their hands to pantomime typing on a computer and snatching money from the air. The details, however, are a mystery to most. In this manner, hacking has become "suffused with symbolic uncertainty as media messages and cultural traces swirl, circulate, and vacillate" (Ferrell, Hayward, and Young 2008, 124).

This chapter thus attempts to fan out the smoke and kick over the mirrors. An understanding of hacking based on mythology is not useful for social science.[2] Definitions are extraordinarily important because "the terms of everyday language, like the concepts that they express, are always ambiguous and the scientist who employed them in the ordinary way without further explanation would lay himself open to the most serious confusion" (Durkheim [1987] 2006, 15). If we are to understand hacker subculture, then it makes sense to ground our definition in the meanings that hackers have created around the concept, particularly as hacker understandings can differ wildly from popular conceptions.

Based on my ethnographic research, hacking is perhaps best thought of as a kind of labor. Many noteworthy studies in criminology have previously found links between deviant, or criminal, activities and work (see Adler 2003; Fagan and Freeman 1999; King and Chambliss 1984; Letkemann 1973; Sutherland 1937; Tunnell 2006).[3] What distinguishes this study from previous works is the *form* of labor that hacking most closely resembles—*craftwork*. Popular conceptualizations often indicate that any singular act—from writing code to data theft—is enough to brand a person as a hacker. Hacking, however, is more a process of *becoming*, much like how Howard Becker (1963) described the dynamics through which a person *becomes* a marijuana user. As a person does not become a craftworker overnight or possess a legitimate claim to such a title by picking up a hammer and hitting a few nails, a deviant act and a few lines of code do not a hacker make. Both craftwork and hacking are processes of development, refinement, and expression.

To make the argument that hacking is a kind of craft, this study draws from three different—yet complementary—theoretical foundations. The first is Richard Sennett's (2008) *The Craftsman*, a sociological work about the process of craftwork and, importantly, how this distinct form of skilled labor is linked to personal and societal dynamics. In other words, the way a person works with their hands helps shape their perceptions and beliefs, which in turn has social implications. Sennett's work then has direct implications for political economic analyses, particularly from a Marxist perspective including Marx's discussions of alienation, species-being, and exploitation. Additionally, as Thomas (2002) has pointed out, hacking as a cultural phenomenon has developed alongside technology, indicating that perhaps the reason for such parallel progression is at least partially a result of direct hands-on work with technology.

The epistemic approach used in this analysis is phenomenological eidetic reduction. This technique of social analysis is concerned with isolating the eidos—essence—of a particular object (Heap 1981; Palermo 1978). An essence is defined as "what is invariant and common to all possible examples of some phenomenon" and it is "what is common to a set of individual items" (Heap 1981, 300, 302). The idea is that the philosopher "'brackets' the natural world and world of interpretation in order to see the phenomenon in its essence" (Finlay 2008, 2). At its core, then, eidetic reduction is about taking an object—hacking in this case—and reducing it to those qualities that are essential for its qualification. This approach is interested in isolating those qualities that, distinct from any individual hacker, compose the *eidos* of hacking. To put it another way, this project seeks to generate a description of the socio-symbolic components that distinguish hacking as a distinct social and cultural phenomenon—to find the essence of hacking.[4]

In addition to eidetic reduction, this analysis engages in what cultural criminology identifies as the *politics of meaning* (Ferrell 2013). Cultural criminology is a relative newcomer to criminology but it has deep roots, drawing inspiration from Chicago School–style subcultural theory, Marxism, anarchism, symbolic interactionism or labeling theory, phenomenology, and theoretical thought on late modernity to create an orientation that situates the immediate lived experience of crime and crime control in the turbulence of late modern capitalism (Ferrell, Hayward, and Young 2008). Though sometimes accused of resulting in a theoretical soup, cultural criminology provides a powerful framework in which to conduct qualitative analyses and connect micro- and subcultural-level dynamics to broader social trends and issues.[5]

In the context of cultural criminology, the politics of meaning refers to "the contested social and cultural processes by which situations are defined, individuals and groups are categorized, and human consequences are understood . . . meaning can be seen to be a constitutive element of human action and a foundation of human culture—an ongoing, everyday process of sense-making, symbolic communication, and contested understanding" (Ferrell 2013, 258). As previously described, hacking is a concept with heavily contested meanings which arise from the hacking subculture, the media, and even agents and agencies of social control (Halbert 1997; Hollinger 1991; Skibell 2002; Taylor 1999; Wall 2012; Yar 2013). These meanings exist in tension with each other, often with the latter two sources dominating public perceptions. The current analysis seeks to cut through these "contested social and cultural processes" to create an understanding of hacking rooted in the subculture from which it emerges—one that pulls itself away from narratives largely manufactured and controlled by politics and the media (Ferrell 2013, 258).[6]

Craft, as understood in this analysis, can be defined as "doing something well for its own sake." According to Sennett (2006, 104), "Self-discipline and self-criticism adhere in all domains of craftsmanship; standards matter, and the pursuit of quality ideally becomes an end in itself."[7] The dynamics of craft run deep in hacking. Eight components of hacking as craftwork will be described. These include: (1) a particular

TABLE 2.1. Components of Hacking*

Theme	Interviewees (%)	Articles (%)
The Hacker Mentality	14 (100%)	124 (64.25%)
Skill	13 (92.86%)	33 (17.10%)
Ownership	11 (78.57%)	118 (61.14%)
Hacking as a Guild	10 (71.43%)	50 (25.91%)
Commitment	10 (71.43%)	25 (12.95%)
Journey over Destination	9 (64.29%)	23 (11.92%)
The Hacker Experience	10 (71.43%)	20 (10.36%)
Hacking as Transgression	13 (92.86%)	86 (44.56%)

* Frequencies from participant observation data are omitted because of the difficulty presented by creating distinct counts from this type of data.

mentality, (2) an emphasis on skill, (3) a sense of ownership, (4), social and learning structures with parallels to guilds, (5) commitment, (6) an emphasis on means over ends, (7) an emotional or phenomenological experience, and (8) an underlying transgressive edge. Following a description of these features, this analysis advances a succinct but arguably comprehensive definition of hacking.[8]

The data from which the conclusions in this chapter are drawn include both ethnographic field research—in the form of participant observation and semi-structured interviews—and content analysis (CA) of *2600: The Hacker Quarterly* (refer to the introduction). Throughout the results, primarily interview and content analysis data are presented to allow the themes to be expressed in the participants' own words, though participant observation did inform the analysis tremendously. Frequencies and percentages for the various themes discussed in this analysis are given in table 2.1.

The Hacker Mentality

In my opinion, you can't be a hacker without a certain mindset . . . It doesn't matter if you are talking about a person who uses that mindset as a 3-D modeler or a security researcher . . . or in cyber espionage offense security . . . they all have the same characteristics. But what we need to realize is that the acts that could be referred to as a hack . . . You kind of need to understand the mindset of the person who performed that act.

In this excerpt from an interview with Keith, a member of Union Hack, he indicates that the mentality—the thought processes—of an individual are vital for being a hacker (interviewees = 14; 100%; CA items = 124; 64.25%). To *be* a hacker, one must *think* like a hacker. In the course of sifting through the ethnographic data, five key components of a hacker mentality were identified including *curiosity, problem-solving, systematic and technical thinking, creative and unorthodox thinking,* and an *orientation towards breaking and creating.* Discussing the hacker mentality is important as such thought processes are shaped by direct work with technology in what Sennett (2008, 9) describes as "the intimate connection between hand and head." By examining the mental components, we can identify hacking as a relatively unique subcultural phenomenon. Through its direct work with technology, hacking permits close parallels to be made between it and craftwork.

Curiosity

The first component of the hacking mentality involves a deep *curiosity*, which serves as a vital link between hacking and craft in the sense described by Sennett (2008, 120): "All of his or her [the craftsperson's] efforts to do good-quality work depend on curiosity about the material at hand." In interviews, observations, and the content analysis data, curiosity was repeatedly described as a feature of thinking like a hacker. For instance, in an interview Russell states, "So, to me, it's more like curiosity of . . . what can it do? What can I make it do to make my life easier?" In his descriptions of hackers, Bruce Schneier (2006, 26) echoes this sentiment in a *2600* article: "A hacker is someone who thinks outside the box. It's someone who discards conventional wisdom, and does something else instead. It's someone who looks at the edge and wonders what's beyond. It's someone who sees a set of rules and wonders what happens if you don't follow them. A hacker is someone who experiments with the limitations of a system for intellectual *curiosity*" (emphasis added). Perhaps stating the point more succinctly, Dr. Zoltan (2008, 57) describes hacking as "exploration, led by curiosity." Curiosity thus seems to be key to thinking like a hacker—indeed, at times this curiosity can be quite intense and lead a hacker onto trouble's doorstep.

In an article written for *Phrack*, The Mentor (1986)—a (in)famous figure among the early hacker underground—wrote an article entitled "The Conscience of a Hacker" (sometimes referred to as "The Hacker Manifesto"). While making a series of claims about the hacker mindset amid a broader social context of increasing scrutiny and mistrust of hackers, The Mentor states: "Yes, I am a criminal. My crime is that of *curiosity*" (emphasis added).

Problem-Solving Orientation

The second feature of the hacker mentality is a *problem-solving orientation*, providing another link between hacking and craft in their ability to identify problems and solve them (Sennett 2008). Hackers, above all things, focus on overcoming some sort of obstacle. These obstacles can include puzzles, problems, or any similar challenge. Hacking, however, is not about *achieving* the goal *per se*; rather, hacking is embedded in the *process* of achieving the goals. Even when hackers have a goal in mind—from developing a program to stealing information—the essence of hacking itself is woven into the process, rather than the goal itself. In sharing his mentality towards hacking, Jensen discussed that he wants to solve projects above almost anything. He admitted that overcoming obstacles could sometimes keep him up at night "obsessing over it."

From *2600*, ternarybit (2012, 26) describes the components of hacking, invoking a problem-solving orientation as a key element. The questions surrounding the nature of hacking are rooted in a false definition that situates hackers primarily by what they do rather than who they are: "Hackerdom, rather, comprises a broad set of faculties and proclivities that I believe everyone possesses to some degree: critical thinking, creativity, inquisitiveness, *problem-solving skills*, and a hunger for knowledge, to name only a few" (emphasis added). Likewise, MS-Luddite (2008, 19) describes the hacker mentality as encompassed almost entirely by the desire to solve problems: "I guess I am a bit biased, but I am a true believer in what I call the 'Hack Factor.' I define this factor as that certain something inside a hacker that simply drives them until a solution to a problem is found." This problem-solving orientation stems from working directly with technology—it allows a person to fumble with an object, find a problem, and then seek out a solution. In this way, the hacker is oriented towards both "problem-solving and problem-finding" in the same way as the craftperson—such as a brick worker or musician—struggles with tasks at hand, yet continues to seek ways to overcome deficits in their knowledge or skill (Sennett 2008, 9).

Systematic and Technical Thinking

Systematic and technical approaches are also part of the hacker mentality. This component perhaps is the most apparent in its parallels to craftwork—with the ability to approach a problem in a manner that is efficient and structured. In this sense, thinking like a hacker is not just about being able to think creatively and critically. It is also important to think in a systematic fashion. For instance, Raj describes the process as similar to an if-then loop approach in programming:

> You are like, "Okay, you know, well, I want to run a brute force attack." And I would try to brute force attack to this port. "Oh, that port is closed so it must be running on something else. Let me do a port scan. You know, to see what port it might be running on. Okay, well, I don't know exactly which one but I've got a pretty good feeling its either A, B, C, D, E, or F. So let me try those." So, I go through systematically those. And all of a sudden I go through, you know, "Okay, well, I think I found one. Let me see what type of response I get." So, it's just kind of like working through an analytical process. In your head like, "This didn't work . . . Okay, well . . ." It's basically, you know, in computer programming, there's the concept of the if-then statement . . . It's one big if-then statement.

Part of the technical component of thinking like a hacker involves valuing efficiency. The mental energies involved in hacking not only dictate that a working solution be developed, but it must be an efficient solution since, as one hacker (Gilbert) told me, there is no sense in doing something if someone else already did it more efficiently and effectively. Harvey describes this mindset in greater detail: "I'm in the PHP configuration file, I'm dicking around . . . [and I think] 'And you know what? I bet I can shave a couple cycles if I use this command instead of that command' . . . or if I write a specialized function that does this this way as opposed to that. I get all excited. And that, that is to me what hacking is." As a result, some hackers tend to think of the hacking enterprise as scientific due to its emphasis on approaching problems and projects in a systematic and efficient manner. As Bill Squire (2006, 26) states, "Don't forget: hacking is scientific."

This process of thinking through problems systematically is important as it streamlines the aforementioned process between problem-finding and problem-solving. Such an orientation provides hackers with the mental facilities to solve problems in a structured and efficient manner. In addition, inefficiency and complexity become problems themselves to find and solve. Problems can be more easily identified and addressed in a systematic manner, but streamlining the process of labor itself for efficiency is a problem worth exploring on its own. Thus, there is a reciprocal relationship between problem-solving or problem-finding and systematic and technical thinking.

Creative and Unconventional Thinking

Creativity and unconventional thinking is highlighted as a component of thinking like a hacker. It is not enough to approach problems in a logical and critical capacity; one has to be willing to think about such problems in an unorthodox manner as well. *2600* author Ninja_of_Comp (2011, 31) describes this creativity as thinking "outside the box" to "look for different ways to solve a problem." This component of the hacker mentality involves looking at "the things everyone else sees, but in a new and different way that's not immediately apparent" (Torrone 2006, 26).

Interviewee Rick also describes this creative unorthodoxy through a metaphor:

> So . . . I mean, you've seen a cage. You've probably seen a jail with all those bars. Some people see the bars. Some people see the *spaces between the bars*. We always saw the spaces between the bars. And we're always baffled that other people didn't see the spaces between the bars . . . It just seemed, like, that in my mind, from when we were in high school and there were gaping, gaping flaws in other people's perceptions. They'd go, "There's bars!" And you'd go, "There's bars this

far apart [places hands about ten inches apart]. Turn sideways and there's no bars." And they say, "No, there's bars." And you're like just . . . [laughs] people refuse to get it.

In "seeing the spaces between the bars," Rick highlights the importance of being able to see things in an unconventional way—an approach reminiscent of Gestalt psychology. The participant elaborates by saying:

> For me it's more of the MIT definition . . . You know, the concept of, you know, you're taking things beyond . . . It's an out-of-the-box kind of mindset. You look at things and go . . . You turn your head sideways and turn your head different ways and you say . . . 'Can I attack this in a different way?' And it's not always an attack . . . like, 'I want to break into' . . . but can we think about this differently? And can we make it do things that we normally wouldn't expect it to? And you can take it above and beyond and it's part of innovating and it's motivated purely by curiosity.

Clearly, then, creativity is a strongly held value for thinking like a hacker. In addition, greater prestige is given towards creativity that inverts standard ways of thinking. As such, this component of the hacker mentality can be summarized as *creative unconventionality*. Such creative unconventionality is yet another feature further connecting hacking and craftwork as well—most notably in the difficulty of separating art from craft, as both seem to be mutually dependent. Additionally, Sennett (2008) also describes the idea that craftsmanship often involves taking tools designed for one specific purpose and using them for alternative purposes instead—*improvisation*, a greatly valued ability amongst hackers, is an example of the value of creativity and unconventionality in craftwork. The problem-solving orientation, systematic and technical thinking, and creative unorthodoxy combine together into what Sennett refers to as "practical creativity" (30).

Orientation of Breaking and Creating

The final component of thinking like a hacker involves a mindset that aims to dissect and disassemble things and then either rebuild them in a new way or create an extension or addition. Aidan summarizes the breaking component of hacking: "[Hacking is] basically taking it apart to see if you can put it back together again. I mean, it's tinkering . . . figuring out what makes it do what it does and . . . ways to break it. That's . . . pretty much what I've always tried to do and that's still what I do . . . try to break things." Echoing this sentiment, *2600* editor Emmanuel Goldstein (2005, 4) asserts, "Computers, telephones, hardware of other sorts, and software of all types exist to be tinkered with, stretched to their limits, modified, taken apart, broken, and fixed. That's all part of the learning process."

The way of thinking about things in terms of their ability to "be tinkered with, stretched to their limits, modified, taken apart, broken, and fixed" also echoes the craftsperson's desire to fix things as a method of learning. As Sennett (2008, 199) states: "Put simply, it is by fixing things that we often get to understand how they work." While the act of simply repairing something and putting it back together is referred to as a *static* repair, it is the *dynamic* repairs that are a key part of hacking culture. Dynamic repairs "will change the object's current form or function once it is reassembled" (200).

To summarize, this research indicates that a hacker is a person who is (a) curious, (b) focused on solving problems or enthused by puzzles, (c) appreciative of systematic and technical approaches to thinking, (d) creative and unorthodox, and (e) focused on dissecting and the art of creation and recreation. This mentality is not only key to understanding hacking as a phenomenon, but it also serves to qualify hacking as a kind of craft. With establishing the role that a particular mentality plays in hacking and how that mentality links to craft, this discussion now turns toward the next component of hacking, an emphasis on *skill*.

Skill

When writing about professional thieves, Edwin Sutherland (1937, 14) stated that "a thief is not a professional until he is proficient." A thief must have developed a degree of *skill* to be appreciated as a professional in his or her trade. Similarly, hacking also heavily emphasizes the development and exercise of skill, particularly in work with high technology (interviewees = 13; 92.86%; CA items = 33; 17.10%) (see also Holt 2010b; Taylor 1999; Turkle 1984). Defined as "a trained practice," skill permeates both hacking and craftwork: "All craftsmanship is founded on skill developed to a high degree" (Sennett, 2008, 37, 20). Skill, as opposed to talent, also implies that such ability to craft had to be honed over time through work and dedication. Hacking places such a degree of emphasis on skill that acts that do not demonstrate such proficiency are often not considered authentic hacks. As Raj demonstrates:

> When a guy posts a piece of code online and says, "Hey, I discovered this . . . the super-user escalation privilege bug . . . in every Linux kernel prior to 26.26," and then . . . So, you log in, you download the source, you compile it, and you're like, "Wow . . . I can get super-user access for any Linux system prior to this kernel." And then you see . . . that this Russian guy wrote a bunch of code that I can't really understand but I can compile it . . . and I can make use of his work. You see, that type of person, to me, is a hacker. The person that spent hours, you know, figuring out that Java sandbox bypass . . . and used it to basically shed the theory that Macs were . . . they were not exploitable.[9] That guy, to me, is a real hacker. The person who is doing social engineering or dumpster diving or asking you when your birthday is and what your kid's name is . . . to try to do a dictionary attack on your system, that's not hacking in my book.

As Raj explains, those who initially took the time to develop and exercise their skill in the creation of a new hack are legitimate hackers, while those who merely perform uninventive attacks and ready-made scripts are not. In these cases, skill is the marker of hackerdom.

Hacking often conjures up imagery of technological wizardry and magic as a mechanism of communicating the raw level of skill a person is able to demonstrate. For instance, Rick describes the early hacking developments of Steve Wozniak: "If you look at the Apple world and the shit Woz did, it was crazy. People cannot even grasp the shit he did. He basically made a color computer out of nothing. Almost magic. Just by changing timing and seeing what happened on the computer. I mean, he used, like, no chips." In fact, the very process of *becoming* a hacker involves both the development of skill and the recognition of such skill by other members in the community. Take, for example, Sutherland's (1937, viii) description of professional thieves: "No one is a professional thief unless he is recognized as such by other professional thieves." Nick Farr (2008, 26) describes this social dynamic among hackers:

> Most of the people in the room, however, are "newbies." They're off to the side, fascinated by these hackers making cool things out of a pile of parts. Through careful observation, some idle chatter, and a few questions about the work in progress, they're getting a clearer idea of what these small components do and how they come together . . . In a few Mondays, after getting a little experience with a soldering iron, a few code samples, a bit of encouragement, and a kit of their own, a few of these newbies will start contributing ideas and hacks of their own—and be recognized by their peers as fellow hackers.

Consistent with the notion that hacking is more about *becoming* than "is" or "is not," the more a person develops and expresses skill, the closer they move toward the subcultural ideal of "hacker." Finding a measurable threshold a person crosses to become a hacker, however, is likely impossible. Instead, members of the hacking community must subculturally and situationally negotiate their position as a hacker through the development, possession, and execution of skill.[10]

Sennett (2008, 20) describes the relationship between craft and skill as one where, "as skill progresses, it becomes more problem-attuned." In this sense, there is a strong relationship between the development of skills for hackers and the problem-solving orientation previously described. In this vein, Joseph Battaglia (2006, 50) describes hacking as the application of skill towards overcoming a challenge: "Working for such entities certainly isn't for everyone but it's full of challenges and, if you can accept the restrictions that go along with it, you'll find that it's a great arena in which to test your skills. It's a new challenge, and we're all hackers. Let's get to work." Further, Sennett (2008, 26) states that "the experimental rhythm of problem-solving and problem-finding makes the ancient potter and the modern programmer members of the same tribe." Hacking involves not just a process of problem-solving but, as skill increases, the ability to find problems to solve. In fact, problem-solving and problem-finding are vital to the process of skill development.

Ownership

When an artisan pursues a craft, there is an intimately close relationship that develops between themselves, their tools, and the
created objects. Through the input of time, skill, and labor, the artisan pours themselves into the object, leaving their mark on it or, in
some cases, literally branding their work (Sennett 2008). In addition,
"craftsmanship requires *mastering and owning* a particular domain of
knowledge" (Sennett 2006, 115; emphasis mine). In this manner, the
craftsperson possesses a sense of ownership over the craft. They are
relatively unalienated in their labor, highly autonomous, and invested
in their work. Through the exercise of what Levy (1984) refers to as
the "hands-on imperative" and by thoroughly investing themselves in
understanding and working with technology, hackers come to possess
a degree of ownership over their craft and its products (interviewees =
11; 78.57%; CA items = 118; 61.14%). For both hackers and artisans, such
ownership can be said to occur in two capacities: ownership over the
act of labor itself and a sense of ownership over technology. As uncovered in this study, hackers, as artisans, take ownership over their craft
in multiple ways.

First, to really own something—to acquire mastery—one should be
intimately knowledgeable about it. Craftspersons spend years honing
their skills and refining their knowledge. Good tradepersons are characterized by their deep knowledge of the items with which they work—
from the raw materials they use to their tools. Similarly, hackers strive
to learn what they can—the deeper the understanding, the better. Part
of gaining this understanding comes with taking things apart. Harvey
describes this aspect of hacking: "If you want to learn to program, you
should learn to hack in some way. I'm not saying go bust into some bank
or whatever but I mean . . . to really know how a machine works, you
have to tear it down." Much like mechanics who possess the skill to take
a car apart and reassemble it, hackers break systems down as a means
of acquiring both skill *and* a deeper understanding of how things work.
In order to fully understand a system, hackers begin by "looking under
the hood."

Hackers also demonstrate ownership over technology through the
breaking of restrictions on software and hardware. Two types of re-

strictions are of importance: technological and legal. In either case, the implementation of restrictions on technology means that a party outside of the relationship between hackers and technology is asserting control on the nature of that relationship. Rick describes going to hacker parties as a youth where the participants created methods for breaking software copy-protection mechanisms. He describes the rationality as such, "The goal is to *make the computer do what you want it to do*. Not what somebody else wants it to do . . . The computer answers to me. Not . . . not to you" (emphasis added). According to Rick, both technological and legislative restrictions—in the form of copy-protection methods and copyright law—were circumvented because both obstructed the relationship between themselves (hackers) and the computer.

Even if we look at computer intrusions instead of cracking, the concept of ownership still applies.[11] When a security hacker breaks into a system and secures control, the system is then said to be "owned." At DEF CON 21, there were two wireless networks set up—one "secure" and one unsecure ("secure" is placed in quotations because, by the end of the convention, that network had been thoroughly compromised). The unsecure network was set up specifically for various hackers to experiment and battle in an attempt to break through each other's security: that is, to "own" someone else's system. In fact, one of the most well-known contests at DEF CON involves Capture the Flag. This game consists of teams of hackers defending and attacking computer systems. Victory is secured when one team can "own" an objective.

The modification of technology also demonstrates an ownership over software and hardware. For Goldstein (2007, 4), hacking is about learning and circumventing restrictions so that one can modify the hardware or software:

> If anything were to sum up what every single one of our articles has had in common over all these years, it's that desire to find out just a little bit more, to modify the parameters in a unique way, to be the first to figure out how to achieve a completely different result. Whether we're talking about getting around a barrier put in place to prevent you from accessing a distant phone number or a restricted computer system, or cracking the security of some bit of software so that you can modify it to perform

functions never dreamed of by its inventors, or revealing some corporate secrets about how things really work in the world of networks and security—it's all about finding out something and sharing it with anyone interested enough to listen and learn.

Even open-source software programming/hacking is tied to the idea of ownership. The very notion that code is open for any and all to comb through, modify, contribute to, splinter from, co-opt, etc. means that each contributor, in a sense, owns the project. In proprietary software, the company owns the software and the source code is closed off to the public. Copy-protection measures are put in place to prevent piracy—thus securing the ownership of the software for the copyright holder. Hackers, however, break the restrictions (as previously described) to prevent the program from being restricted to them. In either sense, hackers seem to desire a closer relationship to the code—a sense of ownership.

Such assertions of ownership also invoke the notions of autonomy, independence, and freedom. These likely spring from the perspective of liberalism permeating hacker culture (Coleman and Golub 2008). As such, the close relationship between the artisan and hacker, their tools, and their objects of labor point towards a greater political struggle occurring within the act of hacking—resistance against control and the value of autonomy (as will be further articulated in chapters 3 and 4 with discussions of technological and economic liberalism).

Hacking as a Guild: Self-Sufficiency and Group Learning

Guilds are groups of artisans who work together to develop and control the practice of their craft. These social structures often invoke images of a bygone era before mass-industrialization and Taylorism where individuals devoted their lives to a craft, working as apprentices and progressing up to mastery status, passing their knowledge onto their own apprentices and so forth. Outside of specialized shops, guild structures seem to have been nearly obliterated in modern times. Guilds, however, seem to persist in small pockets of society, becoming almost subversive in their manifestations. As argued here, one of the areas in which guild social and learning structures seem to have persisted is within the hacker community (interviewees = 10; 71.43%; CA items = 50; 25.91%).

Craftspersons within guilds typically (historically and contemporarily) operate individually or in small groups, and only to come together when necessary to control and develop the trade (Sennett 2008). Hacker social and learning dynamics take on similar qualities. For instance, the activity of hacking often involves a tremendous degree of autonomous motivation and learning. As Miles describes in an interview, "They tend to be introverted, they tend to be self-started. Self-starters. Self-learning." In a similar fashion, Valnour (2009, 32) describes his experience in learning to hack through language borrowed from the Star Wars franchise: "I was beginning to identify with the hacker world, but very much considered myself a padawan [apprentice] without a master. I am sure many of you can identify with me at that age." In this way, there is *some* truth to the stereotype that hackers tend to be loners. Often hacking is a solitary activity involving long hours in front a computer or other piece of technology, working away on a project or problem. The idea of *the individual* is very much valued.[12] This emphasis on the individual is similar to trades, where the craftsperson is at the center. In a factory setting, the task of building a car, for example, is divided between many different workers—emphasis is on the group. For the artisan, the production process is largely in the hands of individual workers.

While there is an emphasis on autonomy in guilds, the individual does not operate within a void. The maker must be trained, typically through a master-apprentice relationship. Additionally, the artisan will learn, teach, and work within the context of the guild. While not conforming to the pre-industrialization image of the craftsperson and the guild, hackers have similar social and learning dynamics modified in the age of the Internet. In this way, the direct relationship between hackers' work with technology and technological progress mediates and influences social interactions as well (Thomas 2002). As Russell comments, these learning mechanisms are vital because learning to hack in complete isolation can be difficult: "It's also one of the problems of knowledge. . . . You've got level one where . . . you are too ignorant to know what you don't know. So, you can't really form the questions. So, you don't know what to ask to advance." In this sense, learning from others accelerates the rate of learning by filling in the gaps in knowledge that

might otherwise take a tremendous amount of time to overcome in isolation. In other words, social learning is important for development as a
hacker (Holt 2010a).

In my own experience as a participant observer, I similarly found
pure self-learning to be difficult and that interaction and mentorship are
important. After my third meeting at Union Hack, I saw a few members
picking locks at a local bar (practice locks, not the bar's). I knew that
lock picking had been practiced in the early MIT days of hacking but
was unaware that the practice was still so prominent. After watching,
I became very interested in learning to do it myself. The problem was,
as Russell stated earlier, I was in a position where I was so ignorant on
the topic that I "didn't know what I didn't know." As such, I had pushed
learning to pick locks onto the backburner. At DEF CON, however, I
had the opportunity to participate in a tutorial at the lock-picking vil-
lage (the convention hosted a number of "villages," which were common areas for the practice and discussion of particular areas of hacking).
After learning some of the basics, I had a firm enough handle on the
practice to engage in more successful and productive self-learning. So
while my individual efforts were still important, I had to learn from
persons more knowledgeable than myself to accelerate my education.

Sharing knowledge is a strong component of the hacker community.
It is not enough to learn individually. Rather, one needs to share the
information one accumulates to benefit the entire community. Prettis
(2009, 28) describes the benefits of such an approach: "Sharing files is
really satisfying and being able to create objects from other people's tried
and true design files will make it easier for folks who are just getting
interested in rapid prototyping to get started. Sharing is something that
makes the world a better place." Sharing is a core component of hacking
culture much like how the exchange of new information and techniques
was key in the function of trade guilds.

On the heels of such an emphasis on sharing, various mechanisms
of knowledge-transmission have developed in the hacker community
akin to apprenticeship. First, more direct one-on-one mentorship relationships can occur. In an interview, Danny describes his early hacker
education experiences. One notable relationship involved a friend he
met online who showed him how to engage in various hacking-related
activities. For instance, he was taught (through having it done on him-

self) how to engage in "dropping dox"—an act which involves breaking through an individual's perceived sense of anonymity by uncovering personal details about them, often ending with the delivery of documents or "dox" to the target. In this way, Danny was directly mentored.

A second manifestation of apprenticeship in the hacker community is group learning. Reflecting on a time before Web 2.0, Rick describes his first encounter with a hacker group. He indicated that his learning accelerated when he was among others capable of teaching him various tricks of the trade, such as bypassing early forms of software copy protections. In one instance, he describes how such group learning dynamics unfolded in this group that he began working with:

> They met like once . . . Once a month or so. And brought all the stuff to somebody else's house who volunteered or had the most plugs and horizontal space. Everybody would swap software and then they taught you about hardware tricks you didn't know. Like, the Apple II was a one-sided floppy machine. Everybody knew that. It had a write-protect slot on the side of the disk so if you punched . . . If it had a hole—a notch—cut in it, you could write on the disk . . . You stuck a piece of tape over it, you couldn't write on the disk. It was protected. And so it turns out, single-sided and double-sided floppy disks are exactly the same. And made on the same lines. They're just not verified on both sides. They ship it on there. But if you turned the disk over, you got a hole punch and you punched a hole in that spot . . . You can write on the back! Nobody told you that! The guys at the computer stores didn't tell you that. Nobody knew . . . These guys do. Everybody knew. Suddenly I had all of these blank discs. They were the backsides of all of my full discs. And I thought I had all these full discs.

This narrative demonstrates the value of group learning for hackers. Rick was able to learn about things he did not even know existed through participation in a hacker group.

Finally, the Internet and other computer networks serve as late-modern mechanisms for *vicarious* apprenticeship. Rick, Harvey, and Miles described learning about computers and hacking by accessing early bulletin board systems (BBSs) where users would upload text files to educate other hackers or would-be hackers. Danny, Keith, and Gilbert described learning from Internet message boards or other repositories such as HappyHacker.net. In this way, hackers write material to be accessed by other hackers, thus providing an indirect form of community mentorship reminiscent of guild trade books (Sennett 2008). Additionally, some of these digital localities are sources for others to ask questions in lieu of more direct mentoring relationships where they often are given the answers they seek or are told to RTFM, or "read the fucking manual" (see also Holt 2010a).[13]

Much like guild systems, hackers stratify the community on degrees of skill. In a guild, crafts are organized in terms of apprentices, journeymen, and masters (Sennett 2008). With increased skill comes a corresponding ascension up the ranks. In the hacking community, a similar stratification method is present. At the lowest skill level there are "script kiddies," "newbies" or "noobs." As one progresses in skill, one comes nearer to being a hacker. Someone can be considered to reach the level of master when they reach the "next level" (as described by Susan) and create an original, clever, and creative hack that required tremendous skill to pull off. In addition, one can gain recognition in the community through the demonstration of skillful and inventive hacks in these group settings—much in the same way as those afforded social rewards in workshop settings: "Organized into a system of guilds, the workshop provided other, more impersonal emotional rewards, most notably, honor in the city" (Sennett 2008, 53).

As demonstrated here, hacking can be considered a kind of late-modern guild. The individual is re-situated closer to the center of production—away from the de-centered model of modern production—while still emphasizing learning occurring in a mentorship and group context. In this space, the individual engaged in relations in two directions. The first involves an engagement with technology as something to be worked with, puzzled over, and learned about. This relationship is often conducted in relative isolation. The second is a social relationship with other likeminded people. Such relationships operate reciprocally and are mutually reinforcing—the stronger both of these relationships become, the stronger the hacker or craftsperson becomes. Additionally, the appeal of hacking also seems to rest, at least partially, in the ability to have one's cake and eat it too. That is, to operate relatively autonomously while also enjoy participating in a cultural learning environment with others who share similar dispositions and experiences. The influence of technology, though, is not only felt at the individual level. It also serves to mediate and influence many social interactions as well (Thomas 2002).

Commitment

To become a master craftsperson, one needs the determination, drive, and devotion to excel in their trade. Sennett (2008, 9) describes this as "commitment." Commitment has also been found to be important for work in other criminological areas (Fagan and Freeman 1999; Letkemann 1973). Likewise, hackers are characterized by a deep commitment towards their activities (interviewees = 10; 71.43%; CA items = 25; 12.95%). Susan summarizes this characteristic of the hacker eidos succinctly when she stated, "The thing about hackers is they love to learn," and "what it means to hack is to just take an interest in how things work." Roger describes hackers as "tech savvy, geeky people with big passionate interests." Further, Roger recognizes that it takes a lot of work and skill to become a hacker but, perhaps equally important, enthusiasm matters as well: "I think it takes actually a lot of study and a lot of homework and a lot of enthusiasm." *2600* author mirrorshades (2005, 50) describes the commitment of hackers in the following terms:

> I do what I do because I love computers. I believe that information is amoral on its own, and that what I do with it is my own decision. "What I do" is whatever I find interesting at the moment; I don't worry about right or wrong, profit or loss, reputation or credibility. There have been countless nights that I have stayed up past 3:00 am working on something that has no inherent value other than the knowledge I gain from doing it. What I do goes beyond interest, beyond hobby, beyond obsession. Can you say the same about anything, *anything* that you do? If you can't, then you have gone through life missing something.

As Turkle (1984, 207) stated in her study of early 1980s tech culture, hackers are "caught up in an intense need to master—to master perfectly—their medium." In this way, hacking and craftsmanship converge through commitment. Sennett (2006, 195) elaborates: "It's not simply that the obsessed, competitive craftsman may be committed to doing something well, but more that he or she believes in its objective value. A person can use the words *correct* and *right* in describing how well something is done only if he or she believes in an objective standard outside his or her own desires, indeed outside the sphere of rewards from others. Getting something right, even though it may get you nothing, is the spirit of true craftsmanship" (emphasis in original).

Journey over Destination

In many ways, the activity of hacking is not so much about technology or the challenge *per se*. Rather, hacking is at least partially embedded in the *process* of working with technology or overcoming an obstacle (interviewees = 9; 64.29%; CA items = 23; 11.92%). This further cements the relationship between hacking and craftwork because, as stated by Sennett (2008, 9), "craftsmanship names an enduring basic human impulse, *the desire to do a job well for its own sake*" (emphasis added). Such a perspective on craft is not unknown, as even C. Wright Mills (1959, 220) describes intellectual craftsmanship where "the satisfactions of working are their own reward." In this sense, as Susan has stated, "hacking is about the journey and the process," not the destination. Similarly, the process of hacking concerns "getting to that end result versus the end result itself . . . the journey being more important than the destination and all that," according to Aidan. Hailing back to the images of the American Wild West, hacker Danny describes hacking as "frontiersmanship"—thus equating hacking to trailblazing and finding new ground. In all cases, hacking is considered to be embedded in the *process* of accomplishing a goal or overcoming a challenge rather than the challenge itself. Such descriptions of hacking parallel the work of Turkle (1984, 201), reinforcing the connection between hacking and this dynamic of craftwork: "What is different for many hackers is that the means-ends relationship is dropped. The fascination is with the machine itself. Contact with the tool is its own reward." In the same year as Turkle's study, Levy (1984, 23) similarly described the "hack" as "a project undertaken or a product built not solely to fulfill some constructive goal, but with some wild pleasure taken in mere involvement."

For artisans, the process of crafting becomes less about the end product of their labor than the labor itself. The craft is in the making rather than the made. Similarly, hacking is more about the process than the end result. In discussing the matter with Keith, he stated that successfully overcoming an obstacle or accomplishing a goal is not necessarily needed to be engaged in hacking: "I might argue that you don't necessarily need the outcome. Because, let's face it, anybody in the community—anybody who associates themselves even loosely with the term hacker—has come up with an inventive, ingenious, absolutely amazing hack using whatever knowledge they happen to have in whatever field they happen to be working in . . . and it didn't do anything. It just doesn't work." Likewise, when engaging in craftsmanship, failure is inevitable in the process of creating works. One learns through these failures. Hacking represents this, as much of the process is trial-and-error. Success is important for advancement as it allows new lessons to be learned and new challenges to be met. The *process* of achieving success or failure, however, is what qualifies an activity as craftsmanship or hacking.[14] If the process of hacking matters so much, then so too must the *experience*. It is toward the relationship between the emotional experience of hacking and craftwork that we now turn.

The Hacker Experience

The deviant experience itself—with all of its emotional passions and perils—is a viable and important area of inquiry (Ferrell, Hayward, and Young 2008; Hayward 2004; Katz 1988). Such an endeavor is dedicated towards moving beyond the 'background' factors of criminality to the 'foreground'—thus illuminating the significance of the immediate experience and participation in crime and deviance (Hayward 2004; Katz 1988). Little academic attention thus far has been given to the emotionality and lived experience of hacking, however. Through the ethnographic data underpinning this analysis, certain experiential components appear to be important for isolating the *eidos* of hacking—components that also mirror craft as well (interviewees = 10; 71.43%; CA items = 20; 10.36%). While some variation exists in these sensational experiences, there are two discrete arrangements of feelings that correspond to different stages of hacking. The first occur during the *process of hacking* and the second manifest upon *completing a hack*.

The Process of Hacking

Upon initial inspection, the described feelings encountered by the participants seem almost discouraging. For many, tedium and frustration are intricately interwoven into the process of hacking. Keith elaborates on the sometimes-mundane nature of security hacking: "Sure, some of it can be automated, some of it can be scripted, but a lot of it is just really tedious and repetitive." The unpleasant experience of frustration can also manifest when failure is encountered too often. "Trying to figure out how something works and not getting the right answer," Susan explains, "is a little bit like being tortured."

Tedium is a result of the often-mundane parts of overcoming a challenge while frustration often comes from experiencing failure. Willingness to fail (and to fully experience these negative stimuli), however, is important for development as a craftsperson (Sennett 2008). Similarly, hackers are no strangers to failure, as *2600* author Altman (2007, 16) elucidates: "The first big system I tried to hack was me. Like many of my first hacks, it wasn't successful." The frustrations experienced in the process of hacking may encourage advancement and adaptation in the act of craftsmanship. "Intuition begins with the sense that what isn't yet could be. How do we sense this? In technical craftsmanship, the sense of possibility is grounded in feeling frustrated by a tool's limits or provoked by its untested possibilities" (Sennett 2008, 209–210).

On the other hand, the process of hacking was also described as fun, thrilling, and adventurous. For Miles, the process of hacking (and playing video games) builds "anxiety and anticipation." Danny describes the feeling of the trespass in hacking as a "jolt" with a "sense of adventure." While tedium and frustration are tied to the process of hacking, a thrill can also be part of it. Of course, the rush seems to be set in the context of two circumstances: (a) when the activity is illegal with proximal chance of being caught, and (b) when the challenge draws closer and closer to resolution.

Another emotional experience, however, may serve to offset the negative emotions experienced previously in the process of hacking. If one manages to endure and find a rhythm, the sensational reward can be profound—resulting in the experience of *flow*, a concept pioneered by positive psychologists and previously used by criminologists (Csikszentmihalyi 1975; Hayward 2004). Flow "involves intense and focused concentration on the activity; action and awareness merge together; the person loses self-consciousness and is no longer aware of self; there is a sense of control over the action; the sense of time is distorted; and the activity is intrinsically rewarding" (Ko and Donaldson 2011, 148).

Flow-inducing activities, in this sense, are said to be "autotelic" (Csikszenmihalyi 1975), in that they are "enjoyable but highly intense pastimes" (Hayward 2004, 183). Many of the hackers in this study describe the process of hacking in a manner consistent with flow—a finding that resonates with Keith Hayward's (2004) connection of flow and late modernity, as few activities are (arguably) as characteristic of late modernity as hacking. Both Jensen and Pete even use the term in their descriptions of the hacker experience, as Pete demonstrates: "In psychology there's a concept called *flow*. And they say that a human being is at his happiest when they are at flow. Like a complete flow state. And when I get into those modes—which I guess would be a hacker mentality mode—my flow is extremely high. It's . . . you know those moments when you get so focused you lose track of time? You look up and you are like, 'Holy crap, look at the time!'" Further, he describes in greater detail the flow process in hacking:

> You start off with the flow of, like, designing it and just doing it and sometimes you're up till six in the morning, seven in the morning doing that kind of stuff and writing code or hacking something and, you know, it's just . . . you lose track of time . . . and it has its downfalls and you're like . . . it has consequences of, like, "I'm lacking sleep and I need to sleep." Right? Your brain can only go so far ahead. But in that moment, it's just . . . It's one of the most rewarding feelings you can have. If you could find happiness . . . [trails off]

As such, one of the emotional payoffs of hacking seems to be flow. This is an important implication as it indicates how hackers can wade through tedium and frustration and still find the process satisfying. Much in the same way that craftspersons find a certain satisfaction in their work, hackers "enter into a realm in which contentment with ordinary things made well reigns" (Sennett 2008, 93). Hackers have been known to call this state "hack mode" or "deep hack mode."[15]

This experience of flow is also noteworthy as a vital part of hacking in its ties to skill. To enter a flow state, one must have their skills challenged (Csikszentmihalyi, Abuhamdeh, and Nakamura 2005). Jane McGonigal (2011, 40–41) states, "Flow was typically the result of years, if not decades, of learning the structure of an activity and strengthening the required skills and abilities." Sennett (2008) makes similar connections with the experience of craftwork. As one hones their skill and expertise, that person becomes more engrossed in the rhythm of their labor, prolonging ones attention span for the activity. The process of flow is tied to the ability to maintain focus for prolonged periods of time—to become engrossed in one's work: "As skill expands, the capacity to sustain repetition increases" (38). As hacking emphases skill so heavily, one can see how flow and hacking would occur in tandem.

Sennett (2008) further describes the development of skill in craftwork in a manner similar to flow in the process of glass making: "She lost awareness of her body making contact *with* the hot glass and became all-absorbed in the physical material as the end in itself." He continues by stating, "If I may put this yet another way, we are now absorbed *in* something, no longer self-aware, even of our bodily self. We have become the thing on which we are working" (174). As such, the process of becoming wholly engrossed in an activity—as is necessary to achieve a flow state—is part of craftwork as well. In both cases, happiness is linked to work that is challenging, intrinsically rewarding, and even playful (Sennett 2008; McGonigal 2011).

Completing a Hack

While the process of hacking comes bundled with its own configuration of emotional ups and downs, separate but related phenomenological sensations emerge upon completion of a hack. These emotions range from a kind of general pleasure to a jubilant euphoria. John had difficulty summarizing how it felt to complete a project. He could only summarize the feeling as follows: "It feels pretty good . . . Whenever I accomplish something, it feels pretty good. So . . . good." He then goes on to describe it as an "a-ha!" moment accompanied by a "sense of accomplishment you get from understanding something." Roger describes the sensation of accomplishing a hack as a sense of confidence tied to intelligence: "You feel like you are smart. At the moment. Like, you are learning all of these intricate things and you are getting around them. And you are solving the problem." Further, he described cracking the digital rights management (DRM) protocol on "Sim City"—the Electronic Arts game reviled at the time among hackers and gamers for its extremely restrictive copy-protection measures—as associated with a sense of victory and accomplishment: "It was a great feeling. It was like, 'I beat you! I beat you Origin!'"[16]

Providing a more detailed account, Pete describes hacking—focusing primarily on how it feels to finish a hack:

> Oh, man . . . It feels good. . . . You know what I love about hacking? It's the ability to create. It isn't necessarily just the high of breaking into something. It's the ability to be able to be creative on how you got in in the first place. Or if it's something that you're looking at and how the creativity of like . . . "Hey, I made [it] this way and it scales." And it's like . . . you make something new. You thought of it a different way. And I . . . I posted once on my Facebook that there is no drug on this planet that a teenager can take that replaces the feeling you get from being . . . [in] your best moments in creativity. And that's how it feels. It's a rush. It feels good. There is still a piece of validation and recognition to it. Sometimes you get to share it with people. That community sense is also—when people get to use the tool that you might've written, when people were using my software,[17] it felt good. You feel useful. And it helped people. It changed lives in some ways.

Pete describes hacking as containing a "rush" and that it "feels good." He also associates a particular "high"—equating the process of hacking with taking drugs and associating that with the desire to do more hacking. Poacher (2007, 11) echoes this association between hacking and a chemical high: "It's the 'hacker high'—that feeling you get from acquiring knowledge that they don't want you to have and getting it without them ever knowing." Pete also associated emotions with the social aspects of accomplishing a hack. Should a hack be made known, a person can gain a sense of "validation and recognition."

Some accounts describe accomplishing a hack as liberating—akin to being released from a prison. Sairys (2004, 46–47) describes the process of breaking through network restrictions in such a manner: "Another check at the network computer made me laugh a little more. TROY_Proxy was the name of the machine [that] housed the friendly BESS [a web filtering program] guard dog. A simple DEL [delete] statement would get rid of it all. Fortunately, none of us had malicious intent. At this point, the network was at our disposal, and even though there was nothing we wanted from all those folders, it was sure nice to know that they were available to us. It was like being released from a prison." Susan describes completing a hack in a similar manner. "When you finally figure it out . . . It's like . . . someone let you out of your cage. And you're like . . . 'I'm free.'" In both of these cases, the catharsis of accomplishing a task feels like one is being freed—a release. The implication here is that when working towards a goal, the hacker feels beholden to the task and even trapped by it until the job is done.

In the process of hacking, one is confronted with tedium and frustration that can, if things align properly, result in a positive flow experience. When one is in a flow state and completes their task, they may be rewarded with positive euphoric sensations, like those previously described. McGonigal (2011, 33) describes this as *fiero*, the Italian term for "pride." "*Fiero* is what we feel after we triumph over adversity. You know it when you feel it—*and* when you see it. That's because we almost all express *fiero* in exactly the same way: we throw our arms over our heads and yell." Miles describes the achievement of a hacking goal as an "epic win," drawing from the work of McGonigal (2011). He also describes the emotional experience of completing a hack:

> It's a success thing. You can, you know, put a bunch of effort . . . cognitive effort into a task and when . . . [snaps fingers] you get done, it's [like] . . . you've won. . . . You'll learn something and it becomes . . . that moment of epiphany, which is sort of a—a transient nirvana . . . because you're not really expecting it to happen exactly when it happens. You think maybe it might happen but you are so busy working on it [that] you are not—there is not really a lot of expectation there . . . When you figured out that, you just get this rush of, you know, kind of endorphins, you know, to varying degrees. You know, it's a win. You won the big game. You've conquered the evil dictator. You know, you've defeated Dracula. . . . It feels good. You gain knowledge from it. You get this happy feeling through acquiring knowledge. You get happy feelings from being able to solve a problem.

Importantly, *fiero* occurs upon completion of some sort of challenge—a problem was overcome. In many ways then, considering the cathartic and euphoric descriptions of hacking provided previously, we can conclude that accomplishing a good and challenging hack provides the sensation of *fiero*.[18] In this sense, *fiero* can be seen as the result of satisfying and challenging work—an emotional payoff apparently beneficial to craftspersons and hackers alike. Considering that craftwork involves similar experiences with flow, it would not be hard to imagine how the violinist, the bricklayer, or the surgeon would gain positive feelings in a similar manner from a job well done. However, such feelings like *fiero* may be more intense through work with high technology (such as through video games and software) because of its relatively immediate forms of reinforcement and feedback (McGonigal 2011).

Hacking as Transgression

The final link articulated in this study between hacking and craftwork is that both are *transgressive* to one degree or another (interviewees = 13; 92.86%; CA items = 86; 44.56%). Transgression is a lived experience laden with emotion—a cultural manifestation and a political act of subversion and resistance (Ferrell, Hayward, and Young 2008). Previous work has discussed craftwork as transgressive because of its tendency to fly in the face of the modern politics of routinization and bureaucratization (Ferrell 2004). While hacking comprises a variety of activities spanning different types of technology and legality, it is always transgressive through its emphasis on resisting and transcending social boundaries. In this vein, Coleman (2012) has noted that the history of hacking is laden with the politics of resistance. Additionally, such subversion is also consistent with Svetlana Nikitina's (2012) characterization of hackers as a sort of creative trickster.

Though the persistent theme of transgression comprises the focus of this section, the reader may unduly gain the impression that such behavior is "negative" in line with the socially constructed perceptions of hacking. Instead, it should be remembered that hacking consists of activities ranging across the moral spectrum—a tendency shared by craftwork as well: "Craftsmanship is certainly, from an ethical point of view, ambiguous. Robert Oppenheimer was a committed craftsman; he pushed his technical skills to the limit to make the best bomb he could . . . The craftsman thus both stands in Pandora's shadow and can step out of it" (Sennett 2008, 11). The same cultural process and practice of craftwork yielded penicillin as well as the atomic bomb. Likewise, hacking can be applied to something as seemingly benign as open-source programming or as harmful as stealing a person's life savings (not all who do either of these activities are hackers, however). In this way, the essence of hacking and craftwork are amoral in that they both stand "in Pandora's shadow and can step out of it" (11). Regardless of morality, however, the transgressive edge persists.

Hacking as Subversive

In the public eye, hacking is automatically associated with criminal computer activity. As previously stated, however, many hacking activities exist that are not criminal, such as open-source programming (Coleman 2013). Even the activities that are *usually* considered criminal are not always illegal. For example, if a hacker breaks into a network system he or she owns, it is often legal. Even in the case of legal hacking, however, the particular activities still often have a transgressive quality or are embedded with the politics of resistance and subversion. When working with technology and software, as Danny states, "if you have to break a few things, you know, that's okay . . . especially rules."

Of course, rules are not the only things that hacking can violate. Expectations can also be broken through hacking. As Harvey suggests: "Hacking has to have that going-outside-what-people-think-you-should-be-doing." Regarding software and hardware, designers are said to not only create the technology, but also create a series of expectations for what can and should be done with it. According to Rick, "When you set up . . . any kind of system . . . computer system, social system, government . . . you set up some rules." Lifeguard (2011, 16) expresses a similar sentiment: "I believe a person is only a hacker if another calls them one. Perhaps a better definition is a person who manipulates a system in ways other than were intended by the system designers and operators. I feel hacking is more than just penetrating systems without permission, but there is definitely an overlap of skills."

Additionally, as previously described, hacking involves breaking and reconfiguring. Part of this breaking process also involves doing new and creative things. As Aidan states, "Hacking is doing stuff you generally are not supposed to be doing or . . . finding new ways of doing something." In this sense, hacking means moving past designer expectations for systems and reinventing what can be done. Such transgressions harken back to the creative unconventionality described earlier as key for the hacker mentality.[19]

Open-source software programming comprises a controversial section of the hacking community. Some members (including some who were interviewed in this study) assert that free and open-source software programming is not hacking; others insist otherwise. For those who claim it is not, the reasons given are typically that F/OSS programing does not involve breaking of some sort. As Aidan claims, "Open-source projects are inherently open so there's no reason to hack them if they are open."

But for those who do consider open-source software to be hacking, the grounds for such are exploration, creation, and defiance of expectations or even subversion of convention. F/OSS hackers are those pushing at the edges of what can be done with programming. To explain this perspective, Miles analogizes such programming to woodworkers who carve intricate and creative things out of wood: "At the same time does that go back to you know, wood carving and stuff like that . . . Those are guys that are . . . They're pushing the edges of what can be done with wood—what can be done with those tools." This sense also heralds back to the understanding of what it meant to be a hacker in the early days of the MIT Tech Model Railroad Club when hackers were known for taking creative and novel approaches toward solving problems while trying to push the boundaries of what could be done with code within the relatively restrictive computational parameters at the time (Levy 1984).[20]

F/OSS programming may also be considered transgressive because its philosophical logic often resists proprietary software and, in many instances, the capitalist notion of intellectual property. The very notion of programming in a manner which is (a) not for monetary gain, and (b) open and available for others contradicts traditional intellectual property arrangements (see also Söderberg 2008). 2600 author glutton (2010, 50) characterizes this resistance to greed as such: "True hackers aren't motivated by a lust for money, and the movie [Hackers] reinforced this by having the villains be money-hungry goons. Historically, hackers have made lousy criminals, simply because they aren't criminal. Sure, a little money was made along the way—for example, Woz and Jobs selling blue boxes [phone phreaking devices]. For the most part, however, hackers pretty much lack the ability to break laws for money. If we were greed-focused, we wouldn't share our findings with others, or contribute to open-source projects." Of course, as admitted in glutton's argument, sometimes hacking *can* be done for gain. What seems to matter is that material gain is not the primary cultural motivating factor.

Hacking and the Criminal Rush

As stated previously, hacking is not always illegal. When a law violation is committed, the criminal component is sometimes thought of as incidental: "I mean the crime was always incidental" (Harvey). In this sense, the criminal act is a stepping stone on the way to solving a problem or completing a project. Sometimes, however, the criminal component of an act can be seductive (Katz 1988). The thrills sought by hackers break away from otherwise mundane and "safe" uses for computational technology—similar to how "skilled craft work produces idiosyncratic designs unimaginable within the repetitions of the assembly line" (Ferrell 2004, 297–298).

For hackers, this seduction seems to largely concern the notion of trespass. To communicate the rush of breaking in and illicitly trespassing into a computer system, Danny compares hacking to another subcultural practice: Urban Exploration.[21] He states, "I mean that kind of first got me interested in this sort of thing. Because there's an adrenaline rush to knowing you are somewhere where you shouldn't be." Similarly, The Piano Guy (2009, 60) states that a quick way to get a hacker to want to trespass is to label something as off-limits, thus creating an enticement to trespass: "Now, if you want to attract the undivided attention of flies, get some dog poop. If you want to attract the undivided attention of a hacker, put a sticker on it that says 'for staff use only.'" As demonstrated here, the injection of trespassing and other criminal behavior can create an additional thrill associated with act of hacking, which can provide a further motivation. Previous research similarly describes excitement as a key motivating factor in hacking: "When hackers are asked what motivates them to write free code or crack computer systems, their answers are many and diverse. A recurrent theme, however, is the thrill they get from doing it" (Söderberg 2008, 2; see also Turgeman-Goldschmidt 2005).

The reader should note that some of the subversive nature of hacking as well as its various thrills might separate hacking from craftwork. Certainly the potential for moral or amoral behavior exists in both, as previously stated. An argument can also be made that certain crafts engage in similar forms of transgression through domain shifts, practical creativity, and other dynamics previously described (Sennett 2008). These links, however, between hacking and craft do not seem to be as strong as they are for other areas. In this way, hacking—particularly illicit hacking— may involve types of subversion and thrills not commonly found in other forms of craft. In this manner, hacking may constitute a unique sort of craft through the intensity of its subversion and its ties to thrill-seeking behavior among some members of its community.

Conclusion

As articulated in this chapter, and central to the political economic arguments presented later in chapter 4, hacking is articulated as a form of labor work similar to previous criminological analyses of other illicit activities and subcultures like professional thievery and drug dealing (Adler 2003; Fagan and Freeman 1999; King and Chambliss 1984; Letkemann 1973; Sutherland 1937). Where previous works have attempted to isolate common themes which unify hacking, such as a hacker ethic (see Brown 2008; Himanen 2001; Levy 1984), the central argument advanced in this analysis is that hacking comprises a kind of craft. Both hacking and craftwork consist of similarities across mental processes, with an emphasis on skill, ownership, commitment, similar social-learning structures, process over results, and emotional experiences. Additionally, both hacking and craftwork are stitched together through the politics of resistance and transgression—though, admittedly, hacking may be more flagrant in its transgressive tendencies. Though the analysis put forth a complex arrangement of characteristics that might be seen as comprising the eidos of hacking, these characteristics may be summarized succinctly. The definition advanced here is that *hacking is a transgressive craft*. That said, craft has two meanings, both of which are equally applicable. The first is that craft is a kind of skill-based productive activity. The second is that engaging in craft can be a guileful and subversive behavior, typically used to describe a person as "crafty." As hacking represents craft in both senses, I posit that the essence of hacking can be distilled into a single term: hacking is *craft(y)*.

In light of these findings, it is abundantly clear that simplistic definitions that identify hacking as any kind of illegal computer intrusion are grossly inadequate (for further explication, see Steinmetz 2015b). Breaking away from such stale perspectives, hacking is articulated here as more than an act or behavior—but instead as a cultural practice tied to work. The very notion of the hacker is intimately linked to the material relationship between labor and the mind (or the development of cultural identity). Additionally, because of its inherently transgressive edge, hacking presents a kind of craft with the politics of resistance running through to the core—resistance against convention, norms, expectations, and even law. As Sennett (2008) declares, the specter of harm looms over craftwork, while the spirit of transgression flows through hacking. Both hacking and craft, therefore, are "never innocent" (294).

Hackers of open-source software craft novel programs; hardware hackers craft inventive new hardware forms and configurations; malware writing hackers craft programs that take advantage of weaknesses in security; and computer security intrusion hackers craft ways to circumvent restrictions on computer networks. These hackers, and others, are defined by their process, their approach, their perspectives—they are defined by craftwork. Making the connection between hacking and this form of labor then opens up this work to consider how hackers are enmeshed in the dynamics of political economy as transgressive intellectual craftspersons. After all, if hacking is a form of labor—as articulated here—then the question becomes: What is being produced and for whom? While this may seem to be a simple question on its face, hacking is drawn into the political economic dynamics of production and consumption as well as deviance and social control. One more piece of the puzzle is absent, however. For a Marxist analysis of hacking to be successful, it will take more than establishing hacking as a predominantly middle-class phenomenon and a form of labor. Indeed, no political economic analysis is complete without consideration of the state to some degree. As such, this examination now turns to hacker politics and philosophy with explicit focus on its perceptions towards government, law, and law enforcement: the focus of chapter 3.

3

On Authority and Protocol

The aim of the project up to this point has been two-fold: to establish hacking as a phenomenon linked to class and to articulate hacking as a kind of labor.[1] This chapter expands on the studies presented in chapters 1 and 2 to examine hackers' perspectives toward the state.[2] Originally, the research involved in this chapter began with the (relatively) straightforward goal of examining hackers' perspectives on government, law, and law enforcement. Because hackers have a reputation for bending or breaking rules and are likely to experience run-ins with institutional authority at some point in their lives, this analysis originally sought to examine their views on such power in detail through field research and content analysis of *2600: The Hacker Quarterly*. The result is the identification of five dimensions of hackers' perspectives toward governments and their institutions. In addition, these perspectives indicate the presence of a broader hacker philosophy of the state, which this analysis describes as *technological liberalism*.

Liberalism has emerged as an enduring yet fragmented philosophical body. While identifying the precise nature of liberalism may be difficult (Rawls 1993), it can be understood broadly as a philosophy that seeks to uphold ethical values such as "freedom, free speech, privacy, the individual, [and] meritocracy" (Coleman and Golub 2008, 256). Further, it does so while also valuing the idea of a rational human actor—a philosophical cocktail with a long history implicated in political economic structures and struggles (Polanyi 1944; Harvey 2014). Reminiscent of the work of early liberal philosophers like John Locke, Rawls (1993, 137) describes political liberalism in these terms: "Our exercise of political power is fully proper only when it is exercised in accordance with a constitution, the essentials of which all citizens as free and equal may be reasonably expected to endorse in the light of principles and ideals to their common human reason." In his definition of political liberalism, values like "free and equal" are conjoined with ideals like "common human reason" and constitutional democracy. Early American liberals—such as Thomas Jefferson and James Madison—advocated for a constitutional republic that would maximize individual liberty while reducing the power of the state to only the minimum required to secure national sovereignty and protect these liberties. Though creating a firm definition of liberalism may be difficult, many of the aforementioned characteristics can be found throughout its various manifestations, from anarchism to libertarianism. In some ways, then, liberalism is like pornography—in the words of the late Supreme Court Justice Potter Stewart, we "know it when [we] see it."[3]

The philosophy of liberalism permeates hacking. The precise appearance of liberalism within the hacker community varies—some hackers are Ayn Randian–style neo-liberals while some teeter towards anarchy. Regardless of its manifestation, the core of liberalism, with its emphasis on autonomy, freedom, and cynicism towards the state, remains. The particular genre found among many hackers is described here as *technological liberalism*—a worldview marked by political liberalism, a technological ontology, and a sense of technological utopianism. Considering liberalism, in general, and economic liberalism, in particular, have a long and storied history within the logics of capital (Polanyi 1944), the conclusion that technological liberalism cuts through hacker culture only further opens the analysis for consideration from a political economic perspective.[4]

Hacker Perspectives on State Authority

This analysis begins with a study of hackers' perspectives of government, law, and law enforcement—proxies for their overall views of states and state actors generally. These perspectives serve as building blocks toward identifying a philosophy of hacker governance. Five dimensions of these perspectives are isolated (see table 3.1). The first is the view that the government is *controlling*, with the second portraying the government as *inept*. Such (over)regulation and ineptitude is then described as leading to various forms of *collateral damage*. Though the previous themes would indicate hackers are exclusively critical of governments, the results here reveal that they are often not entirely dismissive of government and offered a number of positive or supportive perspectives,

TABLE 3.1. Perspectives on Government, Law, and Law Enforcement

Themes	Content Analysis Items (% of Items in Subsample)	Interviewees
Control	180 (75.31)	14
Inept	100 (41.84)	14
Collateral	62 (25.94)	12
Exceptions	89 (37.24)	14
Solutions	79 (33.05)	10

described here as *exceptions* to the hacker critique. Finally, ever the pragmatists, hackers not only offer critiques towards state authority, but rather, also propose a number of *solutions* to perceived problems.

Government as Controlling

A common thread running through the participants' perspectives on government, law, and law enforcement is the idea that the various institutions of the government are used as instruments of control (items = 180; 75.31%; interviewees = 14). There are a number of ways that the government is described as explicitly regulatory and even coercive, almost all of which are negative in connotation. For the purposes of brevity, four are described here through the following categories: *surveillance, secrecy, government as instrument of third-party control,* and *the nanny-state.*

SURVEILLANCE

The most common way in which the government was described as controlling was through the implementation of surveillance and data-gathering infrastructures. Surveillance is a mechanism of state control that seeks to monitor people and amass information to scrutinize and potentially act to control individual behavior. When discussing the controlling nature of the government through surveillance, one of the biggest concerns for hackers is *direct* monitoring by governments. For example, The Prophet (2002, 24) comments on the capability of agencies like the FBI (Federal Bureau of Investigation) to track movements using cellular phones: "If you carry such a phone, the FBI knows exactly where you are at all times. (Of course, J. Edgar Hoover's FBI will only use that capability against criminals and terrorists, right?) [sarcasm]." Goldstein

(2008, 4) also reflects on such concerns in *2600*, particularly as a result of rapid advances made in surveillance technology:

> We've been talking about the increasing amounts of surveillance since we first started publishing back in 1984. Back then, it was more of a "what if" scenario, where most of us feared what could happen if the government had the ability to track us in real time, if there were cameras everywhere, if our private information was no longer so private. As part of the hacker community, we knew full well how fleeting any form of privacy actually was. If there's one thing we've learned over the years, it's that those entrusted with keeping our private information secure aren't really expending all that much effort to achieve this.

Similarly, in response to a question about federal agents confiscating his computer gear, Harvey describes law enforcement efforts to monitor the BBSs that he participated in when he was younger:

> INTERVIEWER: Why were the feds confiscating?
> HARVEY: Well, it was usually [due to] the content of the board and the fact that you had to be careful not to advocate specifically illegal acts. If you said, for example, you normally name in your sub-forums . . . so you name one "codes for dial-up," "long-distance codes," or you name one "warez" for people who trade software, you could have problems, especially if it was an open bulletin board. Back then, one of the most common things that people would do was to protect the new user registration process with a password. And so supposedly you'd get the password from a buddy and that way you'd be in but that was pretty easily bypassed in a lot of cases.

Here, Harvey describes how law enforcement watched these boards looking for evidence of any activity that enabled crime.

Not only are more direct forms of surveillance of concern for hackers, but they also express anxiety over the amassing of private information into datasets by government agencies. Xen (2006, 11), for instance, discusses the implementation of license plate tracking systems in the United Kingdom: "As of Autumn 2005, an ANPR (Automatic Number Plate Recognition) system has been rolled out across the United Kingdom . . . This nationwide system is run centrally from London and is expected to process as many as 50 million number plates a day by the end of 2006. During processing of these number plates, the information of where and when they were seen will be logged and kept on file for at least two years." Xen then goes on to describe the potential consequences of such a surveillance regime: "These systems are wrong on every level and any advantages the government can come up with—or any elaborate 'one in a billion chance' scenario for these systems saving us from a nuclear attack—is just not worth the invasion of privacy and destruction of civil rights" (13). While many hackers have an appreciation for solid security, they also are repulsed by measures of control seen as over-reaching, arbitrary, and or ineffective. Control for control's sake is almost always rebuked, particularly through surveillance assemblages.

While conducting field research, I was able to engage hackers during one of the biggest contemporary controversies in surveillance. In 2013, Edward Snowden—former National Security Agency (NSA) employee—leaked the details about the massive surveillance infrastructure developed by the NSA called the Planning Tool for Resource Integration, Synchronization, and Management (PRISM), in addition to other surveillance programs. Predictably, the hacking community was incensed about this occurrence. In fact, this anger was almost palpable at DEF CON 21. In previous conventions, federal law enforcement agents were at least tolerated among the participants—though many of these officials attempted to hide their affiliations. This tolerance even grew into a relatively good-natured game called "Spot the Fed," where attendees would attempt to find federal agents in the crowd. If correctly identified, the spotter would receive a shirt stating "I spotted the fed!" while the agent would get a shirt stating "I am the fed!" For the 2013 DEF CON, however, the organizers asked federal law enforcement agencies to stay away as a result of the outrage over the Snowden leaks. "Spot the Fed" was cancelled (an Edward Snowden look-alike contest was held, however).

In addition, many of the panels discussed the perceived ethical violations that the PRISM program entailed. They were concerned about just how long the arm of surveillance in the U.S. had extended. The ire took a comical turn when cardboard cutouts of Snowden began ap-

Figure 3.1. Snowden Cardboard Cutouts

pearing throughout the conference (so comical that I could not resist having my picture taken with one) (see figure 3.1). One of these cutouts even featured Snowden as Waldo from the children's book *Where's Waldo*, a jab at the government's inability to capture Snowden at the time. In short, all of the previous examples demonstrate how participants in the study view the government as using surveillance as means to monitor and control—and how such control is often condemned and resisted.

SECRECY

Hackers not only describe governments as controlling through the use of surveillance, but also as a result of their apparent unwillingness to be transparent, particularly the post–9/11 U.S. Federal Government. There is therefore a recognition of a kind of hypocrisy: individuals increasingly lose privacy while government secrecy is greatly amplified. Such feelings are understandable considering that the use of the state secrets doctrine has expanded drastically in the years following the World Trade Center attacks—to the point that "there is a real danger that the government is using the privilege not to protect national security, but to cover up its own wrongdoing" (Ziegler 2008, 692). *2600's* Goldstein (2008, 5), for example, describes not only outrage at the growth of surveillance but also at the lack of transparency surrounding its implementation:

> You may have seen mention of something called "FISA" in the news recently. The Foreign Intelligence Surveillance Act of 1978 may well have escaped the radar of many, as it basically authorizes a "secret court" to approve warrants to collect foreign intelligence information in the United States. Of the nearly 23,000 warrants requested from its inception to 2006, only five were rejected. And yet, this secret court wasn't enough for the current administration. The Protect America Act of 2007 basically removed the warrant requirement, which allowed for an unlimited amount of wiretaps of Americans suspected of communicating with suspicious people overseas. The most outrageous part of all this was that the warrantless surveillance had been ongoing since 2002 as part of a secret cooperative program with the NSA and various major phone companies.

2600 author cbsm2009 (2009, 12) similarly points out the secrecy surrounding certain airport security measures implemented after 9/11: "The names of people on the lists (the No-Fly list and the Selectee list, which doesn't prevent a person from flying but requires him or her to undergo additional physical searchers) are classified by the U.S. government, cannot be challenged in a court of law, and are compiled from unknown sources."

While these are just a few examples, many hackers express a sense of frustration at the power of governments to withhold information on its operations, particularly when government actions are thought to impact personal privacy and other liberties. Such sentiments also breed a degree of cynicism about government operations: "'Information should be free' is not a sustainable tenet of parliamentary democracy. Complete transparency represents, in Landauer's language, a relationship that forms the noose of all governance" (Hurd 2012, 58).

GOVERNMENT AS MEANS FOR THIRD-PARTY CONTROL
Hackers have also described the use of the law as a means of control for non-governmental actors—corporations, individuals, etc. This control can manifest itself through the use of the legal system (e.g., lawsuits) or

even the threat of law enforcement action. For example, PriesT (2008, 31) describes an incident that occurred after dumpster diving in Switzerland: "As one of the guards held me where I was, the other ran off with a phone. I later discovered that he called the police to inform them that I was a terrorist planting a bomb in a dumpster. *Right*. Scared as a wet rabbit, I did whatever the freak they told me to do." Evoking third-party control through copyright law, Rick describes the early Altair BASIC controversy which involved a young Bill Gates calling everyone who copied the paper tapes for his BASIC program "pirates." In this scenario, Gates attempted to use the weight and legitimacy of copyright law to control who had access to his content—thus rendering copyright law an instrument of his control:

> RICK: There's this war. So the war started in '75 when Bill Gates's Altair paper tape got copied. And he called everybody pirates for copying the paper tape. I've got those documents somewhere.
> INTERVIEWER: That was talked about in Levy's book as well, right?
> RICK: And you still find the original documents in the MITS [Micro Instrumentation and Telemetry Systems] newsletter that they sent out, which was a newsletter physically on paper passed around. People scanned it in . . . With Bill Gates's original letter to hobbyists . . . you know, [he was] calling them pirates and telling them there'll never be any good software if you have this. But it separated the world into . . . [as] I call it . . . people who knew how things worked and people who didn't know how they worked (or who wanted it to work). And there was always this pain of figuring out how things worked. Because if somebody didn't want you to know how it worked—because that was their business model—then you're in opposition. So, Bill Gates made this Altair BASIC and how it worked and he solved these really complicated problems. It would be in his best interest for nobody else to every figure out how he did that.

In this way, Gates is said to use copyright law as a way to control uses of code in a manner perceived as largely unfair by Rick. Under this perspective of government as an instrument of third-party control, one of the speakers at DEF CON perhaps summarized it best—"the law is used as a club."

THE NANNY STATE

One problem discussed is a view that the government too heavily regulates behavior that does not need to be regulated—the state acts as a kind of "nanny" or "babysitter." In other words, the state was viewed as overly paternalistic. As Gilbert stated, "It shouldn't be imposing restrictions on what individuals should do that don't affect other individuals." Roger expressed a similar perspective:

> They shouldn't be telling people how to live or how to be safe. I mean, I love to argue about it and people would say, "Why do you even argue about it or care? It doesn't affect you." But way back in the day, they passed a law that you must wear a seatbelt in a car. I find that to be really nanny-state. I have always worn one. It's habit. I actually feel very "off" when I'm not wearing one. But there is this physiological reaction of, "You jackass, put that thing on right now! We are about to go through this windshield." . . . It's just habitual. But I still think it shouldn't be a law. It's flat-out bullshit.

The idea of the government as a "babysitter" or "nanny" was a recurrent theme of frustration in the data. In one Union Hack meeting, the conversation drifted to gun control. John heatedly defended a position that certain things—like gun ownership—should just not be regulated. Instead, the law should only intervene if a *direct harm* was inflicted. He used an example of a child who killed his sister with a shotgun that his parents gave him (the child was about 5 years old). John said that the parents should have the right to decide to give their child a gun but should also face jail time if it "bites them in the ass." In other words, there seemed to be a sense that a babysitter-style government eroded personal responsibility and individual autonomy—two traits deeply valued among many hackers.

Government as Inept

Hackers, in a perhaps unsurprising finding, largely depicted the government as inept in its operations (items = 100; 41.84%; interviewees = 14). An ideal is held for effectiveness and many governments—the U.S. government in particular—is often viewed as falling short. Four ways in which governments are said to fail in their duties involve governments portrayed as *dysfunctional, ignorant and misguided, subject to manipulation,* and *corrupt.* Perhaps capturing the perspective most adequately, author Bill Squire (2006, 29) describes the ineptitude of policy makers: "As real hackers we solve problems, while the law and politicians only make matters worse."

DYSFUNCTIONAL

One particular description given by hackers of government ineptitude or inadequacy involves the view that the government is somehow broke, inefficient, or somehow impaired, particularly when compared to other forms of regulation. Aidan summarizes the general perception of the state as dysfunctional when he describes his perspective on the U.S. government: "In general, [it] is broken. Nothing can be done, everything is always gridlocked, people make decisions based on . . . if it was brought by their own party of not. Our dual party system is fundamentally flawed in that regard. And it's become more so as the divides have become greater between the two over the past twenty years. And what the solution is, I don't know. But what we have isn't working. It's broken. Other governments are also broken. I mean, they have the same issues involved as our government." Aidan describes his perception of governments as "broken" due to the irrationalities of bureaucracy and politics—particularly is alleged inability to accomplish anything.

In another example, governments were perceived as dysfunctional because their implementation of controls were seen as ineffective compared to informal or cultural regulation; formal social control is lacking compared to informal social control. For instance, Rick described how communities should be free to solve their own problems and the government should only step in as a last resort:

> Criminal justice steps in to—[fill] this odd gap that we've created for ourselves . . . So, when I was in school and it's not . . . totally uncommon now . . . kids bullied each other. And people would tell you, they'd go, "Okay, well, you're just gonna get in a fight and you're going to punch him and then they're not gonna bully you anymore." . . . And most of the time that solved the problem. I got in one fight . . . I got the scar here [he

reveals the scar on his hand] where I hit a guy in the mouth with braces who basically otherwise pummeled me but then he never bothered me after that. His braces, like, sliced my hand and I ended up with a bunch of stitches. And after that . . . the problem went away. Now we've reached a point where we say . . . There is a problem that you used to be able to solve amongst yourselves but we've [the government] declared nobody can solve that particular problem anymore. Now you're to call the experts to solve that particular problem. Because we've declared . . . ourselves the experts and you can't solve that problem anymore. And so [the] government keeps inventing problems that only it can solve—and the reasons that only it can solve the problems. And that's usually where I fall afoul of governments.

In this scenario, Rick describes how informal social control is being encroached upon by governmental control. His words echo the late Nils Christie's (2004, 51) descriptions of the erosion of informal control in society: "We have constructed societies where it is particularly easy, and also in the interest of many, to define unwanted behavior as acts of crime—this in contrast to being examples of bad, mad, eccentric, exceptional, indecent or just unwanted acts. We have also shaped these societies in ways that encourage unwanted forms of behavior, and at the same time reduce possibilities for informal control." In doing this, the government is seen as creating a problem where there originally was not a problem needing government intervention. The government is seen as dysfunctional because it meddles with perceptibly superior mechanisms of informal social control.

IGNORANT OR MISGUIDED

In both interviews and *2600* articles, hackers were prone to describing governments as ignorant, naive, or somehow misled about social problems they attempt to address. One way this occurs is through governments having a false perception of hackers and hacking. Goldstein (2003b, 4) demonstrates this perspective when he talks about the transition in public perceptions towards hacking:

Hackers were no longer just kids playing around. In the eyes of main-stream society, hackers had become definable as actual criminals, along with thieves, murderers, rapists, etc. In some cases, hackers were viewed with *more* fear than violent criminals and even received greater sentences. And again it seemed incredibly absurd. While such abuse and illogical thinking proved to be a lot harder for us to get used to, a good number of politicians, judges, and members of law enforcement seemed to have no trouble with the concept. They could envision sending a hacker to prison for life for crimes that in the real world would hardly merit an overnight stay in the county jail.

Here, Goldstein (2003b) is expressing a viewpoint that casts various government actors as conducting their duties in a fallacious fashion, having an image of hackers disjointed from reality. Phocks (2003, 54) describes the U.S. government as fundamentally misguided about the nature of the Internet and computing in generally: "Imagine a world, if you will, plagued by terrorists and evildoers, whose weapons is the personal computer. It has powerful encryption used to block anyone from reading plans of how to destroy structures vital to a country's survival. It contains a slew of programs designed solely for destroying security and rendering the world helpless to attacks—and anonymously connecting to a terrorist network consisting of tens of thousands of systems just like it, bringing together all who oppose a country to share information and formulate plans of attack. Welcome to the government's view of the Internet." The perception here is that law enforcement is generally not well-equipped or educated enough to deal with issues—perceived or otherwise—with technology-related activities.

SUBJECT TO MANIPULATION

Another way that governments are described as inept is through vulnerability to manipulation either by businesses, hackers, or even everyday persons. For instance, The Prophet (2007, 14) describes the process of "SWATing"—essentially manipulating the 911 emergency phone system to call in Special Weapons and Tactics teams onto unsuspecting persons: "VoIP [Voice over Internet Protocol] services in particular have illustrated practical vulnerability in the E911 system. Recently, a group of highly unethical phreaks [a hacker of telephone systems] (one of whom was known years ago as "Magnate") was arrested [*sic*] for engaging in an activity called 'SWATing.'"[5] SWATing can be extremely dangerous for all parties involved. While many view this activity as juvenile on the part of the caller, concern is expressed about how a system can be constructed in such a way to allow such potentially detrimental manipulation to occur.

In another example, Rop Gonggrijp (2007, 26) discusses how the government of Amsterdam could be easily manipulated through weaknesses in their privately owned electronic voting systems:

> At the polling station, I had to use a brand new electronic voting machine that the city was renting from a company called SDU. In fact, Amsterdam had contracted the entire election as a turnkey service. SDU was even training the poll-workers. This "voting machine" was in fact a computer with a touch screen running Windows. To make matters worse, inside each computer was a GPRS [general packet radio service] wireless modem that sent the election results to SDU, which in turn told the city. I had not been blind to the problems of electronic voting before, but now I was having my face rubbed in it. And it hurt.

In both given instances, governments and related institutions and systems—primarily through their ignorance and ability to be misled—are described as being at risk of potentially detrimental manipulation by outsiders. This point is related to the idea of state institutions being used as instruments of third-party control. The distinction here is that not only are governments used by others to control for "legitimate" purposes (as in sanctioned through law or policy), but also be manipulated for *illegitimate ends*, thus creating an image of the state as a puppet on strings.

CORRUPT

A final example of hacker views of government as inept is through corruption. As used here, corruption indicates that a government cannot control its own institutions or actors in a satisfactory manner. For The Prophet (2010, 13), the inability of the United States to compete with other countries in broadband penetration (availability of broadband Internet connections) is a result of crooked politicians: "The U.S., frankly, isn't even on the radar screen. It's globally ranked twentieth in broadband penetration, and I've given up on policy makers there to think beyond their own corrupt self-interest." Similarly, Goldstein (2003a) asserts that ". . . now we are at a point where those already in power have grown impatient with such things as due process, civil rights, and public perception. In some disturbing and almost comical examples, we see exactly how little the law actually means to them." Finally, Leviathan (2011, 57) authored a short story in 2600 offering a cautionary tale about government authority involving brutality and corruption: "Investigation by the BBC's Washington Bureau has uncovered more circumstantial evidence that President Martera's [the fictional U.S. President] administration ordered the brutal murder of two American journalists in May of last year, evidently for reporting on the military kickback scandal, which implicated Martera's chief of Staff Joel McLaren and his deputy Lawrence Young. Further, there is evidence of a detailed, complex chain of command between the assassins and the President himself." In each of these instances, the government and its actors are viewed as operating in a manner inconsistent with their legitimate duties and operations often by perpetuating their own self-interests over the interests of their constituency.

Government as Creators of Collateral Damage

As previously described, governments are seen by the participants to be controlling in a number of ways in addition to often being inept. These traits—while being seen as negative in and of themselves—are often thought of as detrimental due to the collateral damages they yield, which may include, but are not limited to, diminishing *privacy* and *civil rights, miscarriages of justice,* as well as *physical harms* including deaths or torture (items = 62; 25.94%; interviewees = 12). These damages were largely considered the result of efforts to control, incompetency, inadequacy, or otherwise dysfunctional attempts to implement policies and practices.

DESTRUCTION OF PERSONAL PRIVACY

One of the more prominent collateral damages that participants discussed concerned diminishing privacy.[6] Gilbert describes his view on the relationship between law enforcement and privacy: "They're [putting] security cameras up everywhere in some places already. . . . I mean, I guess the proactive policies make some people feel safer but it's really not worth it. . . . I think there is usually plenty of evidence even after the fact in most cases that they can still do what they need without . . . the monitoring of everything and doing all kinds of proactive stuff." Here, Gilbert is expressing concern about the use of proactive policing and how that diminishes the amount of privacy people are reasonably able to expect. Xen (2006, 13) echoes this sentiment when s/he discusses the increasing surveillance state in the United Kingdom, which is alleged to become increasingly intrusive and harmful to privacy and civil rights: "These systems are wrong on every level and any advantages the government can come up with—or elaborate a 'one in a billion chance' scenario for these systems saving us from a nuclear attack—is just not worth the invasion of privacy and destruction of civil rights."

When the Snowden leaks were released in 2013, the hacker community reacted with vitriol—unsurprised that the invasion was occurring but upset about the privacy violation. At DEF CON, one of the more heavily attended panels involved the Electronic Frontier Foundation discussing privacy issues. Whenever a negative or pejorative statement was made about the NSA, the audience would cheer and applaud. A couple of persons stood, nodding vigorously and clapping their hands together. In both of these cases, efforts by the U.S. government to control through surveillance were considered detrimental to privacy.[7]

EROSION OF CIVIL LIBERTIES

Various civil liberties—aside from the penumbra right to privacy—are also said to be eroded through governmental actions. Sam Bowne (2011, 55) claims that Fourth Amendment protections (freedom against unreasonable searches and seizures) have been imperiled in recent times in the wake of the expanding security state: "The temptation to become an outlaw is very strong right now. For a decade, our government has used its propaganda machine to make us all very afraid, so we no longer expect Fourth Amendment protections. The 'emergency' is so dire that our leaders cannot afford the luxury of ethics." Rick describes how copyright law is used to restrict learning and jeopardize the First Amendment's clause regarding freedom of speech. He discusses an idea for a program he had but, should he actually create it, the project could be silenced through law (remember, for many coding is considered a form of speech):

This is where you have to think like a hacker. But funnily you have to think like a hacker because this is one of the most fundamental . . . weird crazy problems now that you're going to hear about for the next decade . . . So, I said, "Okay, I can't build this because they're suing everybody and if I go out and build this and start the project to build this, somebody is going to decide they don't like it and they're going to sue me and I don't have the time or the money or anything to deal with this." It needs to be built. How do you make it? Where do you go? You can't talk about some of this shit now because people will sue you for talking about shit that they don't like now. It's very creepy. They make up these laws [referring to loose interpretations of copyright law], so I went, "Holy crap! What the fuck do you do? Does free speech exist?" It wasn't clear that it did.

To cope with this problem, he suggests the creation of such a program through a fictional story because, as he argues, one of the last bastions of free speech resides in fiction:

> You know, you could be held liable for knowing it? And not telling. I mean, it's crazy shit. There's only one place that I could argue that free speech exists—completely unencumbered free speech—in fiction. I can say any fucking thing I want in a novel. I mean, in a fictional story about stuff. Because it's a fucking story.

In short, various liberties (as identified in liberal philosophy and often codified in the liberal U.S. Constitution) are viewed as almost perpetually endangered—either by a metaphorical death from a thousand cuts or the quick drop of a guillotine. As will be explored further in this chapter, the loci of hacker concerns about harms to liberties is a key point in the broader hacker philosophy of technological liberalism.

PHYSICAL HARM

Efforts to control, particularly those that are viewed as inept, are also said to lead to various types of physical harms. The ever-quotable Goldstein (2003a, 5) states that the U.S. government's War on Terror has not only undermined due process but has also permitted the use of torture: "By being defined as an 'enemy combatant,' the rules on due process can be suspended. Not only that, but torture is increasingly seen as a valid way of obtaining information from a suspect." While conducting field research, some members of Union Hack and DEF CON attendees discussed the events surrounding Aaron Swartz—a hacker who illegally acquired numerous academic journal articles from JSTOR (Journal Storage) and was subsequently charged with a number of crimes which amounted to a maximum of one million dollars in fines, thirty-five years in prison, and a number of other penalties. The circumstances surrounding Swartz's case are said to have contributed to his suicide. For many, the perceived penalty-to-harm ratio was seen as grossly disproportionate and unfair. Swartz's death was perceived as the consequence of criminal justice actions. John summarizes his perspective on the Swartz affair: "[It was a] ridiculously disproportionate assignment of responsibility through prosecution. . . . I think I might have to look at . . . liability in terms of damages and things like that. Who was the victim there? Who was actually hurt? And . . . I don't even know the case, but my gut tells me that there wasn't enough damage there to really warrant . . . the charges he was assigned." Additionally, a number of the participants at DEF CON lamented the death of Swartz. The Electronic Frontier Foundation described multiple attempts to advocate legislation designed to prevent the type of perceived overcharging implicated in his suicide.

MISCARRIAGES OF JUSTICE

The death of Swartz also highlighted another perceived collateral damage from state control—miscarriages of justice. While the erosion of civil liberties and death were viewed as problematic enough, the case of Aaron Swartz was also lamented because it created a perceived *injustice* through a system that is supposed to be pursuing justice. Because his suicide followed the announcement of the charges against him, the raw volume of charges is popularly thought to have contributed to his suicide. His death thus represented more than a loss of life; a greater moral ideal was believed to have been assaulted as well. Rights were not only potentially infringed upon, the case also triggered a more abstract and visceral moral indignation. Even at DEF CON, Swartz's name was regularly heard throughout the corridors. His case was frequently described, in conversation and in convention presentations, as a symptom of government control and incompetence. Instances of overcharging have been similarly lamented in techno-culture across many other cases where hackers—or "security researchers"—have been arrested and charged for studying security and intellectual property protection protocols (Doctorow 2008; Lessig 2004; Thomas 2002). These cases not only infringed on autonomy and liberty; in many ways they were viewed as a greater affront to the very idea of justice.

These alleged miscarriages of justice have also been described when the justice system perceptibly failed to properly find guilt and carry out punishments. Miles describes the incident surrounding the infamous Casey Anthony case, which involved a mother accused of murdering her children:

> So, yeah, you've got all these private investigators out there with zero computer forensics knowledge but they are all authorized to conduct computer forensics investigations and, you know, that type of thing. I think we are going to see a lot more of the issues like Casey Anthony where the computer forensics guy didn't bother to look at her Firefox history and didn't see that she had been Googling how to like . . . "fool-proof suffocation methods," I think was the search string. Which would've convicted her in a heartbeat if they had presented that, you know, in court but they didn't so . . . She's free! Now, whether she's guilty or not, I don't know. That's . . . guilt or innocence that's . . . that would've probably gotten her convicted . . . And considering that law enforcement didn't do it right, she probably should have gotten off by letter of the law.

According to Miles, a potential miscarriage of justice occurred because law enforcement—through improperly trained digital forensics technicians—did not properly investigate the murder. The result was said to be a potentially guilty person deemed innocent due to faulty investigative work. Overall, one area of collateral damage wrought by allegedly excessive control efforts or through perceived incompetence or inadequacy are miscarriages of justice.

Exceptions to the Hacker Critique

Hackers tend to be stereotyped as anti-authoritarian contrarians who buck the system for the sake of bucking the system. If one were to stop reading this analysis at this point, it would be easy to garner the impression that the current study lends credence to these stereotypes. Rather than simply offer a critique, however, the majority of the participants in this study—in addition to a number of authors in the content analysis—do not wholly detest the *idea* of governments, only poorly functioning or harmful ones (items = 89; 37.24%; interviewees = 14). As Sam Bowne (2011, 55) demonstrates, a desire for at least some form of oversight is not wholly absent from the hacker community: "I want a world of law and order, in which people must be tried and convicted before they are punished."

Within the interviews, a number of the participants—while being critical of the government—claimed a need for such regulation. For example, Jensen discusses law enforcement as an institution that is often fraught with corruption, brutality, or other abuses of power. That said, he states that law enforcement is "necessary but it has to be watched." According to him, law enforcement is not a problem *per se.* Rather, its abuses of power are the issue. Similarly, Miles describes government as problematic in general for similar reasons but recognizes it has value: "Government is necessary, you know. I think we need to be doing a better job of who we are hiring in the bureaucracy and I think we need to be doing a better job of who we pick to design the bureaucracy." Russell further elaborates by stating, "There is a need for it. Laws and order and everything." He continues by defending the necessity of law enforcement: "To deny that it is needed is just a fallacy. They are needed. It's just a question of how it's currently being implemented." In these instances, the idea of governance and law enforcement are not the problem. It is simply a matter of implementation.

Further, for some hackers the *size* of the government was seen as the primary problem rather than the existence of the regulatory body itself—thus articulating a more libertarian perspective consistent with previous work on hacker politics (Barbrook and Cameron 2001; Coleman and Golub 2008; Jordan 2001; Jordan and Taylor 2004). Roger explains: "[I] may be young and naïve talking but I don't think it [the government] should be big. I don't like it really at all. I find it's wholly unnatural. I see why it exists. So many people trying to get peace. Though it bothers me a lot. I think it should be smaller. Not anarchy but . . . I don't think it shouldn't be as big." In essence, government itself is not the problem but its magnitude is seen as a key source of social woes. This particular perspective, though, may be just as much a result of the geography in which the research took place (Texas) as its affiliation with the hacker community.

Previously, this analysis discussed the negative view the participants largely adopted towards government efforts at control. Not all control was viewed as a problem, however. In one conversation with a hacker—who is also a photographer—he described getting into a legal dispute with someone who allegedly violated his copyright by using one of his photographs without permission. In this scenario, copyright was actually valued and the weight of the law was used to protect his intellectual property from being used to make someone else profit without proper recompense. Regarding control for the purposes of national security, Harvey supported the notion of government secrecy to at least some degree in response to the WikiLeaks disclosures from Chelsea Manning: "Even in my wildest days as a hacker, the thought of releasing military documents would have turned me pale." Toni-Sama (2007, 49) also appreciated the potential capacity for regulation through legislation when he described problems with cellular phones and VoIP networks: "It could also be easily spoofed from a cellphone. In addition, most consumer VoIP networks don't support encryption, so phone calls could be intercepted and even changed. This should be legislated soon, since government is extremely interested in regulating this new form of communication." In sum, not all efforts at government control were seen as problematic.

Additionally, not all government actions are viewed as inept. Raj, for instance, commented on law enforcement competency generally: "I think, in general, law enforcement is doing an adequate job." When asked about how well federal law enforcement handles technological crime issues, he further reinforced his view, saying, "I would say about appropriately." *Sometimes* governmental action, particularly law enforcement, may be viewed as, at the least, sufficient and suitable. Many times, this competency is said with a tone that may as well be a pat on the head. The impression is given that law enforcement are catching up and 'doing their best' like a child earning a participation ribbon for effort in a three-legged race. That said, others seem to still view law enforcement as extraordinarily competent in certain regards, explaining why some go to extreme measures to protect their privacy and obscure their activities.

Occasionally hackers describe institutional policies or actions to be detrimental but differentiate their thoughts on individual actors within the system—recognizing that employees may be forced to enact bad policy but that does not mean they are bad people *per se*. Harvey explains, "I've known a lot of good cops. I know a lot of people with bad cop stories but I've known a lot of good cops." He also shared his views on the War on Drugs, arguing that the policy creates more problems than it solves. He continues by discussing how it erodes police discretion, and states, "It puts law enforcement officers in a terrible position. And it's getting worse because of the dashboard cams. In the old days, when things weren't on film, they could excuse stuff. And, you know, I've seen it happen. Where cops are just like, 'Hey . . . you are doing something stupid but you are fundamentally not malevolent so we're going to let you off the hook. Go forth and sin no more.'" Here, Harvey is discussing the idea that police officers can do good work if given discretion but policies constrict their abilities to act fairly.

Not only did a number of the participants discuss government as necessary, functional, or even beneficial in certain capacities, a few have worked for or with the government at some point during their lives. Both Jensen and Russell were in the Navy and have worked as government contractors. Pete regularly works as an information security contractor for certain agencies. Miles has helped with federal law enforcement investigations. In fact, it is interesting how many hackers seem willing to work with law enforcement depending on the circumstances. At DEF CON, one presentation involved quizzing the audience participants on ethical questions through a show of hands. Approximately 30 to 50 percent of the participants in the room raised their hands when asked if they would help federal agents in at least a limited capacity (depending on the context).

Solutions

As previously discussed, one of the central features of being a hacker is an orientation towards problem-solving. In this sense, hackers' perspectives on government law and law enforcement not only include critiques but also solutions to any perceived problems (items = 79; 33.05%; interviewees = 10). These fixes generally fell into two categories. The first involve approaches that seek to work within the system, so to speak. Appealing to the sense of politicians, the act of voting and proposing and supporting bills, among other methods, are all ways of licitly seeking change and solving the social problems described throughout this chapter. We will call these *conventional* tactics. The second arrangement of solutions includes strategies that are more subversive. These attempt to circumvent and resist various forms of government control and oversight. Some of these fixes may be illicit while others may be legal but potentially obstructive for government agencies (specifically for surveillance attempts). These strategies are perhaps best described as *circumventional*. Examples of each are described below.

CONVENTIONAL

The participants in the current study suggested numerous ways to solve problems, which would involve using the system to create changes but leaving the overall system intact. An example of a *2600* author suggesting a conventional approach to social change is provided by Pat D. (2011, 54): "The last and final thing you can do to protect your anonymity and privacy in the digital age is to stay informed and lobby the lawmakers. Let them know that you are not happy with the changes they are trying to make in regards to your online privacy." At DEF CON, I listened as presenters discussed proposing bills and other legislative fixes for perceived problems. To prevent the type of overcharging that faced Aaron Swartz, bills were proposed to lessen the maximum penalties and fines with which a person could be charged. As a measure to bolster personal privacy from the NSA and other government agencies, legislation was suggested in numerous states and also at the federal level. In essence, using the ideally self-corrective properties built into the U.S. government, members of the hacking community advocated for change.

Another configuration of conventional solutions involved downsizing the influence of the government and reducing its role in everyday life. Rick argues for reduced government involvement in people's activities: "So, I used to call it pragmatic libertarianism. You know, I don't want there to be *no government* and hands off everything . . . Let's be decent and sensible and pragmatic but most of the time people can solve their own damn problems." Harvey echoed these sentiments when he called for government to be minimized in favor of informal control: "I tend to prefer rule by things other than government. I tend to prefer government by men and rule by culture. Meaning, you know, informal type stuff." Russell expressed a similar view on minimizing governmental influence: "I'm a minimalist in that sense. I believe that government has a very limited basis . . . I mean, they are there to protect the people and to provide . . . I'm trying to think. I'm pulling a blank right now but there is a phrase that I use . . . 'very limited government.' They are there for police, for maintaining a military, stuff like that." Under this perspective, the participants are not calling to "tear down the system" or else reconfigure it entirely. Rather, they are simply saying that the government reaches too far and needs to be scaled back. If the government were a plant, the argument would be to prune the bush rather than replace it entirely.

Another conventional solution involves upholding a particular set of standards for government officials. Miles describes his perspective on police abuse of force and power: "You know, people say, you know, police need to be held to a higher standard . . . I don't think it's really right. I think they need to be held to the same standard. They are not." What he is articulating here is that he believes police officers are given too much latitude and, rather, they should be held up to similar standards regarding use of force that the general population is. The solution is essentially to alter the standards applied to law enforcement. The overall system would remain untouched and police would still exist; they would just be judged differently.

Approaching the problem from an angle that could be considered neoliberal, Pete argues that a solution to law enforcement's difficulty handling computer crime issues is to work more closely with private industry:

> I don't think the government is anything [worth] bad mouthing. The good news is, the industry . . . the info sec [information security] community is becoming aligned with the government because we have to get intelligence and to defend our corporations and our banks and we all kind of work together now—with all the stuff because of the Internet is intertwined. Your economy or corporate banks . . . your financial institutions are a heavy part of that. They go down and it affects the economy. . . . We aren't all sitting by ourselves with the governments in a black box in their own little room doing their own secret stuff anymore. It's bidirectional now—which is great. It's a good start.

From his view, the solution is not to lessen the power of the banks. Rather, the solution is to collaborate with the private sector to maintain stability.

CIRCUMVENTIONAL

Conventional solutions involve working within the system. Circumventional strategies, however, involve more direct forms of resistance. These approaches often involve, as the label implies, circumventing government oversight and control. Of note is the use of technological and cryptographic solutions to avoid government control through monitoring. Pete discusses using encryption to protect one's privacy not just from the government but from any prying third party: "I'm all for it. I encourage cryptography. I encourage, like, your emails being encrypted. I try to encrypt as much of emails as I can if people have encryption. Just because I like to feel that this stuff is most likely private to me. And it may not be the government that I have to worry about but I like to know that most likely I've done my best job on my own to keep my expected privacy private." In a similar fashion, WillPC (2007) advocates for the use of encrypted "darknets," which are "closed networks used for file-sharing" (McGuire 2010, 511). He states that "this new wave of totalitarianism calls for the next generation of file-sharing technologies, darknets" (WillPC 2007, 15). These circumventional tactics, and their politics, will be discussed in greater detail toward the end of this chapter.

In sum, there are predominantly two types of solutions advocated for by the participants. Conventional approaches, which involve working within mechanisms designed into the system of governance to create change, were advanced. These methods implicitly or explicitly adhere to the notion that governments can be self-corrected through a vigilant and careful populace. Circumventional approaches were also described, primarily in the form of resistance and circumvention—notably through cryptography (though two anarchistic participants in the field research indicated that obliterating the system may be the necessary rather than just bypassing state control). An important distinction between these two approaches is the *type of problem* for which they typically advocate. For substantial change to the system, conventional approaches seem to be preferred. For immediately coping with the problems wrought by an out-of-control government, resistance and circumvention are generally preferred until conventional approaches take effect. Importantly, this finding, while it may apply to many hackers, may not be applicable to *all* hackers.

Thus far, this chapter has focused on hackers' attitudes, beliefs, and perspectives on governments and their institutions, agencies, and actors. The reader has likely notice some commonalities among the various themes discussed throughout. A common spirit seems to course through these perspectives—a relatively consistent philosophy and ontology. As argued here and elsewhere (see Coleman and Golub 2008), these views are congruent with liberalism—but manifests as a somewhat unique variant thereof. It is toward this philosophy the analysis now turns.

Hacker Philosophy

The purpose behind presenting hackers' perspectives on government, law, and law enforcement is to provide the tools with which to dissect and articulate broader hacker philosophy. Reflecting on these findings and prior scholarship, three separate but related themes are explored in this section—all of which coalesce into a kind of hacker political orientation. The first is already familiar to the reader but will be further linked to the previously described results concerning hackers' perspectives on government, law, and law enforcement: *liberalism*. The second consists of a worldview impacted by direct work with technology described here as a *technological ontology*. Finally, a belief that all problems are solvable through technology—*technological utopianism*—is explored. Each of these dimensions coalesces into what I term *technological liberalism*. These themes are discussed in turn.

Liberalism

The first three themes presented—government as controlling, inept, and damaging—demonstrate that hackers are, by and large, cynical toward governance and authority. In particular, government control and its corresponding incompetence or inadequacy are viewed as detrimental, bordering on calamitous. We can already see the ghost of liberalism haunting these views. Since the state is frequently a cause for worry, there is often an emphasis on minimizing the size and effect of the government. From the hacker perspective, therefore, government is seen as often going *too far* in efforts to control. Combined with a perceived inability to properly perform many of its functions, hackers then describe collateral damages wrought by the state. These damages included fears of miscarriages of justice, erosions of civil liberties, and loss of privacy, among others. Notice how many of the described damages concern threats to the individual in terms of loss of autonomy and liberties. These concerns are wholly consistent with the philosophy of liberalism.

Hacker perspectives, however, are not wholly dismissive of governance. In particular, governments are viewed favorably when they uphold individual liberties. The original architects of liberalism thought much the same way, viewing the creation of the state as necessary to uphold liberal values for the majority of the population. The state would act to ensure that one person's exercise of freedom does not potentially impact another person's freedom. Thus, some individual's freedoms would be curtailed by the state to preserve individual freedoms at the societal level. Hackers appear to appreciate the state in much the same way. When the state acts to protect individual liberties, particularly those associated with technology such as freedom of speech, the state is viewed as beneficent.

In this manner, both hackers and liberalism view the state as inherently problematic but potentially useful if deployed correctly. Liberal philosophers devised a number of mechanisms to ideally ensure that the state was managed optimally. In the U.S., an example would be the drafting of the Constitution with a number of checks and balances to prevent one side of the government from gaining too much power. The creation of the Bill of Rights was also an attempt to protect individual liberties to the greatest degree possible in an effort to curtail government control. Likewise, hackers have also devised a number of ways to address overextensions of government control and the problems such control creates. Conventional approaches are advanced which largely advocate for using mechanisms built within the system to seek redress for the problems created, such as through soliciting new legislation or contacting legislators. Circumventional solutions are also given which typically advocate subversion. The political economic dynamics of liberalism, particularly technological liberalism as described throughout the remainder of this chapter, will reemerge in chapter 4.

Technological Ontology

Liberalism, however, is not enough on its own to wholly explain hacker perspectives towards state authority. What makes the hacker perspective unique—along with other related subcultures—is a particular emphasis on technology. In particular, two characteristics seem to dominate. The first is a *technological ontology* (Warnick 2004). Using Lakoff and Johnson's (1980) conceptual metaphor theory, Warnick (2004) argues that hackers perceive the world through the ontological metaphor which states that the world functions like a computer system. An ontological metaphor is one which serves to shape a given persons perception of reality and, importantly, what the ideal conditions for that reality are. In the case of the "world is a computer system" metaphor, this perspective advances the notion that the world, and all of its various systems (social, economic, political, etc.) operate best when conditions ideal for computational performance are met. These conditions include, for example, a lack of restrictions on the flow of information. A computer would not function well if data were prevented from moving in the most efficient way possible through the computer system. Other systems—since they are viewed to function similar to computers—must also then perform optimally under such conditions. Aside from the influence of liberalism, this ontology may be one reason free speech is a concern for hackers and other technologists. According to the technological ontology, social systems may operate best when information can flow freely through networks. Liberalism and the technological ontology may therefore be mutually reinforcing.

A link also exists between Warnick's (2004) technological ontology and craftwork. Under this metaphor, hackers use computers as a means to understand the world surrounding them. In describing metamorphosis in craftwork, Sennett (2008, 127) details the concept of a "domain shift," which "refers to how a tool initially used for one purpose can be applied to another task, or how the principle guiding one practice can be applied to another activity." Once developed within a trade, tools, skills, and principles can be transferred and applied to other crafts. These shifts are often unconventional. The transferal requires perceiving one craft through the view of another. For hackers, competency in computational craftwork allows for conceptual understandings developed through direct work with computer technology to be transmitted to other areas. In the instance of Warnick (2004), the domain shift would occur allowing social life, politics, and so on, to be understood in terms similar to those applied to computing technology.

The technological ontology is linked to the particular form (or forms) of liberalism found among hackers. The "world is a computer" metaphor and skepticism about the power of government are mutually reinforcing. If the world works optimally under the conditions best suited for computer operations—free-flowing and efficient communications between parts—then of course governments will be viewed negatively. Governments, by design, regulate; they control. These beliefs becomes further intensified when consequences are envisioned as a result of government regulation interfering with ideal social configurations, a feature of the hacker philosophy toward which this analysis now turns.

Technological Utopianism

The third characteristic of hacker perceptions tied to technology is a sense of technological utopianism (Barbrook and Cameron 2001). Technological utopianism is similar to the notion of technological determinism associated with theorists like Marshall McLuhan. The latter consists of a belief that individual and societal change is dependent upon relationships with technology. For some, this means that there is little escape from tech's physical *and* symbolic confines. McLuhan (1964), for instance, argued that meaning was fundamentally altered—and in some ways, dictated—by the medium of communication. In this manner, *the medium is the message*. Technological utopianism shares this belief about the power of technology. Utopian thought, however, is future-oriented. Involved is the active envisioning of a future distinct from current circumstances, which "gestures to other possibilities and other times" (Yar 2014, 3). Not only can technology change society, but these changes are viewed as a stepping stone toward an imagined future. Technology is thus viewed as a means toward broad sweeping social change. For hackers, utopian thinking manifests in beliefs about the fantastic possibilities of technology. Every problem becomes an engineering problem and better living is possible through science.

Technological utopianism therefore holds that computers and other forms of high technology are potential panaceas for society's woes. "Techno-scientific utopias" are therefore conjured in the imagination (Yar 2014, 11). For instance, while sitting in plastic chairs in a parking lot outside of a bar at two o'clock in the morning, some members of Union Hack and I held a late-night discussion about BitCoin and other forms of digital currency. I was skeptical about the long-term viability of "eCurrency" and made my concerns known. The members of Union Hack certainly saw problems as well but where my concerns were with the idea in general, theirs concerned implementation. From their perspective, if one could figure out the right way to implement eCurrency, then economic troubles associated with standard currency could be alleviated. Technology could be made to work progressively. While they acknowledged the complex nature of money and economics, a technological fix like eCurrency was envisioned as a relatively simple and elegant solution—a goal that hackers often strive for. The complications presented by eCurrency were viewed as problems to be circumvented rather than intrinsic issues. The implications such technology posed for an envisioned utopic future were too great. The only problems with eCurrency that seemed worth considering were technical and engineering challenges. Issues of value and abstraction, for example, were not real problems and, if they were, they could be engineered away.

Utopian thinking also includes the imagining of dystopian alternatives (Yar 2014). Books and movies—like *1984, Brave New World, The Matrix, Equilibrium, Terminator*, and others—show a future where technology has wrought detrimental societal consequences, often on a global scale. While hackers generally seem to lean towards optimistic forms of utopian thinking, dystopian possibilities also orient their imaginations as well. In particular, these images tend to emerge when state and corporate powers intervene in the deployment and use of technology in ways that are seen as threats to privacy (and other liberal values). Once again, the discussions around the NSA's PRISM program at DEF CON 21 and in other venues are examples of such cognition. While PRISM in its contemporary form was often described as dystopian, worries were also saddled on the idea that government expansion in surveillance would continue on into an envisioned future. Orwell's Big Brother figure and other dystopian metaphors were deployed to describe the trajectory of technology and privacy under state control. Of course, such concerns are not new in tech circles. Longstanding fears and mysticism among hackers have historically surrounded government programs like Carnivore and Echelon, which preceded PRISM (Yar 2014). In this way, "far from offering freedom from state intrusion, the Internet would appear to be at the heart of a digital Panopticon that gathers anyone using the technology in its grasp, and . . . matches anything projected in dystopian fiction" (Yar 2014, 62; citations omitted). Dystopian visions thus lurk throughout the hacker cultural imaginary, though most of these pertain to the co-optation of technology by state or corporate interests rather than anything dystopian about technology in itself.

Both technological ontology and utopianism intermingle with the philosophy of liberalism. Building from the work of Coleman and Golub (2008), such a perspective can perhaps best be summarized as *technological liberalism*. In the previous discussion of hacker perspectives on government, law, and law enforcement, the liberal perspective runs throughout but it is important to note that the issues involved were often technological in nature. Perhaps such an emphasis is unsurprising as hackers primarily work with high technology. As a result, it should be expected that many of their concerns and solutions should also be technological in nature. The contention made here is that such a perspective is not merely from an *emphasis* on technology but that direct work with computers and other forms of machinery—building from Sennett's (2008) arguments for the relationship between the head and the hand—serve to help shape the subculture's ontological perspectives and beliefs (Warnick 2004). In fact, these three components of technological liberalism are mutually reinforcing. For instance, computers operate best when information can flow freely between parts. Thus society must operate best when information can flow freely between persons and institutions. Such an orientation reinforces liberal beliefs in free speech. The connection between the liberalism and the technological ontology also encourage utopian/dystopian thinking. When technology can guide humanity toward utopian or dystopian futures, for example, then the preservation of liberal values becomes ever more pressing to ensure society moves progressively.

Technological Liberalism in Hacker Thought: Crypto Anarchy and Technolibertarianism

To further demonstrate how technological liberalism manifests in hacker culture, two bodies of thought that originated from hackers and similar subcultures are explored here. The first is what Jordan and Taylor (2004) refer to as *technolibertarianism*. This perspective views technologist culture (including hackers) as often adopting a libertarian or even neo-liberal flair. Specifically, technolibertarianism advances the position that the social, political, and economic spheres of the Internet are capable of self-regulation and do not need state control. For example, John Perry Barlow (2001, 28), a key figure in technolibertarianism and a techno-activist, wrote the following in reaction to the creation of the Telecommunications Act of 1996: "On behalf of the future, I ask you of the past [governments] to leave us alone. You are not welcome among us. You have no sovereignty where we gather. We have no elected government, nor are we likely to have one, so I address you with no greater authority than that with which liberty itself always speaks. I declare the global social space we are building to be naturally independent of the tyrannies you seek to impose on us."[8] In Barlow's dismissal of state sovereignty, invocation of "liberty," and declaration of independence from tyrannies, the influence of liberalism is clear. Even the title of his writing heralds back to the language of American liberal architect Thomas Jefferson: "A Declaration of the Independence of Cyberspace."

Thus what Jordan and Taylor (2004) refer to as technolibertarianism has helped shape hacker and other technologist subcultures. This analysis, however, disagrees with their work in that technolibertarianism is not broad enough to encompass the various streaks of liberalism that run through hacker culture (Coleman and Golub 2008). Libertarianism is but one manner in which liberalism can manifest, often taking a social Darwinist, Ayn Randian slant of extreme *laissez-faire* meritocratic market governance. With many hackers emphasizing meritocracy and a disdain of regulations, it is understandable why the label of libertarianism might be embraced. Some hackers, however, express views that contradict libertarianism, valuing community and cooperation more than stark individualism. Indeed, some manifestations of liberalism in hacker culture lean towards what may be characterized as anarchistic rather than strictly libertarian, as Jordan (2001) has previously acknowledged.[9] As a result, the association with a broader ontological perspective, particularly towards the state, running through hacker culture may be more appropriately described as a form of liberalism, rather than libertarianism.[10]

Crypto anarchy comprises the second example of technological liberalism's impact on hacker/technologist thought. The crypto anarchists arose from the public key cryptography movement, which was a push by technologists in the 1980s to make encryption easier and more accessible (Levy 2001). One of the reasons public key cryptography was advocated was that (ideally) individuals could use such technological measures to protect themselves and their privacy, particularly against intrusions by the state (Frissell 2001; Hughes 2001; Levy 2001; May 2001b). Cypherpunk Eric Hughes (2001, 82) describes the perceived liberal potential of technology held by crypto anarchists: "People have been defending their own privacy for centuries with whispers, darkness, envelopes, closed doors, secret handshakes, and couriers. The technologies of the past did not allow for strong privacy, but electronic technologies do." In this, we can see that the liberal values of privacy and autonomy are in full display. Crypto anarchists, however, perfectly demonstrate a sense of technological utopianism—the best way to solve problems wrought by state control, particularly surveillance, is to use the technology of encryption. As such, crypto anarchists aptly display the orientation of technological liberalism.

Conclusion

While perhaps taking the long and winding path to its conclusion, the argument advanced in this chapter is that hacking is underpinned by a philosophy of technological liberalism, a combination of liberalism, a technological ontology, and technological utopianism. To demonstrate this, the results of an ethnographic content analysis and ethnographic field research were discussed concerning hacker perspectives on government, law, and law enforcement. Five themes readily manifested themselves through the data. The first three present a kind of "hacker critique," in which governments are viewed as controlling and inept, often capable of creating collateral damages through their (dys) functions. The fourth presents some exceptions to these critiques. The state, while viewed as problematic, is not worth discarding outright as there are some appreciated aspects, such as its perceived ability to protect civil liberties. Finally, potential solutions to the hacker critique are offered. Discussing these five themes establishes a foundation on which to advance the argument for the existence of a broad hacker philosophy: technological liberalism.

The impression may have been given that *all hackers* subscribe to technological liberalism *all of the time*. To make this assumption, however, is a mistake. Much like Coleman and Golub (2008) caution against the canonization of a "hacker ethic" that encompasses the entire hacker community, it would be a mistake to say that technological liberalism flows through all hackers and their activities consistently. That said, the argument made here is that *many* aspects of the hacker community seem to coincide with technological liberalism. As such, it may serve as a reasonable political philosophy for understanding dominant perceptions in the hacker community, but may fall short in explaining the activities of some individual hackers or those who work in the margins of the hacking community.

With this caveat in mind, the notion of technological liberalism will resurface again as a key point dialectically situating hackers within the context of capital accumulation, production, and consumption. Having now established that hacking is (1) a class-oriented phenomenon, (2) a craft, and (3) underpinned by a philosophy of technological liberalism, this analysis now builds from this foundation to advance the argument that hackers are located firmly within the dynamics of capitalism as both a creative and destructive force—as both a boon and a bane to capital.

PART II

The Radical Turn

4

The (Hack) Mode of Production

Thus far, the approach adopted in this book has been careful—examining multiple facets of hackers and hacker culture. While initially separate analyses, the chapters included in part 1 all point toward a common end. Proceeding from the individual level to the subcultural to the philosophical, this analysis has attempted to deeply explore hackers and hacking culture in a way that builds toward a broader structural understanding. Since hacking has been identified as (1) a class-based phenomenon, (2) a kind of labor (craft), and (3) linked to technological liberalism, the evidence indicates hacking is best understood from a *political economic* perspective. In particular, radical criminology and the Marxist theoretical tradition provide a robust body of knowledge from which to situate hackers in the broader dynamics of capitalism and the forces of crime control.

Before proceeding, we should revisit the definition of hacking developed in chapter 2. Hacking was determined to be a kind of late-modern technological transgressive craft or, in other words, *craft(y)*. As such, the hacker is a laborer (either working for themselves or others) in the technological sphere (particularly in programming) who engages in creative, skillful, and often transgressive computational feats. Included are various free and open-source software programmers, security hackers, hardware hackers, and other members of the hacker community. Hackers can be hobbyists or professionals, criminal or non-criminal, but in all capacities they are laborers. In recognizing hackers as a collective of intellectual laborers, it thus makes sense to adopt nomenclature previously suggested by Wark (2004), to recognize hackers as a particular class of worker, which he refers to as "the hacker class." The use of such a term, however, may be mystifying in that it aggregates widely variant forms of labor ranging from the cubicle-confined-yet-virtuosic programmer to the underground security hacker. The reader, therefore, should bear in mind that "hacker class" is meant to represent a *diverse* pool of technological labor.

The following discussion is divided into six sections, which situate hacking in the dialectical nuances of capital accumulation from a Marxist perspective and thus present "a searing cultural assault on the accepted meanings of crime, law, and justice" (Ferrell 2013, 262).[1] First, the implications of hacking as a middle-class phenomenon are discussed in the context of Marxism. Then, hacking is discussed as a craft, filtered through Marx's discussions of skill, social structures, and labor experiences. Third, narratives concerning a split from the Protestant ethic called the *hacker ethic* are explored as they potentially contribute to the immiseration and the exploitation of the hacker class. Specific ways in which hackers are exploited are then explored. Fifth, technological liberalism is situated in the greater history of economic liberalism with particular attention to liberalism's entrenchment in the contradictions of capitalism. Finally, hacking is briefly discussed as a blurring of production and consumption in late-modern capitalism. Chapter 5 then expands on this analysis, providing what is perhaps the most radical criminological component of this analysis, exploring how the image of hackers, technology, and intellectual property are arranged in such a way to permit the implementation of legal mechanisms towards hackers and the technological realm generally.

Hacking as Middle Class

Early in chapter 1, hacking was established to be a largely a middle-class phenomenon (though, by no means, exclusively). While this conclusion may be obvious to some, as Karl Polanyi (1944, 133) has stated, "The emphasis on class is important." The middle classes, for Marx, were a group precariously situated in capitalist society. They reap relative benefits from their class positioning in society, yet are constantly in peril of trickling into the proletariat. As capitalism has evolved over time, the distinction between middle and working classes have only become more blurred and permeable. Because of their relative privilege over other members of the proletariat or non-bourgeois classes, they are often willing to defend capitalism. When they confront the political economy, they "fight against the bourgeoisie, to save from extinction their existence as fractions of the middle class. They are therefore not revolutionary, but conservative. Nay more, they are reactionary, for they try to roll back the wheel of history" (Marx and Engels [1848] 2005, 20).

Hackers find themselves in similar class positioning under late-modern capitalism—caught in the wheels yet often relatively privileged compared to lower and working classes.

Many previous analyses of hackers and other social and cultural issues surrounding the rise of the information economy have fallen into what Michael Perelman (1998, 9) has described as a "willful disregard for the nature of class." Class helps shape the narratives of peoples' lives. The analysis of hacker background and developmental factors showed that, while the cost of technology is rapidly declining, there are particular advantages afforded to hackers as largely members of the middle class relative to the working class and poor including (1) the ability to readily access computers, (2) surplus time to spend learning the ins-and-outs of programming and other computer-related tasks, and (3) existing in an environment that is more likely to nurture behaviors conducive to learning about computers and programming. These advantages matter as much in their early stages of development as they do in adolescence and adulthood.

From a Marxist perspective, the early exposure to technology that such class positioning affords is vital in learning to work. In *Capital Volume 1*, Marx ([1867] 1967, 421) describes that to be an effective machinist, it is best to start young: "To work at a machine, the workman should be taught from childhood, in order that he may learn to adapt his own movements to the uniform and unceasing motion of an automaton." Of course, Marx was writing at a time where the machine was being used to deskill labor and reduce the worker to a simple cog in the productive process. While deskilling still occurs—most notably with advances in artificial intelligence—there is a strong need for skilled laborers in the technological domains, particularly computers. Even in these circles, there is a pressure to start young as exemplified through efforts to pull children into computer programming training or "coding camps" and other related programs.

In describing the rise of knowledge and technology workers in the current era of capitalism, David Harvey (2014, 188) states: "They needed, however, to be well educated in analytic and symbolic skills and much of this begins in the home where, loaded down with electronic gadgets, children learn at an early age how to use and manipulate data and information adequate for an emergent 'knowledge-based' economy." Then, connecting such early development with technology to middle-class status, Harvey (2014, 188) continues: "This group forms the core of a relatively affluent though highly mobile upper-middle class within capitalism." The ability to access technology early and often—found more often among middle and upper classes—is thus associated strongly with developing proclivities into hacking.

Though the cost of technology is continuously declining, and many hackers have engaged in practices to overcome cost barriers, pricing and availability still constitute a barrier for large swathes of the population. For instance, even if one were to fully take advantage of F/OSS software, acquiring hardware alone could make things difficult. If one is poor then practices like dumpster diving or "trashing" for old computers and components are available to circumvent cost barriers. These practices, however, indicate that additional (and sometimes significant) efforts are unnecessary for middle or upper classes.

In addition, as chapter 1 previously indicated, the relative privilege of middle-class status also is conducive to a pre-adolescent environment that favors learning and interest in technology. "Middle-class households," Perelman (1998, 9) explains, "can offer their children access to powerful new learning opportunities, such as computers and online services, which families of poorer children cannot dream of affording." Much of this learning happens within the context of play for the young and "the economics of play works in favor of the well-to-do" (12). Children in relatively affluent environments are not only more likely to have access to computers but also to people who offer instruction and advice in technology—poor children are often at a disadvantage in this regard. As a result, "class status is crucially relevant in understanding the role of information within the information economy" (13). In other words, many hackers have the advantage of various environmental, intellectual, and material resources indicating economic class as a key variable.

Hacking, Craft, and Marx

All human beings want the satisfaction of doing something well and want to believe in what they do. Yet at work, in education, in politics, the new order does not and cannot satisfy this desire.
(Sennett 2006, 194)

The second chapter of this book explored the essence of hacking. In doing so, this work found that hacking is perhaps best thought of as a kind of labor—craft. This finding points to the necessity of a political economic analysis. Craftwork has a conflicted history with the progression of capitalism—a conflict that Marx ([1867] 1967) himself noted while describing how machinery further intensified the exploitation of the worker through reducing the number of laborers necessary (thus increasing the surplus population and also deskilling work). This, in turn, increased dependency on the capitalist for employment and perpetuated the alienation between the worker and him/herself.[2] He perhaps best summarizes this relationship by stating, "The number of tools that a machine can bring into play simultaneously, is from the very first emancipated from the organic limits that hedge in the tools of a handicraftsman" (374). Sennett (2008, 80) echoes this sentiment: "The greatest dilemma faced by the modern artisan-craftsman is the machine. Is it a friendly tool or an enemy replacing work of the human hand?" Three components of craftwork are discussed here as relevant from a Marxist perspective—useful for situating hacking in the dialectics of capital accumulation. The first concerns skill, followed by hacking and guild structures, and ending with the experience of craftwork and hacking.

Skill

One of the key features that qualifies hacking as a craft is an appreciation of skill. Skill is the marker of a true hacker and craftsperson. No legitimate claim to either can be made until one accrues the skill necessary to be recognized by one's peers as such and, even so, there is always the lingering impetus for greater skill development. Marxist analyses of labor, however, have long noted "capital's penchant for deskilling," thus pitting the elements of craft against the interests of capital (Harvey 2014, 119; see also Braverman 1974; Marx [1867] 1967; Perelman 1998). In the early periods of industrialization, craftwork was eroded, giving way to the efficiency and control demanded under advocates for Taylorism, Fordism, and similar deskilling regimes. For these laborers, "their specialized skill is rendered worthless by the new methods of production" (Marx and Engels [1848] 2005, 16). To increase the ability of capital to extract greater surplus value from the worker, labor had to be broken into its constituent tasks, which could then be efficiently strung together along a series of "specialists" and machines to accomplish the manufacture of a product more rapidly than any single craftsperson could. Such approaches did make many goods affordable for the masses—indeed, such has been one of the canonized social goods wrought through industrialization.

There are problems with the industrialized labor process, however, which Marx was more than keen to point out. One is that these processes—particularly the inclusion of machinery—makes it so the worker has to spend less time generating the value it takes to pay their wages for material subsistence or, as Marx describes it, to reproduce their labor. This process then means that more of the time the worker toils at the machine is more *surplus value* generated which the capitalist gets to reap. In this way, the worker is said to be *exploited*. Another consequence of this process is that the worker becomes *alienated*. While this alienation occurs in various ways, one is that the worker becomes alienated from their work. In other words, in the era of craftwork, the laborer was in greater control of the process of production and this process was also more internalized. The movements of the craftperson, the skill developed, and the knowledge acquired through time and effort were all integral to the process. Thus it was difficult to separate *labor* from *laborer*. Under industrialized capital production, however, the skill and knowledge of the craftperson are removed. Skill is replaced by task specialization, such as screwing on a single bolt to a car chassis *ad infinitum*, and through machines capable of performing intricate tasks with relatively little human input. Knowledge is replaced by a concentrated caste of machine builders and designers. In this way, the worker is *alienated from their labor* in that it is now something external to them and, through the process of exploitation, hostile.

Of course, the emphasis on deskilling has not been total. Indeed, there have been many forms of skilled labor that have endured. After all, if skilled labor were completely eradicated, who would design and build new technologies? This presents a contradiction for capital because it has a vested interest in the products of skilled labor but there is "a direct relationship between the degree of skill required to perform any given task and the scarcity of that skill," according to Ursula Huws (2014, 28). Further, skill possession increases "the ability of the workers who possess it to negotiate with employers . . . for high wages and decent working conditions." While machinery has been traditionally used to resolve this problem, until artificial intelligence advances sufficiently, machines cannot replace the skilled and creative labor necessary to design new technologies.

Where capital cannot eradicate skill, it instead attempts to reduce its monopolization. Harvey (2014, 120) describes the abolition of monopolizable skills in computer programming:

> When new skills become important, such as computer programming, then the issue for capital is not necessarily the abolition of those skills (which it may ultimately achieve through artificial intelligence) but the undermining of their potential monopoly character by opening up abundant avenues for training in them. When the labour force equipped with programming skills grows from relatively small to super-abundant, then this breaks monopoly power and brings down the cost of that labour to a much lower level than was formerly the case. When computer programmers are ten-a-penny, then capital is perfectly happy to identify this as one form of skilled labour in its employ, even to the point of conceding a higher rate of remuneration and more respect in the workplace than the social average.

In this way, capital is said to deskill the domains that provide the best return on surplus value without the need for skill and to proliferate skill in areas where it is necessary. This strategy is, as Harvey (2014) describes, to essentially saturate the market with skilled labor so as to prevent its monopoly power.

Hacking then presents a two-folded reaction to capital's efforts. First, it is a clear reaction to the deskilling of labor generally. By embodying many characteristics of craft, hacking runs against the banality of modern work environments and seeks a return to a time when the craft was worth pursuing in and of itself—developing one's skill in a trade and seeking satisfaction through that labor. From the hacker working on the edges of programming development to the security researcher seeking new and innovative ways to bypass or obliterate digital security systems, the phenomenological objective is to find satisfaction in ones work—through flow, excitement, or other emotional outcomes. In many ways, it is a struggle against the tedium and banality of late modernity.

The other reaction is to the erosion of monopolizable skills. Hacking is not just about developing skill. In its emphasis on doing inventive and unorthodox things, it pushes ahead—each hacker thus developing a kind of niche, a specialty. The problem is the moment they solve a particular problem or figure out a new approach *and* that knowledge becomes shared, it is open to proliferation among other programmers. For instance, the moment an innovative new program in Linux is created, others may be similarly crafted for proprietary operating systems.[3] In the domain of security, when one person finds and publishes a new exploit, it can be appropriated into the literature used to train new security engineers and programmers.[4] Or when a malware writer codes a new and inventive virus and releases it into the wild, that code is open for study by security researchers and potentially replication by other enterprising coders. When considered in tandem with the ever-expanding body of knowledge in these domains and the need for workers to continuously keep abreast of current developments in their fields—lest they fall victim to "skills extinction"—it becomes clear that the skills hackers develop are not "durable possessions" (Sennett 2006, 95). The continual emergence of new technology similarly threatens to antiquate accrued skills. In this way, hackers and similar laborers are always in a rush against their own obsolescence, seeking to stay on the cutting edge. In the workplace, this approach could be seen as a way to prevent their skills from becoming devalued through the mass training of other programmers. Such efforts are also necessary for hacker-laborers to prevent being rendered useless in late-modern capitalism and thus be relegated to the ranks of the surplus population (Marx [1867] 1967; Sennett 2006). These threats are all the more intense when considering that the growing pool of skilled labor domestically in the West is increasingly displaced by cheaper skilled labor in the areas of programming and human services elsewhere in the world through globalization of the market (Fuchs 2014; Sennett 2006).

To summarize, then, hacking and craftwork can be seen as ways to overcome the alienation of deskilled labor by internalizing the labor process through skill development and knowledge attainment. In addition, hacking also finds itself caught in a dilemma as the threat of *deskilling* is replaced with that of the *devaluation of skill*. Where the elimination of skill is not practical—such as in the domain of programming—capital strives to devalue skills through the proliferation of avenues for training. Hackers, as craftpersons, prevent total devaluation as they push for continual skill development and the creation of new and innovative tricks and solutions. The dilemma, however, is that the more hackers expand what can be done with computers (and share that knowledge) they potentially contribute to the pool of knowledge which can be used to train others. Thus, hackers are caught in a race against their own devaluation.

Guilds

Capital and hacking have a relationship erected around the use, development, and control of skill and knowledge. Skill, however, is not just a relationship between a worker (or a machine) and the object of labor. It is also inherently a *social relation*. One such manifestation of this, as previously described, is alienation. Skill can also be a mechanism for erecting and stratifying social groups as evidenced among both craftpersons and hackers. Social learning structures are built based on the accruement and demonstration of skill and are thus stratified to some degree along those lines. Before capitalism, production was dominated by craftpersons often organized under guilds which "conferred monopoly power over access to a skill that was based on a specific technical expertise" (Harvey 2014, 117). As evident in the social relations of skill, guilds were important because they allowed workers to ensure at least a small degree of prestige and higher rates of compensation for their labor. One point of tension between craft and capitalism was in the destruction of guilds, thereby allowing capitalists to seize control of "labour processes in industrial production" from "a division of labour and skill structure that were strongly rooted in the trades, resting on artisan labour" (116–117). Thus the social relations of skill were transformed from guild structures to the logics of industrial capitalism.

In a late-modern resurgence of guild-like social relations of skill, the hacking community further indicates a kind of backlash against the productive powers of capitalism. Previously, in most occupational environments, capital sought to tear down the power of workers in collectives—first as guilds, then as unions—to ensure the greatest returns on investment through surplus value. While the hacking community has arisen with similarities to guilds, this subculture does not necessarily help secure the wages and the nature of technological work from capital. What the hacker community does accomplish, however, paralleling guilds, is to create *social structures* to control and propagate learning and the development of skills. While advances in artificial intelligence and other areas of technology may eventually render various technological positions relatively deskilled (Harvey 2014), hackers—through the constant emphasis on creativity, novelty, and skill—race ahead of such advances. In turn, hackers secure a position as craftpersons, and the hacking community then serves as a guild to promote the spread of such skills.

Hacker Experience, Flow, Craft, and Capitalism

Skill, however, is also a trait intimately tied to the phenomenological experience of both craft and hacking. The feelings of satisfaction and excitement—through such mechanisms like flow—stem from a deeply engaging process of trial-and-error, learning, honing, and development (in some case, such as security hacking, risk plays an increased role in the emotional experience). In this sense, the labor process is largely internalized within the individual. This internalization is even evident in Marx's ([1867] 1967) definition of labor-power: "By labour-power or capacity for labour is to be understood the aggregate of those mental and physical capabilities *existing in a human being*, which he exercises whenever he produces a use-value of any description" (emphasis added). Alienation occurs when those mental and physical capabilities are externalized from the individual labor through industrialization and machinery. This alienation provides insights into capital's effects on hackers' relationship to skill, as previously discussed, but it also—through externalizing the process of labor—serves to augment the *experience* of labor as well.

Throughout his work, Marx highlights that, in the unalienated form, the laborer gains satisfaction from the labor process. He asserted that it was not work itself that was the problem but the particular form of labor and the social relations that manifested around it. Alienation therefore generates a negative psychic experience for workers. The augmentation of the labor process through capital comes "at the cost of the mental, emotional, and physical well-being of the workers in its employ" (Harvey 2014, 125). Such alienation can create a deep sense of dissatisfaction with one's work. For instance, Sennett (2006, 106) describes programmers who were frustrated by their company's practice of pushing for early releases of software: "These programmers resented the firm's practice of shipping out incompletely formulated software in versions then 'corrected' through consumer struggles and complaints. While deeply antithetic to unions, the programmers were developing a loose professional movement called craft in code, demanding that the company desist from this highly profitable but poor-quality practice. They wanted the time to get the programs right; their sense of meaningful work depended on doing this job well for its own sake." The company pushed to streamline the production process while the programmers wanted to work intimately with the code—to perfect it. It is in this investment of time and themselves that they found meaning in their work. When software development is sped up and decoupled from the interests of the programmer-laborer, meaning begins to trickle away. These programmers were experiencing a degree of alienation from their labor.

As previously stated, both skill and knowledge are components of the labor process that were once deeply internalized within the individual, becoming increasingly externalized through changes in production, particularly the introduction of machines. Of particular importance, skill and knowledge—collectively called "intelligence" (Harvey 2014)— once removed, eliminate parts of the experience vital for intrinsically satisfying work: "To the degree that intelligence is increasingly incorporated into machines, so the unity between mental and manual aspects of labouring is broken. Workers are deprived of mental challenges or creative possibilities. They become mere machine operators, appendages of the machines rather than masters of their fates and fortunes. The loss of any sense of wholeness or personal authorship diminishes emotional satisfactions. All creativity, spontaneity and charm go out of the work. The activity of working for capital becomes, in short, empty and meaningless. And human beings cannot live in a world devoid of all meaning" (Harvey 2014, 125). In other words, the alienation process in labor deprives the worker of those elements that give work meaning— namely creativity, mental challenges, and autonomy. We can understand then why Marx ([1867] 1967, 427) noted that "only since the introduction of machinery has the workman fought against the instrument of labour itself, the material embodiment of capital."[5]

Some of this may sound familiar to the reader. When previously describing hacking as craft, the experiential components of craftwork were discussed. In particular, craftwork was described as an intimately satisfying process of labor where the person would eventually be able to lose themselves in the activity. The ability to exercise skill, be creative, and develop oneself alongside the product is what makes both craftwork and hacking meaningful. Under capital production, efficiency and mass production are favored over the aspects of labor that give it significance for the worker. In this way, hacking can be seen as a kind of reaction to industrialized production—a sort of sanctuary for satisfying labor and flow in late modernity. In its continual race to avoid the monopolization of skill, hacking also becomes a craft-like process of labor that preserves the innate satisfactions of work.

As stated earlier, in his descriptions of industrialized capital, Marx ([1867] 1967) indicated that machinery—technology—was one of the primary mechanisms used to deprive the laborer of the satisfactions of meaningful work: "The lightening of the labour, even, becomes a sort of torture, since the machine does not free the labourer from work, but deprives the work of all interest" (423). It is interesting, then, that technology does not destroy the satisfactions found in the experience of working for the hacker *per se*. Instead, work with technology *becomes* a source of meaning. The way this happens is through the craftwork dimensions described previously, allowing satisfaction through work *with* technology rather than *through* technology. Through the method of craft, hackers attempt to push the limits of what can be done with technology through skill, knowledge, and creativity. Conversely, industrialized labor uses technology to *deprive* these qualities to the worker. As such, hackers are able to maintain the satisfactions of labor through the very devices used to strip labor of meaning elsewhere. This experience, however, becomes an issue when it contributes to the exploitation of hacker labor (as described later in the discussion of the hacker ethic).

Through capital, labor has become devoid of meaning for many workers. Hackers and other technologists may struggle against this by finding satisfaction in working directly with technology, flipping the relationship between labor and technology on its head. In this manner, hackers and similar technologists challenge what Max Weber ([1905] 2002) refers to as *the Protestant ethic*. For Weber, this ethic stemmed from a widespread Calvinist anxiety that a person could do little to alter their fate for the afterlife—one's post-death destiny was predetermined. The method for resolving such dread was to labor toward prosperity. Consistent with the biblical passage that "for there is no good tree which produces bad fruit, nor, on the other hand, a bad tree which produces good fruit" (Luke 6:43), laborers who subscribed to the Protestant ethic believed that it would be impossible for a damned person to thrive in the living world. Wealth became a sign of Godliness. Under the Protestant ethic, work is not a source of satisfaction in and of itself; enjoyment of labor was of little concern. Rather, labor and wealth are valued first and foremost as measures of afterlife predestination. In recent decades, scholars have argued that this Protestant ethic has been supplanted as the dominant ethos of work in late modernity, particularly in tech industries, by *the hacker ethic*. Much as the Protestant ethic promoted the exploitation of labor, so too does this hacker ethic in the context of late-modern capitalism. It is towards this ethic the analysis now turns.

Marxism and the Hacker Ethic

In the introduction of this book, the idea of *the hacker ethic* was briefly explored. If the reader will remember, numerous writers have attempted to detail a common subcultural ethos permeating the hacker community. These attempts have described this ethos in multiple ways such as a do-it-yourself orientation (Levy 1984), underpinned with a sense of liberalism (Coleman and Golub 2008), laced with a technological ontology (Warnick 2004), and filled with a sense of technological utopianism (Barbrook and Cameron 2001). Of particular importance, some authors argue hacker culture embodies a break from the Protestant ethic, which mandates a divide between time at work and time spent at recreation (Brown 2008; Himanen 2001; Kirkpatrick 2002). Instead, hackers are said to implode this ethic and engage in labor and leisure simultaneously. Such a perspective on work has been referred to as "the hacker ethic."

As previously demonstrated, these authors are correct in their assessment of hacking as a form of labor. These writings on the hacker ethic, however, are theoretically and conceptually myopic in that—loosely drawing from Weber—they often view the hacker ethic in a manner that can be considered utopian. Indeed, if these writers are to be believed, the hacker ethic is a beacon of hope against the droll mundanities of everyday labor under the Protestant ethic. Now the worker is to *enjoy* their productive time. What these arguments fail to see is that the hacker ethic—from a Marxist perspective—does not stop the exploitation and alienation that occur under capitalism. Instead, these relations only shift while maintaining their hierarchical rigidity.

In their work, these authors wax poetic about the liberating potentialities of the blurring of labor and leisure (Brown 2008; Himanen 2001; Kirkpatrick 2002). The problem is that, for workers under the hacker ethic, their labor is not simply blurred with leisure—this blurring creates an exploitable pool of additional surplus value for capital. During the work day, part of the time spent laboring is dedicated towards labor paying for itself, generating enough value to maintain its material existence—which Marx calls *necessary labour time*. Once that is taken care of, the rest of the time spent producing is value the capitalist pockets, as Marx ([1867] 1967, 217) explains:

> During the second period of the labour-process, that in which his labour is no longer necessary labour, the workman, it is true, labours, expends labour-power; but his labour, being no longer necessary labour, he creates no value for himself. He creates surplus-value which, for the capitalist, has all the charms of a creation out of nothing. This portion of the working-day, I name surplus labour-time, and to the labour expended during that time, I give the name of surplus-labour. It is every bit as important, for a correct understanding of surplus-value, as nothing but materialised surplus-labour, as it is, for a proper comprehension of value, to conceive it as a mere congelation of so many hours of labour, as nothing but materialised labour.

In this process, while the worker can commit more of their time to the capitalist for increased wages, they must give more of themselves as well. As Marx ([1844] 1959, 4) explains in *The Economic and Philosophic Manuscripts of 1844*: "The raising of wages gives rise to overwork among workers. The more they wish to earn, the more must they sacrifice their time and carry out slave-labor, completely losing all their freedom, in the service of greed. Thereby they shorten their lives." Part of the sacrifice for the worker is time in which they are in control of themselves; time given over to the capitalist. Additionally, if the worker does *not* give their time over and, instead "consumes his disposable time for himself," then through the denial of surplus value, "he robs the capitalist" (Marx [1867] 1967, 233).[6] While machinery and other forms of technology work together to alienate the worker, as previously discussed, it also then amplifies the exploitation of labor: "Thus we see, that machinery, while augmenting the human material that forms the principal object of capital's exploiting power, at the same time raises the degree of exploitation" (395).[7]

It is easy to see how the blurring of labor and leisure can be framed positively; the worker no longer must toil for the bourgeoisie. The "toil" is somehow mitigated because labor takes on an enjoyable quality. Productive time, to some extent, becomes recreational time. Recreational time, however, also becomes productive time. Hours previously spent doing tasks unrelated to one's occupation are now spent developing skills and potential intellectual commodities which will make them more valuable workers: "There are no clear boundaries any longer between work time and leisure time, between the inside and outside of the factory, and between wage and volunteer labor" (Söderberg 2008, 4). For example, a programmer working on a personal project at home is not just enjoying their occupation; they are also becoming more skillful workers for their day job. This may be one of the greatest tricks of capitalism in the late twentieth century and into the twenty-first century: if the laborer is allowed to enjoy their work, *they will surrender more of their productive time to the capitalist.*

For many, this may not be an issue—after all, should not the worker enjoy their labor? Certainly the notion that labor should be something satisfying and meaningful to the worker is agreeable to most. Hackers and programmers, however, are not undergoing satisfying and meaningful labor in a void.[8] According to Marx ([1844] 1959, 29), when labor is sold under capitalism, they pour their life into the object and that life becomes something external to the laborer:

> The worker puts his life into the object; but now his life no longer belongs to him but to the object. Hence, the greater this activity, the more

the worker lacks objects. Whatever the product of his labor is, he is not. Therefore, the greater this product, the less is he himself. The *alienation* of the worker in his product means not only that his labor becomes an object, an *external* existence, but that it exists *outside him*, independently, as something alien to him, and that it becomes a power on its own confronting him. It means that the life, which he has conferred on the object confronts him as something hostile and alien.[9]

In the blurring of labor and leisure, the life poured into the object is equally "hostile and alien" as it acts to immiserate. Labor is still separated from the worker and given to the capitalist (the financial fruits of the labor are reaped almost entirely by the techno-capitalist). The difference between this relationship of life and its objectification under the *Protestant ethic* and the so-called *hacker ethic* is the manner in which work is given emotional and moral value. For the *Protestant ethic*, work was intimately tied to the idea of religion, conferring value onto work through its implications of delayed gratification. For the *hacker ethic*, however, the work is given emotional and moral value through the association of pleasure and fulfillment in the act of labor itself. In both instances, life is still surrendered for the sake of the capitalist. While the relationship (or the perceived relationship) between the laborer and work has changed, the process of capital accumulation is left relatively intact and the worker is still immiserated.

In this way, the transition from the Protestant ethic to the hacker ethic further facilitates the exploitation of the hacker class. Direct work with computers through the hacker ethic thus fulfills one of the key problems surrounding machinery for Marx ([1867] 1967, 403): "If machinery be the most powerful means for increasing the productiveness of labour—*i.e.*, for shortening the working-time required in the production of a commodity, it becomes in the hands of capital the most powerful means, in those industries first invaded by it, for lengthening the working-day beyond all bounds set by human nature. It creates, on the one hand, new conditions by which capital is enabled to give free scope to this its constant tendency, and on the other hand, new motives with which to whet capital's appetite for the labour of others." Under the hacker ethic, the technologist surrenders more of their time over to the capitalist willingly. In this way, the hacker ethic embodies what Julian Kücklich (2005) refers to as *playbour*, a port-manteau of *play* and *labour*. Christian Fuchs (2014, 124) explains the exploitative measures of playbour in a manner similar to the dynamics underpinning the hacker ethic: "The exploitation of digital playbour is based on the collapse of the distinction between work time and play time . . . workers are expected to have fun during work time and play time becomes productive and work-like. Play time and work time intersect and all human time of existence tends to be exploited for the sake of capital accumulation." Thus, the blurring of labor and leisure under the hacker ethic—the collapse of the divide between work and play—seems to make hackers and other technologically skilled workers vulnerable to exploitation on a major scale, with capitalists able to further colonialize workers' time. Indeed, this is part of a broader trend within business, particularly among white-collar and technological occupations that seek to capitalize on the voluntary efforts of workers (Fleming 2013). The problem with playbour and the hacker ethic, however, is that the worker is often gleeful at such immiseration and exploitation since labor becomes almost indistinguishable from play. As Fuchs (2014, 133) states, "Exploitation tends to feel like fun and becomes part of free time."

Under trades, the worker could engage in deep and fulfilling labor in a way which gave them monopoly control over the product and the process (though the craft/tradesmen system was by no means free of flaws itself). Under industrial capital, both of these characteristics—the fulfillment and the control—were removed from the laborer. The capitalist then extracted surplus value from the worker and constantly searched for ways to intensify the percent of surplus value to be had. Under playbour and the hacker ethic (and a resurgence in the craft of technological work), some sense of fulfillment is returned to the labor process as well as some degree of autonomy/control. The ability to extract value through surplus labor, however, still seems to be in the hands of capital. The dynamics underpinning the relationship between *the worker* and the *process of labor* thus seem to be shifting in late modernity while the relation between *workers* and *capital* appear to have remained relatively constant. Whether in the form of profession, hobby, rebellion, or even criminality, hacker labor appears vulnerable to immediate commodification.

The Exploitation of the Hacker Class

Not only does the rise of the hacker ethic, which is endorsed in various tech industries (Fuchs, 2014), perpetuate a gleeful immiseration of the worker, there are specific ways in which hackers—as technological laborers—are exploited, particularly related to their creative tendencies because "it is more or less axiomatic, at least in a capitalist economic system, that growth depends on innovation" (Huws 2014, 104). The ways in which hacker labor is exploited are numerous and, as such, a comprehensive explication is avoided in favor of a representative discussion. Key contradictions and points of exploitation will be detailed beginning with the relationship between free and open-source software (F/OSS), proprietary software, and commercial interests. Remember that the F/OSS movement is directed towards collaborative programming experiences designed to generate software free for the public and open for others to contribute. Tension exists in the programming community about the appropriate philosophy to guide F/OSS. One side holds F/OSS should contribute to the market place and has no problem with the appropriation of F/OSS for capitalist interests. The other opposes this relationship, though typically not on radical grounds but on liberal terms. As F/OSS guru Richard Stallman (2002) has stated, free in this sense means "free speech" rather than "free beer." For such views some have labeled Stallman a communist or socialist. Stallman himself has denied these claims, asserting that capitalism itself is not the problem but proprietary ownership of software is, namely that it restricts access to source code which is considered a form of speech—potential radical resistance is neutralized through the language of liberalism.

Regardless of which philosophy is held in the F/OSS community, free and open-source software has become intimately connected with vectoralist production. For example, one of the largest enterprises in F/OSS programming is Linux, an open-source operating system based on the UNIX architecture, which comes in numerous varieties tailored for different user experiences and demands. Such efforts are said to resist proprietary operating systems like Microsoft's Windows and Apple's Mac OS because of their free and open nature.

Currently, however, Linux is being absorbed into capital production. For instance, it is used as the primary operating system in many business servers, thus providing a low-cost platform for companies. Industry giant IBM boasts of using Linux in many of its servers (Vaidhyanathan 2012). Google has also appropriated Linux in its Android operating system, which is currently the most widely used smartphone platform (Calia 2013). While Google does not profit directly from the operating system itself because of the copyright requirements dictated by the Linux community, it does profit from sales from the Google Play store—a marketplace where users can purchase applications and other media for their Android electronics. In this sense, Google profits from Android, which was chiefly built from decades of development from the Linux community—a legacy of labor that it got for free. Similarly, the video-game distribution platform, Steam (owned by the Valve Corporation) has appropriated Linux to create its own "distro" (distribution) for computer gaming called SteamOS. Steam thus gets to release video games through its service (of which it gets a cut of the sales) on an F/OSS platform. While Valve must pour capital into altering Linux to meet their needs (similar to Google with Android), much of the foundational labor did not cost the company a red cent.

The lines between the F/OSS movement and capitalist production are permeable. In the early days when the F/OSS movement was simply the free software movement, key figures in the hacker community gathered to determine how to encourage corporate involvement in free software (Söderberg 2008). The term "open source" was adopted to appeal to businesses worried that free software would undermine profits. In addition, they also developed an alternative to the GPL software license, which makes all works accessible and modifiable and subsumes any subsequent works automatically under the same license, thus making proprietary ownership of code difficult. The summit decided to create an "open source license" that performs the same functions as the GPL but allows for derivative works to be copyrighted, allowing corporations to make their own proprietary versions to make open-source software (and its associated labor) profitable (Söderberg 2008). It would seem, then, that the hacker class assists in its own exploitation. To put the situation bluntly: "Open-source licenses can be described as an organisational principle for systematising 'primitive accumulation,' by which is meant theft, of the social labour taking place in developing communities and in the commons" (Söderberg 2008, 38).

Such forms of exploitation echo Barbrook and Cameron (2001) in their description of the "Californian Ideology": "The existence of a 'gift economy' among hobbyists was a necessary precondition for the subsequent success of products made by Apple and Microsoft. Even now, shareware programs still play a vital role in advancing software design" (370–371). They continue by stating, "The history of the Internet also contradicts the tenets of the free-market ideologues . . . many of the key Net programs and applications were invented either by hobbyists or by professionals working in their spare time. For instance, the MUD [multi-user dungeon] program, which allows real-time Net conferencing, was invented by a group of students who wanted to play fantasy games over a computer network" (371). The infrastructures and various technologies these companies use are not created through capital alone. Rather, such advancements often involve using products developed through the free labor of "hobbyists" or "professionals working in their spare time." Thus, while F/OSS can be said to resist commercialization through collaboration and openness (meant to stand in opposition to proprietary ownership and direct control of labor), capital re-calibrates itself and absorbs F/OSS as an area of extractable resources, particularly intellectual labor—winning "the ultimate prize for companies involved in the hacker movement is to engage a pool of gratis labour in one end of the balance sheet and to sell the output in the other end with no discount" (Söderberg 2008, 40).

In this fashion, F/OSS serves as a kind of digital commons—a collective pool of labor intended for the benefit of society at large. Capital, however, "consumes the commons for free . . . The essence of the commons is its social character, but in capitalism the commons are individually appropriated as proprietary goods by capital" (Fuchs 2010, 189). An additional consequence is that obtaining free labor from open source drives down the wages of employed programmers: "Not only do corporations thereby cut labour costs in individual programming projects. They also impose an overall downward pressure on the wages and working conditions of in-house computer programmers" (Söderberg 2008, 40; see also Dafermos and Söderberg 2009; Fuchs 2014).

The appropriation of such fruits of hacker intellectual labor constitutes expropriation bordering on what Marx ([1867] 1967) termed *primary* or *primitive accumulation* and Harvey (2010) describes as *ac-*

cumulation by dispossession. Under this method of accumulation, capitalists actively seek to take resources away from laborers. Early capitalist land grabs is one example of this phenomenon. The bourgeoisie devised methods, often deploying the state, to claim rights to landed resources, thus *dispossessing* laborers of their access to these resources. Once capitalists had control of these resources, it became much easier to force workers to sell their labor, as a vital means of subsistence was now converted into property and restricted from public use.

Of course, under traditional forms of primitive accumulation, the worker is entirely deprived of access without submitting to the will of the now legally sanctioned owner or becoming an outlaw (Hobsbawm 1965). Under this contemporary form of informational primitive accumulation, the worker is not wholly cut off. Such is the nature of computational technologies—information is only copied rather than stolen outright. In this sense, then, it is not so much the intellectual resources themselves that are subjected to primitive accumulation but the labor used to develop these software programs as resources. Indeed, under the ethos of the "gift economy," members of the hacker class—while working towards noble ambitions of creating software for the common good— have their labor appropriated by vectoralists. Perelman (1998, 78) thus distinguishes this form of accumulation as "advanced accumulation."

This accumulation occurs because of the capitalists class' *"collective monopoly over the means of production (or, in its updated version, the means of financing)"* (Harvey 2014, 135; emphasis in original). In the case of intellectual property, such as F/OSS programs, however, *means of production* and *means of financing* also includes a near monopoly on the *means of distribution*—that is, control over the *vectors* (Wark 2004). Of course, the Internet has been said to provide a level playing field for distribution—everyone can contribute and share their content. Numerous success stories exist for individuals getting their messages out to the public for relatively little investment. These cases, however, do not represent the general predilection of Internet consumers. Most people want an easy-to-use product from a known vendor or brand, similar to how many users prefer familiar news sources on the Internet over independent media sources (Hess 2009).

In this way, capital possesses an advantage due to its tremendous resources. It can erect its own distribution channels and advertise its services in a way that most F/OSS software networks cannot. Fuchs (2014, 302) similarly addresses the how this disparity in finance capital perpetuates this disjuncture:

> Within capitalism, free software development requires time and time is a scarce resource. So many free software developers have a day job for earning a living and contribute to software development voluntarily and unpaid during their spare time. Facebook and other commercial platforms in contrast have a revenue stream that stems from Internet prosumer commodification, which allows them to employ software engineers and other operational personnel, to buy servers and other goods that are necessary for operating and to engage in public relations by running ads and campaigns that promote Facebook usage. Platforms like Facebook and Google also have reputational power and political influence because they are huge organizations that control access to a large global user community.

In this manner, F/OSS programmers provide a large pool of free labor while capital can invest additional resources to retool F/OSS software to its needs and then use its resources, power, and influence to penetrate the market and garner attention. To provide an example, recall that for many Linux was not a popular computer operating system despite it being free and open for many years. Google, however, streamlined the user interface and then engaged in mass marketing through packaging the OS in smartphones. Android now dominates the smartphone market—Linux is widespread. Most users of Android, however, do not use Linux as a traditional operating system and may not even be familiar with free and open-source software.[10] That is the power of finance capital in the vectors: "This means that alternative online platforms in capitalism are facing power inequalities that stem from the asymmetric distributions of money and other resources that are inherent in capitalism" (Fuchs 2014, 302).

Additionally, capitalists not only appropriate free and open-source software projects but also use the ideological values like "openness" and "freedom" as marketing tools.[11] For instance, IBM invested in F/OSS development and marketed the enterprise through the slogan, "Peace, Love, and Linux" (Söderberg 2008, 5). Such strategies are essentially ventures of cultural capitalism, as Slavoj Žižek (2009, 52) describes: "At the level of consumption, this new spirit is that of so-called cultural capitalism; we primarily buy commodities neither on account of their utility nor as status symbols; we buy them to get the experience provided by them, we consume them in order to render our lives meaningful." Similar to Žižek's (2009) description of Starbucks and the "coffee ethic," which packages abstract values into the consumptive experience, companies like Google benefit from some users who consume Android (and its other open source-based software like its web browser Chrome) because of its associations with free and open-source software.[12] Thus, the hacker class' labor is abstracted into liberal values, which, in turn, contribute to the consumer experience. The only party that comes out ahead in this scenario are corporate owners, while the hacker class continues to be immiserated and exploited.

Even underground, black market or otherwise illicit forms of hacking do not escape at least *some* form of exploitation under the auspices of capital accumulation. While gains may be had for hackers engaged in data theft, virus writing, and other forms of technocrime, capital has reoriented itself to these threats. Indeed, these threats have sparked a massive multi-billion dollar computer crime control industry (Yar 2008a). Technocriminals, including some hackers, thus provide a pool of labor that generates real and perceived levels of risk for individuals, businesses, and government agencies, among others. This risk is then transformed into a market gap that security and insurance companies can remedy. Even threats posed by technocriminals are thus exploitable. In addition, hackers may also form the ranks of the technosecurity industry, thus providing a pool of skilled labor for these companies. Hackers are therefore on both sides of the threat-security divide—providing, in many ways, both the illness and the cure for techno-woes. Capital, however, seems to be the primary beneficiary. Thus, according to Yar (2008a, 190), security has become "inextricably entwined with the circuits of accumulation in contemporary capitalism."

Technological Liberalism and Capitalism

Recall that in chapter 3, hacker perspectives on government, law, and law enforcement were examined. The analysis pointed towards a particular philosophical perspective on the state—and potentially in other domains—permeating hacker culture, described here as a *technological liberalism*. Involved is the ethical underpinnings of liberalism, a technological ontology, and a sense of technological utopianism. Two examples of technological liberalism were then given, crypto anarchy and technolibertarianism. Much like the other analyses presented in this work, this examination has direct implications for hackers' relationships to capitalism from a Marxist perspective, particularly through its liberal philosophical roots. In particular, the history of liberalism and capitalism—economic liberalism, as Karl Polanyi (1944) refers to it— operates in a dialectical contradiction, capable of both oppression and liberation (Harvey 2014; Polanyi 1944).

Liberalism, with roots dating back to the Enlightenment, has arisen as a philosophical perspective intricately intertwined with the development of capitalism (Losurdo 2014). Polanyi (1944, 135) states: "Economic liberalism was the organizing principle of a society engaged in creating a market system." The creation of private property and the ability to produce, buy, and sell goods on the market garnered strong legitimacy from liberal notions of autonomy, meritocracy, freedom, and liberty among others. With its emphasis on personal freedom, this philosophy abhorred state power and control. This liberalism, in all of its forms, usually maintains a wary and cynical perspective towards the state.

With economic liberalism came the idea of *laissez-faire* economics. Under this notion, the state would ideally refrain from meddling in the affairs of the market and only intervene when life, liberty, and property were at stake. Thus, as capitalism took off in various countries like England, "laissez-faire was interpreted narrowly; it meant freedom from regulations in production; trade was not comprised" (Polanyi 1944, 136). In other words, the state's role became to protect political economic relations, but not to interfere with trade and the market. It was not until the 1830s, however, that "economic liberalism burst forth as a crusading passion, and *laissez-faire* become a militant creed" (136).

Economic liberalism and *laissez-faire economics* presented a kind of utopian ideal. Persons would be free to engage in market relations. As each person exercised freedom across the market—both in selling and purchasing—the market would maintain itself. The state would only be necessary to curb the impulse of others who would use their freedom to infringe on the liberty of others, either through violence, coercion, fraud, or theft. In this way, "*laissez-faire* or freedom of contract implied the freedom of workers to withhold their labor either individually or jointly, if they so decided; it implied also the freedom of businessmen to concert on selling prices irrespective of the wishes of the consumers" (Polanyi 1944, 148). While such practices could be engaged in, the ideal was that it would be irrational for persons to do this as the shifting forces of the market would punish that behavior. Polanyi (1944, 148) elaborates: "But in practice such freedom conflicted with the institution of a self-regulating market, and in such a conflict the self-regulating market was invariably accorded precedence."[13]

Despite cooperative efforts between liberal and radical criminologists, radical criminology has long recognized the problems of liberalism, particularly with how such perspectives can easily become the hand-maidens of power. Indeed, such wariness of liberalism is built into the core of radical criminology, as even Marx's critiques of capitalism were reactions to the stark realities of economic liberalism and other histori-cal circumstances. The idea of the utopian free market regulating itself with little intervention from the state for the betterment of all became a problematic affair for Marx. While capitalism did serve to advance hu-mankind in terms of technological development and mass production, Marx was struck by the barbarity of the system towards its workers. How could such a supposedly utopian system of freedom and equality ravage entire portions of the population while other albeit smaller segments were afforded vast riches? From an extreme *laissez-faire* position, since all parties are capable of exercising their freedom, some chose more wisely and were awarded in the market place for it. Under this explana-tion, the causation for social stratification is internalized—often mani-festing in rhetoric casting such diparities as results of moral or biological defects of the individual (Losurdo 2014). Resisting liberalism's tendency to transform social issues into personal problems, Marx (and other radi-cals of the time) chose to view the problem as an illness of capital rather than an illness of character.

An example of one such issue presented by economic liberalism—particularly its vision of freedom—is articulated through Marx's ([1867] 1967) descriptions of freedom and labor. He notes that workers under capitalism are simultaneously freed of ownership over the means of production—thus losing their capacity to make a living outside of wage labor—and also free to sell their labour-power to anyone they wish. Thus, through disparate ownership over the means of production (remember that current notions of private property were products of economic liberalism), the worker was subordinated in the market place, forced to subsist through wage labor. What this example demonstrates is the dual character of freedom—it is a source of liberty *and* a source of domination, one of the key contradictions of capitalism noted in Marx's work. There is, as Harvey (2014, 203) states, "a whale of a contradiction here. Freedom and domination go hand in hand. There is no such thing as freedom that does not in some way have to deal in the dark arts of domination."

Polanyi (1994, 257–258) points to the source of this contradiction between freedom and domination in the meaning of freedom itself: "Clearly, at the root of the dilemma there is the meaning of freedom itself. Liberal economy gave a false direction to our ideals. It seemed to approximate the fulfillment of intrinsically utopian expectations. No society is possible in which power and compulsion are absent, nor a world in which force has no function. It was an illusion to assume a society shaped by man's will and wish alone. Yet this was the result of a market-view of society which equated economics with contractual relationships, and contractual relations with freedom." Under this perspective, economic liberalism pretends as if "power and compulsion" as well as "force" are not problems for the liberal market.[14] In forgetting these notions, power and coercion are then allowed to run roughshod over the populace through liberalism's blind eye toward such forces. Only force or coercion of the state seems to be of concern. This dynamic can easily be seen in the neo-liberal economic policies of contemporary Western nations, most notably the United States, which have led to massive social inequality and also contributed to the expansion of institutions of social control, such as the U.S.'s corrections commercial complex and its military industrial apparatus (Lilly and Knepper 1993; Harvey 2014).

Even in the early days of liberalism, the contradiction between freedom and oppression was evident. Marxist philosopher Domenico Losurdo (2014) investigates such contradictions throughout the infancy and adolescence of liberalism, particularly in America and Britain. He describes how the rhetoric of liberalism was often paradoxically used to justify racial domination. The same Americans who were ardently trying to protect themselves from the perceived tyranny of British rule were also the ones deeply invested in maintaining chattel slavery and the relocation and extermination of the indigenous peoples (Losurdo 2014). To sustain this paradox, narratives were fashioned to exclude non-whites as full persons who would normally be protected under liberalism.[15] For instance, British philosopher John Locke is quoted as denigrating the resistance of Native Americans against the expansion and domination of the colonists: "When he [the Native American] sought to challenge the march of civilization, violently opposing exploitation through labour of the uncultivated land occupied by him, the Indian, along with any other criminal could be equated with 'one of those wild savage beasts with whom men can have no society nor security,' and who 'therefore may be destroyed as a lion or a tiger'" (cited in Losurdo 2014, 24). Under this strategy, non-Whites are reduced to the level of animal—as subhuman—and therefore categorically excluded from liberal protections. Animals were thought incapable of acting with the rational and moral mind of humans and, as such, were not considered able to appreciate their liberties nor act to protect them sufficiently in a civilized society.

Liberalism also holds that private property is necessary for the sustainment of liberty—people need to be able to own things and do with them as they please without interference from others. Once non-Whites were reduced to the level of animals, which could be owned as property, their ownership through means like chattel slavery became seen not as a form of domination but as an *exercise of liberty* (Losurdo 2014). Post-abolition, the narratives that sustained the contradiction between freedom and oppression shifted. Workers were brutally subjugated by capitalists. One justification for such exploitation was a belief that the workers did not deploy their liberty to the fullest extent possible (Losurdo 2014). If they had, then they would be owners rather than workers. Instead, they *chose* such conditions. Blame was internalized as social issues were transmogrified into personal problems. Such methods are reminiscent of contemporary political rhetoric surrounding wealth inequality and other social welfare issues. Thus, through liberalism, the denigration of the laboring classes under capitalism finds a legitimating mechanism that sustains the contradiction between freedom and oppression—the oppressed either are not deserving of liberty categorically or they fail to exercise their liberty adequately.[16]

It is in such a context of economic liberalism and the contradiction between freedom and domination that we find hackers and technological liberalism. In particular, there are aspects of *technological* liberalism that reflect broader beliefs in *economic* liberalism. Involved first is a rejection of state regulatory power. Recall two examples of technological liberalism provided in chapter 3, crypto anarchy and technolibertarianism. In both of these areas of thought, state scrutiny and control is thoroughly rejected (Frissell 2001; Hughes 2001; May 2001b). As John Perry Barlow (2001, 28) stated in his "A Declaration of the Independence of Cyberspace," "Governments of the Industrial World, you weary giants of flesh and steel, I come from Cyberspace, the new home of Mind. On behalf of the future, I ask you of the past to leave us alone. You are not welcome among us. You have no sovereignty where we gather." In this work, he goes as far as to reference the Boston Tea Party, a favored historical moment for the contemporary hyper-libertarian American political group, the Tea Party: "I decided it was a good a time as any to dump some tea in the virtual harbor."

The primary problem with technological liberalism—particularly as expressed through the "Californian Ideology" (Barbrook and Cameron 2001)—is that, while they both reject state power, the emphasis on economic deregulation roughly parallels Polanyi's (1944) description of economic liberalism and *laissez-faire* and Harvey's (2005) descriptions of neo-liberalism. Technological liberalism thus "stresses individualism, personal responsibility, competition, private property, and consumerism, lacks consciousness of inequality and exploitation, and is in line with the basic ideas of neo-liberalism" (Fuchs 2014, 122; citation omitted).[17] As my friend Gary Potter described it, "You are as free as our profit-margins allow."

For instance, according to crypto anarchists, one of the perceived virtues of cryptography is that encryption can protect privacy in the market place, thus preventing state control from obstructing the flow of money and commodities (Hughes 2001). Timothy May (2001a, 67) declares that cryptography will allow corporations, along with other "virtual communities," to effectively be "on a par with nation states"—an outcome he finds agreeable. Likewise, in attempting to cast-off the perceived oppression of the state, Barlow (2001, 28) defends online capitalist marketplaces by stating, "You [governments] have not engaged in our great and gathering conversation, nor did you create the wealth of our market-places." Barbrook and Cameron (2001, 373) summarize this state-centric political perspective in the following terms: "The California ideologues preach an antistatist gospel of high-tech libertarianism—a bizarre mish-mash of hippie anarchism and economic liberalism beefed up with lots of technological determinism. Rather than comprehend really existing capitalism, gurus from both New Left and New Right much prefer to advocate rival versions of a digital 'Jeffersonian democracy.'" In other words, the digital philosophies that have emerged from the hacker class are, by and large, unreflexive of issues surrounding capitalism. For them, the problem is state authority alone. As a result, any political action on the part of the hacker class only addresses part of the problem and, in total, protects the interests of capitalism.

The hacker class does have a history of resisting corporations but these entities are not largely seen as the problem in and of themselves—only their attempts to exert control on technology and hacker activities are viewed in such a manner.[18] In this sense, members of the hacker class are fans of *laissez-faire* economics as long as the market stays in sort of a utopian ideal—markets that maximize the liberal notion of free trade and ownership without resulting in control and domination. Hackers by and large remain fairly uncritical of capitalism as a power structure, however, thus rendering this ideal fantastical. To essentialize these hacker philosophies, then, we can assert state *and* corporate efforts to exert control are resisted but the idea of the capitalist marketplace is left intact—and it is here we find the critical oversight. A liberalist bent saturates the hacker class, which views capitalism as an ideal so long as its undesirable outcomes are suppressed. From a Marxist perspective, the system cannot be regulated in such a manner, as the problem is the system *itself*. Thus the hacker liberal philosophy finds itself being absorbed into the contradictions of capital accumulation through a pre-dominantly state-centered critical perspective.

The Blurring of Production and Consumption

Beyond blurring labor and leisure, the hacker class muddies the division between production and consumption. As high-capitalism has pro-gressed from a production-based society to one based on consumption, the hacker class engages in a contradictory relationship with the consumption of intellectual property in addition to its role as content producers (Baudrillard 1970). As previously discussed, hackers often produce and endorse the use of free and open-source software. This practice, however, does not mean that proprietary software and other content are not used at all. The particular way that many (but not all) members of the hacker class consume software and other proprietary intellectual property presents a contradiction worth noting.

The piracy (or "warez") scene has been intimately connected with hacking since early hackers shared Bill Gates's proprietary Altair BASIC software (Décary-Hétu, Morselli, and Leman-Langlois 2012; Holt 2010a; Levy 1984). Interestingly, pirating content is an act that is simultaneously subversive towards capitalism and intellectual property ownership while also upholding the institution. In a study of an online piracy group that I co-authored with Ken Tunnell, we found that pirates often engage in copyright infringement as a way to undermine copyright ownership (Steinmetz and Tunnell 2013). For some, in true technological liberalist fashion, the perception is that intellectual property is intangible and inherently "wants to be free" (59). Bruce Schneier (2006) summarizes this perspective when he states that "trying to make digital files uncopyable is like trying to make water not wet." In other words, the very ease with which intellectual property is replicated presents problems for proprietary intellectual property (Söderberg 2002). Pirates are also said to resist the current capitalist mode of intellectual property distribution and control because they believe this approach is outdated in the era of the Internet (Steinmetz and Tunnell 2013). In this vein, hackers and pirates can be seen as subversive in their consumption of content.

This type of consumption, however, also supports capitalism. In the previous study, "many participants treated piracy as an alternate mode of content distribution apart from traditional for-profit methods. After all, the 'Sharing is Caring' ethos is communal and has some semblance to a socialist worldview. The practice, though, is offset by members' hyper-consumption. It involves both sharing and downloading volumes of content. Others have alluded to pirates' contradictory positions situated between a culture of consumption and a culture of communalism. It evidently is possible to both care-and-share and satiate oneself through consumption" (Steinmetz and Tunnell 2013, 63–64). The primary problem springing from consumption of proprietary content, even if it subverts the direct payment process, is that "this contradiction is widespread among pirates—loathing the industry but loving the high-budget content that can only be generated by it" (64). While certainly more independent and low-budget projects have spread through piracy channels, the act typically involves the consumption of content that has been created by capitalist productive mechanisms. In essence, even while subverting capitalism, hackers uphold capitalism by desiring the intellectual property that it generates. Even with pushes to support and use F/OSS software, consumption in other domains (including many other areas of software) seems to be relatively unabated. The very cultural practices of hacking and piracy, then, can be said to provide some measure of resistance against the market-ends of capitalist production but not necessarily the consumptive.

Conclusion

In many accounts, hacking is portrayed as an utterly transgressive, resistant phenomenon to structures of social and technological development. Certainly there is tremendous truth to these accounts. Hackers have a long history of bucking trends, bending and breaking rules, and challenging authority. In the same paradoxical fashion that freedom can be oppressive, hackers operate within a dialectic that co-opts their various forms of labor—even when it is resistant and transgressive—into capital accumulation. Other mechanisms, however, exist which manage hackers as an exploitable class. In the tradition of radical criminology, the following chapter examines the role of the state and ideology in the maintenance of late-modern capitalism and its relationship with hackers.[19] In particular, this analysis now turns to understanding how ideological apparatuses are erected, which ultimately legitimate forms of social control on the less-than-desirable aspects of hacker culture while bolstering the power of capital in the increasingly abstracted technological domains of accumulation.

5

Crafting a Crackdown

In the previous chapter, hacking was shown to operate as both a *bane* and a *boon* for capital production in the information economy.[1] Working classes throughout the years have endured similar relationships to the political economy. When populations in the working or underclasses pose a threat to capitalism they become a "problem population." Steven Spitzer (1975, 640–642) states that, "Although these groups may victimize or burden those outside of the dominant class, their problematic quality ultimately resides in . . . the fact that their behavior, personal qualities, and/or position threaten the *social relations of production* in capitalist societies." These groups thus endanger, in some form or fashion, capital accumulation. Problem populations, however, cannot be wholly disregarded as they also serve as a valuable pool of labor for capitalism. Spitzer (1975, 645) describes this quality as the "utility of problem populations."

Hackers comprise a key problem population for the information economy. They are an indispensable source of productive and creative energy. As Jordan and Taylor (2005, 5) declare, "Hacking and hackers [have] become integral to multi-million dollar businesses; the microserfs [have] arrived." They also imperil ensconced methods of production, distribution, and consumption, however, through craft-like approaches to labor, challenges to network/information security, and defiance against intellectual property configurations, to name only a few examples. Societal reactions to political economic resistance have historically differed. Spitzer (1975) argues that reactions largely vary between groups designated as *social junk* and *social dynamite*. The former are populations labeled deviant because of their "failure, inability or refusal . . . to participate in the roles supportive of capitalist society," but are not disruptive enough to warrant "rapid and focused expenditure of control resources" (Spitzer 1975, 645). For example, hackers that participate in petty forms of digital vandalism, small-time security intrusions, and other forms of negligible malfeasance may present a "costly yet relatively harmless burden to society" in this manner (Spitzer 1975, 645). These small-time technologists may be a nuisance, but do not pose a significant enough threat to the relations of capital production to warrant significant coercive intervention. Official deviants acting as *social dynamite*, on the other hand, are more likely to trigger a major social response because of their potential to "call into question established relationships, especially relations of production and domination" (Spitzer 1975, 645). Hackers who actively transgress against intellectual property configurations, conduct major security breaches, and openly articulate political resistance are thus met with calls for coercive control specifically because of their potential to disrupt the operations of capital directly or indirectly. This chapter largely concerns itself with the development of social reactions to the social dynamite within the hacker community—though such fallout bears implications for all hackers. As with many of the laboring classes throughout the history of capital production, capitalism struggles to suppress the potential disruptive power of hackers—particularly those acting as social dynamite—while trying to maximize their utility.

Creating the conditions necessary to implement legitimate forms of control on social dynamite and other problem populations is no small task. Hearts and minds must be primed to accept such measures. This conditioning is primarily accomplished through *ideology*. While Marxist thought often seems preoccupied with the material conditions of society, tremendous attention has been given to the manifestations of power in the mental, social, and cultural imagination. Drawing from the radical criminological tradition as well as insights from labeling, moral panics, and the social construction of crime, this chapter describes the formation of an ideological apparatus that legitimizes the mobilization of state coercion and other measures against the threat hackers pose to capital accumulation.

According to Marx and Engels (1947, 37), ideology is the "rule of thoughts." From this perspective, consciousness is shaped by the material circumstances within the given political economy. In particular, the power relations of the time are ensconced. As Marx and Engels (1947, 64) explain: "The ideas of the ruling class are in every epoch the ruling ideas, i.e., the class which is the ruling *material* force of society, is at the same time its ruling *intellectual* force." The classes that disproportionately control the productive and consumptive methods of society shape much of the imaginative components of the social order. Harvey (2014, 127) summarizes this dynamic by stating that "ideological controls upon the flow of knowledge and of information become essential, along with schooling in the right ideas supportive of capital and its requirements for reproduction." Material life thus shapes the *ontologies* of subjects within the political economic order. Perceptions of social reality are configured in such a way to be largely compatible with the mode of production. Of course, that is not to say the effects are totalizing. The "means of mental production" produce their own contradictions within the broader mode of production.

Within the confines of ideology, not only do problem populations present threats to the means of material production under capitalism, but they also become symbolically associated with social maladies. For instance, the Irish, particularly the Irish working classes, have historically been stereotyped as drunkards. In *Condition of the Working Class in England*, Friedrich Engels (1958) describes the condition of the Irish immigrant working classes in Britain. His descriptions are no doubt products of their time, painting the Irish as "uncouth, improvident, and *addicted to drink*"—adding that they "introduce their brutal behaviour into a section of English society by no means noted for civilized habits or moral principles" (104). Rather than relate these traits to some intrinsic flaw in the Irish character, he instead points to their material circumstances. Engels chastises Thomas Carlyle for his description of the Irish working class, stating "Carlyle's description is a perfectly true one, if we overlook his exaggerated and prejudiced defamation of the Irish national character" (105). Instead, Engels points to social sources for the condition of the Irish working class: "What else is to be expected? Society treats him in such a way that it is virtually impossible for him to avoid becoming a drunkard. Society neglects the Irish and allows them to sink into a state bordering upon savagery. How can society complain when the Irishman does, in fact, become a habitual drunkard?" (106–107). Ideology helps construct the Irish as drunkards *by nature* rather than as a *result of historical circumstances*. If the Irish are viewed as deficient by national character, then the Irish can themselves be more easily blamed for social ills by the British working class instead of the antecedent structural conditions.

In other words, the creation of ideology within the political economy largely rests on *social construction*. The theoretical tradition of social constructionism has enjoyed a strong legacy within the social sciences, influencing symbolic interactionism, feminism, postmodernism, Marxism, neo-Marxism, and others. Its impact within criminology has been profound with various strains of critical criminology. Concerned with fundamental questions of ontology and epistemology, social constructionists, like Peter Berger and Thomas Luckman (1966), contend that our comprehension of the social world is created through a reciprocal process of meaning creation and interpretation. Such meanings are not created and processed in a void, however. Social structures and other relations shape the encoding and decoding of meaning in significant ways. In this fashion, social construction is intimately tied to ideology, a "hidden mechanism that regulates social visibility and non-visibility" (Žižek 1994, 3). Ideology structures our ontology in such a way that we can only imagine particular ideas, structures, forces, etc., within the realm of possibility. Social construction is an instrumental process in regulating "social visibility and non-visibility" in the social and cultural imaginary. In other words, the process, which culminates in ideology, is wrought largely through social constructions of reality.

In crime and criminal justice, there is nary an issue untouched by social construction. As Victor Kappeler (2011, 186) explains, "Criminal justice, like crime, is a social construction that shifts with intellectual perspective, political influence, social sentiment, cultural values, and the interests of powerful groups in society." The influences of media, politicians, culture, and other forces help craft our understanding of the world around us. Often, particularly in the areas of crime and crime control, these understandings are mired in myth and misconception (Kappeler and Potter 2005). Many of these myths, however, are shaped by power relations within society. For example, mythologies often portray the marginal and the downtrodden as dangerous while white-collar and corporate offenders' crimes and other social harms are downplayed, even though they are far more damaging physically and financially (Kappeler and Potter 2005; Reiman and Leighton 2012). In their interaction with power relations, such mythologies become intrinsically ideological.

Social constructions are seldom benign. They not only reify power relations within a given context but they also influence action, often against the marginalized and dispossessed. Take, for example, Howard Becker's (1963) *Outsiders*, a foundational study on the social construction of crime. In his study, Becker (1963, 3) challenged research that "accepted the common-sense premise that there is something inherently deviant (qualitatively distinct) about acts that break (or seem to break) social rules." Instead, he was interested in, among other things, the social process by which acts and, importantly, *people* became labeled as deviant. In his research, Becker revealed that the prohibition of marijuana (or "marihuana") was largely a result of changing social circumstances. At the time, marijuana was connected to marginalized racial populations, violence, sexual promiscuity, suicide, etc. Key figures also garnered public attention as they drew connections between marijuana, moral degradation, and populations on the fringes of society. Becker (1963) refers to these individuals as "moral entrepreneurs," or persons with strong moral beliefs who seek to influence others and change social policy to be consistent with such beliefs. If the social context is primed to react to these moral crusades, the public may intensely rally behind the cause out of fear, believing that the problem, if left unresolved, will result in moral decay and social decline. Criminologists Stan Cohen (1972) and Jock Young (2011a) refer to this phenomenon as a "moral panic."[2] Within political economy, many of these moral panics manifest during times of crisis for capitalism (Hall et al. 1978). Thus, for marijuana and other issues, social construction changes perceptions of reality and primes the public for social policy changes. As Marxist policing scholar Hall and colleagues (1978, 221) explain: "To put it crudely, the 'moral panic' appears to us to be one of the principal forms of ideological consciousness by means of which a 'silent majority' is won over to the support of increasingly coercive measures on the part of the state, and lends its legitimacy to a 'more than usual' exercise of control."

The social construction of crime has implications from a radical criminological perspective. Social constructions like crime and justice mythologies can provide legitimacy for the creation of new laws and policies as well as crime control efforts by various wings of law enforcement. In Becker's (1963) study, the labeling of marijuana as deviant and criminal permitted a crackdown on its users, predominantly racial minorities. In Jeff Ferrell's (1993) ethnography of graffiti artists, local elites campaigned to portray graffiti as a cultural blight, which lead to a crackdown on the art form and its artists. Various laboring classes have also not been immune to these effects as well. Many operations of the criminal justice system are thus directed downward toward controlling what Randall Shelden (2008) terms *dangerous classes*, reminiscent of Spitzer's (1975) discussion of problem populations. While Shelden is reluctant to provide a formal definition, the dangerous classes generally consist of the underclasses, racial and ethnic minorities, and laboring classes that pose a threat to the operations of capitalism. "Many of the daily activities of the American criminal justice system," Shelden (2008, 14) states, "have revolved around controlling, regulating, containing, or in some way keeping tabs on those groups deemed dangerous" (see also Platt et al. 1977). In this capacity, criminal justice includes not only law enforcement, courts, and penal institutions, but legislatures and private corporations (including the various security industries). Social construction and ideology provide mechanisms useful for legitimating the application of crime control on certain populations while leaving others, like political elites and the wealthy, relatively untouched.

Such ideological mechanisms have historically permitted the use of formal social control against laboring classes. For instance, the perception that laborers were ungrateful layabouts, among other things, permitted the use of law enforcement, the military, and militia forces against industrial laborers in the late 1800s and early 1900s (Harring 1983; Zinn 2005). The social construction of persons of African descent as subhuman ideologically allowed the creation of slave patrols during U.S. chattel slavery (Losurdo 2014; Platt et al. 1977). Ideology thus creates an environment where criminal justice and other forms of coercive control can be successfully implemented to reduce the threatening qualities of particular classes while maximizing their utility toward production and accumulation. Spitzer (1975, 640) refers to this process as *deviance production* which "involves the development of and changes in deviant categories and images." Problem populations are thus officially branded as deviants and subjective to coercive forms of control, most likely through state action. In this fashion, deviance production is a method of enclosing acts deemed threatening to the state or capital, but perhaps not necessarily the public—the creation and suppression of "social crime" (Lea 1999).

Hackers are subjected to the same forces of ideology and coercive control as many other crime "problems," becoming perhaps one of the most prominent dangerous classes in the information economy. Hackers are responsible for a myriad of economic threats while also providing *utility* through their potential as a creative laboring class (Spitzer 1975). Thus capitalism relies on the state and the creation of a technosecurity industry (among other mechanisms) to control these threats while taking advantage of hacker labor. Ideologies are erected to justify the concentration of power in this regard in the interests of capitalism. Drawing from Hall et al. (1978), Christian Fuchs (2014) explains that when both the mainstream media and political/law enforcement authorities argue for similar policies in the wake of a moral panic, a reification of the "control culture" and "signification culture" occurs that acts to ensnare the issue. In this fashion, the media and state actors cooperate in the creation of an "ideological state apparatus." In the articulation of such an apparatus, both the media and state authorities give legitimacy to the process of social control (Fuchs 2014). The remainder of this chapter is dedicated to explaining how such an "ideological state apparatus" forms around hacking.

The campaign to secure technological infrastructure and intellectual property for capital from the threats posed by hackers involves what I describe as three *fronts of social construction*. First, hackers are constructed as dangerous. Second, intellectual property is reified. Finally, technological infrastructures are construed as vulnerable. These fronts combine into an ideology that lends legitimacy to social control efforts toward hackers and related technologists. The development of such an ideology is necessary so that capitalists can maintain or gain control over the vectors. As a result, this analysis continues in a long line of works that analyze "how culture and ideology are manufactured and manipulated in order to further elite interests" (Bell and York 2010, 116).

The Construction of the Hacker as Dangerous

As previous research has demonstrated, the image of hackers has morphed over time into a rather sinister visage by media, political rhetoric, and the other forms of popular discourse (Halbert 1997; Skibell 2002; Thomas 2002; Wall 2007, 2008, 2012; Yar 2013). In recent years, hacking has become synonymous with *technological danger*. It would be untenable to assert that such an ideological endeavor was instrumental in nature, though undoubtedly some individuals purposefully cast hackers negatively for such purposes. Rather, the social construction of hackers as a dangerous class is most likely structural through the power of ideology—the social and political economic configurations of capitalism work in such a way as to encourage such portrayals. The public is particularly susceptible to these messages because they have "little direct contact with computer hackers," which makes the hacker image "particularly susceptible to shifts in public perception" (Skibell 2002, 343). In addition, for many, hackers' "actions are difficult to understand, have overtones of adventure and action, and make for good publicity" (Halbert 1997, 366).

In the media, whenever a computer network crime is committed, the term "hacker" is frequently used (with little consideration for its historical and cultural roots) (Holt 2009; Turgeman-Goldschmidt 2011; Yar 2013). Following the results of Operation Sundevil, a secret service sting on computer crime, Assistant Director of the Secret Service—Gary M. Jenkins—stated hackers were "no longer misguided teenagers, now high-tech computer operators using computers to engage in unlawful conduct" (as cited in Halbert 1997, 361). Such constructions are so potent that the hacker has now come to represent the "archetypal 'cybercriminal'" (Wall 2008, 47). As a result, the only substantive popular culture representations of hackers we tend to experience are those that involve various computer misdeeds and crimes. As Coleman and Golub (2008, 256) state, today's dominant public perception of hackers is that they are typically "young men whose pathological addiction to the Internet leads to elaborate deceptions, obsessive quests for knowledge, and bold tournaments of sinister computer break-ins."

Popular culture provides a litany of examples of the social construction of hackers. As David Wall (2012, 12) points out, these characterizations are not a recent development. In the Victorian era, the "savant" character archetype emerged, "a learned person of profound knowledge who could utilize technology to his or her (usually his) advantage for good or bad." Classic monster stories used this archetype including Mary Shelley's *Frankenstein* and Robert Louis Stevenson's *The Curious Case of Dr. Jekyll and Mr. Hyde*. Like most fiction—horror, science fiction, or otherwise—these depictions are products of their time. The particular image of the technology-wielding scientist using nigh magical knowledge and skill to control the forces of nature, themselves, and others emerged in a period of "great social upheaval caused by technological innovation" (Wall 2012, 12). Much like the Frankenstein Monster or Mr. Hyde, these horrors were the result of scientific discovery run amok. Hackers, it would seem, are the contemporary versions of Drs. Frankenstein and Jekyll—technological masters capable of (willingly or unwittingly) causing devastating consequences through their experiments. In this way, the savant was "a Victorian prototype of the hacker" (Wall 2012, 12).

Perhaps the earliest popular media representation of hackers in the contemporary sense was in 1983 with the movie *WarGames*. In this movie, David Lightman (played by a young Matthew Broderick) is searching for the video game company called Protovision. Using a modem and a computer program that randomly dials numbers until it finds a connectable server (since termed "war dialers" following this movie's release), Lightman inadvertently accesses the supercomputer WOPR (War Operation Plan Response) (Thomas 2002). Under the impression that the system is a video game rather than a U.S. Department of Defense computer built to simulate outcomes of a nuclear war, Lightman nearly causes World War III. While the movie does not portray hackers as overtly sinister, Lightman's technological knowledge is portrayed as hazardous. Through the combination of intelligence, skill, and blissful ignorance of the ramifications of his actions, Lightman—as just one person—jeopardizes the entire world. The impression gleaned is that no malice is needed on the part of the hacker; their knowledge and skill is dangerous in and of itself.

WarGames was a watershed moment for hacking. For some, the movie would act as a calling to hacker culture (Coleman 2012; Thomas 2002). The movie drew in novices to hacking while some seasoned technologists were introduced to the concept. *WarGames*, however, was also pivotal in bringing public attention to the idea of computer crimes: "The movie helped problematize computer hacking as an issue, and just as the underground exploded in the wake of the movie, so did stories about them" (Skibell 2002, 341).

In 1995, the movie *Hackers* was released. The film opens on a preadolescent Dade Murphy (Jonny Lee Miller) facing consequences for a major computer security hack that resulted in a legal mandate barring him from computer use until he turned eighteen years old. The movie then flashes forward to Dade moving to New York City with his mother after his parent's divorce. Here, he falls into the local hacker scene. The plot centers around Dade's hacker group running afoul of a criminal hacker (Eugene, aka The Plague) working for a major corporation. This hacker attempts to frame Dade's crew for a virus he created as the crew comes increasingly close to uncovering a multi-million dollar scam run by Eugene and a high-level corporate administrator. The movie ends with the scam thwarted and the hackers cleared of charges. As is typical of Hollywood movies, a romantic subplot runs throughout the movie, and culminates in Dade going on a date with Kate, a fellow hacker played by Angelina Jolie.

Hackers was one of the first mainstream pop culture representations of hacker subculture, often described as *the scene*. The film showed the scene as a combination of nerdy technological enthusiasm, cyberpunk style, and youth countercultural sensibilities. The movie also played on the tension between hackers and the U.S. Secret Service who, at the time, was the key law enforcement agency cracking down on hacking activities. Capturing the animosity felt by members of the community, the Secret Service were portrayed as out-of-touch and overly aggressive, with their raids of middle-class urban and suburban homes appearing comical in their excess.

Despite the campy writing and visual effects, the movie made genuine attempts to pay homage to its subcultural roots. References were made to notable hacker sayings (like "hack the planet!") and figures. One character was even named Emmanuel Goldstein as an homage to the editor of *2600: The Hacker Quarterly* (himself adopting the "handle" from the pseudo-antagonist of Orwell's *1984*). What the movie also did, however, was play into the mythos of hackers as omnipotent technological wizards. There is seemingly little hackers cannot do in this movie. For instance, Kate and Dade engage in a competition to see who can make Secret Service Agent Richard Gill (Wendell Pierce) the most miserable. Together, they cancel his credit card, create a fake personal ad in his name for various sexual services (which results in a deluge of explicit calls to his work phone), place a warrant out for his arrest, and fake his death by altering his payroll accounting information to "deceased." In another example, antagonist The Plague unleashes a virus that threatens to cause a worldwide ecological disaster by capsizing numerous oil tankers. As such, the movie portrays hacker abilities as farcically powerful, regardless of their moral underpinnings.

Six years after *Hackers*, popular culture continued using the hacker as both a character archetype and a plot device, though the criminal connotation became stronger over time. In 2001, *Swordfish* further advanced perceptions of hacker-power while also emphasizing the illicit qualities becoming more associated with hacking. In one scene, Gabriel Shear (John Travolta) attempts to recruit Stanley Jobson (Hugh Jackman), a hacker recently released from prison, for a criminal endeavor. To test his skills, Gabriel gives Stanley sixty seconds to break into a U.S. Department of Defense network with a (literal) gun to his head while receiving oral sex. Despite the ludicrously unrealistic task set before him, Stanley manages to succeed.

The practice of showing hackers as simultaneously antagonistic and heroic technological juggernauts continues today. In a post–9/11 era, media has portrayed hackers on both sides of terror conflicts. In the 2007 movie *Live Free or Die Hard*, the antagonist is a sort of "cyberterrorist" that the hero, John McClane, must stop with the help of a hacker who uses his skills to thwart the terror plot to cripple critical technological systems on which American society has become dependent. In 2015, *Blackhat* was released. This film features Chris Hemsworth as Nick Hathaway, an incarcerated hacker furloughed to help stop another "black hat" hacker from crippling major infrastructures and markets in conjunction with an organized crime syndicate. The definitional boundary of hackers in these films sticks firmly within the realm of technocrime and security. In these depictions, hackers are featured on both sides of the battle, indicating a sort of destructive (or protective) metaphorical strength regardless of moral or nationalistic orientation. In other words, even when they are on the side of "good," their skills are still represented as powerful through their utility to defeat an enemy.

These portrayals are haunted by the threat of potential destruction if the hacker's moral alignment wavers. As Wall (2008, 50) explains, "The mythology surrounding the omnipotent hacker assumes that once the ethical hacker's moral bind has eroded and they go over to the 'dark side' then they become a danger to society." Seldom is the term "hacker" used when describing a dedicated programmer working on an open-source project—these representations yield poor dramatic tension and audience interest, particularly as audiences now come to expect danger and subversion from hackers. Couple the aforementioned constructions of hackers with the fact they are often portrayed as conflated with organized crime, all powerful, anonymous, and unpunished, it is easy to see how hackers have been erected into an omnipotent cyber-specter haunting the digital plane, regardless of how much these portrayals may differ from reality.

To some degree, there are hackers who have been complicit in this construction. Though I urge the reader to avoid confusing "hacker" with "criminal," there are indeed hackers who engage in illicit and harmful behaviors. As the general population is already primed through media and political rhetoric to view hackers generally as criminals, these events serve as a kind of confirmation bias, reaffirming public perceptions. "A steady stream of media reports in which vandals, burglars, thieves, terrorists, and trespassers are labeled as hackers does more than shift our focus, it establishes a new prototype," as Helen Nissenbaum (2004, 208) explains. "The more times people hear about hackers in these terms, the more they are led to see these hackers not as the exceptions but as the rule. A category shift occurs not as a result of revised formal definitions, nor at the edges where boundaries are carved, but at the center where the *typical* hacker is drawn. The accumulation of stories constructs the prototype of a newly defined category" (emphasis in original). While identifying precise estimates of stereotypically illicit hackers is impossible, it can be safely stated that not all hackers are criminal. As one hacker stated in an interview, these hackers "are a minority, but a *loud* minority." Through these constructions, however, the public equates technocriminal hackers as prototypical hackers.

Recently, one particular activity that drifts between licit and illicit has substantively contributed to hacker demonization. Though hacking has historically enjoyed a proud legacy of pranking and similar behaviors (McLeod 2014; Peterson 2011; Thomas 2002), one genre of tricksterish hi-jinxes has seized the spotlight: *trolling*. With its origins stemming from early phone phreaks and other hacker/prankster traditions, trolling involves "the targeting of people and organizations, the desecration of reputations, and the spreading of humiliating information" (Coleman

2014, 19; see also Nikitina 2012). Almost always outlandish, vulgar, and offensive, trolling is practiced by many persons across the Internet—with hackers comprising some of the most dedicated and infamous of all—to solicit "lulz," or laughter, at the expense of others.

Some trolling activities are relatively small-time such as making controversial statements in an online discussion forum to trigger volatile social reactions (like telling a message board for feminists that women "belong in the kitchen"). The troll does not have to believe in their claims—the objective is to incite a reaction. Recognizing that the point is to trigger hostility, some persons attempt to deflect attention away from such provocateurs ("don't feed the trolls!"). Other such pranksters are more ambitious and pursue a larger audience. For instance, the hacker organization Anonymous is known for combining their trolling expertise with political activism. In 2008, they famously targeted the Church of Scientology for attempting to remove an interview with Tom Cruise from the Internet. Anonymous used denial of service attacks to take down the Scientology website, made prank calls, "declared war" on the Church, and arranged protests outside of various church centers with the protestors wearing Guy Fawkes masks, to name a few such lulzy strategies.

Many of the more notable trolling efforts have involved barrages aimed at security systems or, more importantly, perceptions of security, like website defacement. In this way, the pursuit of lulz shows "how easily and casually trolls can upend our sense of security by invading private spaces and exposing confidential information" (Coleman 2014, 19). Trolling hackers simultaneously challenge taken for granted notions of Internet security (and social decorum) while also contributing to dominant perceptions of hackers as dangerous digital others.

As previously stated, trolling is part of a broader legacy of prankster tendencies in hacker culture. Steven Levy (1984) describes the early MIT hackers engaged in numerous pranks. Indeed, MIT continues to enjoy a tradition of noteworthy pranks, many of which performed by local hackers and have been cataloged over the years by T. F. Peterson (2011) in his book *Nightwork: A History of Hacks and Pranks at MIT*. In fact, one of the definitions of "hack" provided by *The Jargon File* is "to pull a prank."[3] These types of acts, while often humorous and well-intentioned, can result in what Kembrew McLeod (2014) calls "prank blowback," or collateral consequences. Major trolling events are often theatrical and designed to blur truth and fiction in a manner that can send others—including the public and the media—into a panic, unable to clearly discern threat from spectacle. These acts may thus create fear and distrust of hackers across the spectrum. Anxieties about technology and hackers prime the public and media to view any activities affiliate with "hackers" as threatening. Lulzy behavior of any kind then may be interpreted as a confirmation of such anxieties, contributing to what moral panic theorists term a *deviancy amplification spiral* (Cohen [1972] 2002).

Persons who perform acts others do not understand have historically been viewed as witches, warlocks, sorcerers, magicians, and other supposed conjurers of dark power. Similarly, persons who can manipulate technology in ways laypersons cannot fathom are viewed as dangerous for their forbidden knowledge. Indeed, this is why hackers and other technologists are sometimes described as magical or "wizards." As science fiction author Arthur C. Clarke once declared, "Any sufficiently advanced technology is indistinguishable from magic." While part of this mystification may result in awe-struck wonder at what a hacker can do with technology, it may also encourage a sense of fear and danger. Such imagery can be used to invoke tension and drama, as recently demonstrated in the best-selling 2014 video game *Watch Dogs*, a Grand Theft Auto–like game featuring hackers with superhuman abilities to manipulate their environment, predominantly through the exploitation of a city-wide surveillance infrastructure called ctOS.[4] While participating in a digital bank heist in the opening cutscene of the game, your partner-in-crime and future antagonist Damien Brenks invokes these images of wizardry by declaring, "We are the modern day magicians—siphoning bank accounts out of thin air." Some hackers, however, embrace the connotations of magic and wizardry to describe hackers with immense skill. Thus the general lack of knowledge concerning technology among many in society creates a space for a warped folklore of hackers to develop.

Combine such mystification with dystopian visions of the technological future and the stage is set for widespread fear of hackers as technological others waiting to bring ruin upon an increasingly technologizing world; their power viewed as increasing with corresponding technological changes in society (Yar 2014). Society seems equally capable of supporting seemingly contradictory views of technology—that is, technology will be the savior of civilization while also being a tremendous source of anxiety (Thomas 2002; Yar 2014). Hackers, as seemingly magical purveyors of the technological realm, stand "at the nexus between the danger and the promise of the future of technology" on whom "we can heap all of our anxiety about technology" (Thomas 2002, 26, 45).

These perspectives have only intensified over time as hackers have become more incorporated into popular culture and their activities given increased airtime in news media and political rhetoric. Reid Skibell (2002, 336) perhaps best summarizes the demonization of hackers when he explains that "the rhetoric surrounding computer hacking consistently reinforces the potential catastrophic economic and national security threats posed by malevolent intruders, and at the same time attaches the subject of this threat to young, obsessive, self-trained computer aficionados." According to Debora Halbert (1997, 362), "Although arrested hackers are few, they are remarkably visible as harbingers of a possible future where computer crime and terrorism run rampant." Portrayals of hackers range from hyper-intelligent nerds to sinister cyber-madmen. Regardless of the image, the lurking specter of power and potential danger is present. "The media, law, and government offer different perspectives on the hacker," states Halbert (1997, 368), "but when taken as a whole, a sinister character emerges—an enemy."

Such portrayals become more problematic in light of a recent trend in hacker characterizations. In an effort to understand the intensity and devotion of hackers to their craft, some have turned to psychopathological or medical explanations (Sterling 1992; Yar 2005). For instance, early hacker discourses often portrayed these individuals as pathologically addicted to computers (Skibell 2002; Yar 2005). In a time period where few people had access to such devices, those who spent large portions of their time on computers were seen as hooked, much like a drug addict or alcoholic. Indeed, some psychologists have explained alleged hacking behaviors as a result of an "Internet Addiction Disorder," which is "an addiction akin to alcoholism and narcotic dependence, in which the sufferer loses the capacity to exercise restraint over his or her own habituated desire" (Yar 2005, 392). In a Foucauldian sense, then, the social context of the time demarcated boundaries of socially acceptable, or "healthy," behavior that hackers fell outside of—thus permitting a discourse that branded hackers as abnormal and deviant (Skibell 2002). Currently, an increasing percentage of the American populace spends sizable portions of time on personal computers and smartphones. Determining individual addiction to the Internet is becoming harder to discern in the age of the "Internet of things." As a result, the idea that hackers are addicts has perhaps waned, though not disappeared entirely.

Other pathological explanations have been given for hacking behaviors, however. One that is currently popular is an emerging discourse casting hackers as *autistic*. Investigative journalist Misha Glenny (2011), for example, utilizes Asperger's syndrome (a form of autism spectrum disorder) as a way to explain hacker criminality—suggesting that autism reduces the ability for the predominantly male population to empathize while also encouraging intense skill development. Social science researchers have similarly explored connections between autism and hacking, finding that hackers tended to score higher than normal on autism-spectrum quotient instruments (Schell and Holt 2010; Schell and Melnychuk 2010). The connections between hacking and autism exploded further when Julian Assange, noted hacker and head of the (in)famous WikiLeaks organization, drew this connection in 2011 in an op-ed he penned for the British newspaper *The Independent*. While Assange focused on his initiation into hacking, the paper targeted the connection he drew between hacking and autism with a headline reading, "I am—like all hackers—a little bit autistic" (Assange 2011). The full quote, however, reveals more nuance and a bit of tongue-in-cheek disdain for those viewing hackers from the outside: "I was beginning to get the hacker's disease: no sleep, bottomless curiosity, single-mindedness, and an obsession with precision. Later, when I became well-known, people would enjoy pointing out that I had Asperger's or else that I was dangling somewhere on the autistic spectrum. I don't want to spoil anyone's fun, so let's just say I am—all hackers are, and I would argue all men are a little bit autistic." In this discussion, Assange points out that *others* described him as autistic and that he is just going along with it for the sake of discussion—neither fully agreeing nor disagreeing with the characterization. When converted to a headline and passed around through other news sources, Assange's statements were made into admissions about the connection between hacking and autism.

Such characterizations undoubtedly contributed to a conversation I had with a self-described "cyberpsychologist" at a conference a few years ago. When she found out that I was studying hackers, she immediately wanted to tell me about her insights. Amid the din of the bar, she excitedly explained her views on hackers as criminal deviants who engage in security penetration as a mediated form of rape. She also described hackers as *categorically* autistic. I was taken aback by the audacity of the generalization (among other things). While not to diminish the possibility that hackers may disproportionately exhibit features associated with various forms of autism (though, you would likely find these same tendencies among members of STEM fields as well), it is a far leap between incommensurate representation and the conclusion that *all* hackers are autistic, or that only the autistic can be hackers. Though this researcher was likely an extreme case, this view in addition to recent connections in popular discourse with hacking as autism made me worry that the image of hacking was changing once again. Hackers and other geek or nerd subcultures have long been characterized as socially awkward and intense in their interests. This discourse—much like the longer-standing addiction rhetoric—threatens to change hackers and the like from "different" to "pathological."

The pathological view of hacking also lends itself to policy implications. Hackers have now been constructed as technological wizards and criminals who may also be autistic. They are different and that difference is a result of something internal to them—not anything sociological or cultural (Wall 2012). In a Foucauldian sense, then, the discourse makes possible particular strategies for dealing with the hacker problem, which often take the appearance of legal action. But such characterizations also indicate that a medical model may also be appropriate to stem to future dangers that hackers may pose, as Glenny (2011, 271) explains: "With further research, this could mean that it will be possible to identify hacker personality types among children who are still at school. In this way, peers and mentors could encourage their skills while, at the same time, offering them ethical guidance so that their abilities can be channeled in positive directions." In other words, kids can be screened to "identify hacker personality types" and treated accordingly. Thus hackers are something that we potentially can—and apparently *should*—identify and monitor, lest they go rogue. The fear of hackers turning to the "dark side" thus becomes a biological or psychological matter. Hackers are viewed as aberrant others worthy of public fear and legal scorn—regardless of if they are considered monsters by design or by choice.

Whether viewed as sinister, collateral-inducing, pathological, or any combination thereof, the notion that hackers are culturally envisioned as frightful and dangerous is difficult to refute. The urge to stigmatize hacking in popular culture and political rhetoric only increases as economic interests becoming increasingly dependent on the Internet and related technologies. As the Internet becomes increasingly secured for corporate interests, as will be discussed in this chapter, "behavior once considered normal and legal becomes abnormal and dangerous, hence the demonization of hackers" (Halbert 1997, 369). (As an aside, notice how hackers are portrayed as constant threats to data and personal privacy and how relatively little time is spent questioning the legitimacy of corporations amassing such data). These characterizations are notably reminiscent of Becker's (1963) work. Hackers, like marijuana-smokers, graffiti artists, and other deviant subcultures, are caught in the wheels of labeling and social reaction. Having established the social construction of hackers, attention is now turned to an ideological front where hackers find themselves in constant conflict—the reification of intellectual property.

Constructing Perceptions of Intellectual Property

"It is no accident that intellectual property rights are as strongly contested in the twenty-first century as land rights were in eighteenth-century Scotland."
Ursula Huws (2014, 75)

The second ideological front used to secure ideological dominance is through *social/legal constructions of intellectual property*. Intellectual property is a curious creation. While information has existed throughout history, the idea of *ownership* over information as *private property* is a fairly recent development coinciding with the rise of capitalism, taking on more perverse forms as society becomes more networked and information-dependent. As Perelman (1998, 30) explains, "This approach to information is indeed revolutionary." The growth of intellectual property has coincided with the growth of information industries (Callahan 2014; Perelman 2002). The expansion of such industries is not exactly surprising. Computer technology has permitted data transmission and storage on a scale the world has never seen. As such, it makes sense that control over digital communication vectors would become a key point of economic interest. In addition, as economic growth is stymied in other sectors like manufacturing, capital turns to increasingly abstract economic domains for expansion, notably the financial and information sectors (Harvey 2014; Perelman 2002).

While copyright and patents existed previously, their current form is a relatively recent creation springing from the vociferous desire of corporations to protect their expanding repositories of informational content including movies, television shows, music, video games, software, designs, and other forms of intellectual property. As with other forms of private property under capitalism, however, intellectual property becomes dependent on the state to support and provide legitimacy to the idea of intellectual property as well as provide legal means to protect such property. In private (physical) property, for example, Marx (1842) explains- the process whereby the practice of wood collection in common forests was converted to wood *theft* in his newspaper, *Rheinische Zeitung*. According to Marx, it is only possible for the theft of wood to occur if trees and their constituent parts are (1) constructed as private property and (2) that such property is considered sacred and protected under law. Both of these conditions are only enacted when economic interests are in place that benefit from maintaining exclusive rights to resources. Forests are thus transformed from commons to property where ownership is given to one party over others—an inherently coercive power relationship. The law then acts as a weapon to uphold these exclusive rights (Turk 1976). Governments thus confer *monopoly* rights to patent or copyright owners (Perelman 2014).[5] State power reinforces the legitimacy of the economic interests underpinning the trees as private property.

The notion of intellectual property arose in much the same fashion—economic interests were present for the creation of a legal apparatus that recognized and legitimated the idea that information could (and *should*) be owned. Intellectual property, however, was not always treated as analogous to private property. For long periods of time, secrecy was the primary mechanism to protect and control knowledge (Perelman 2002). Craftspersons in previous eras (and even today) would refuse to share their trade secrets with outsiders. Religious leaders obscured their methods to produce so-called miracles and magics. Information was recognized to be important, but such knowledge was generally not considered protected through legal rights as property. The onus was on the information-bearer to protect the data; society in general was not responsible. Once information was no longer secret, any power that a person had accumulated through its control was lost.

The creation of intellectual property rights, however, provided an alternative to secrecy as a method to control information. Now, information could be widely known but the state would act to regulate and protect the economic interests of those who claimed ownership. Even early forms of intellectual property, however, were not totally analogous to private property of the tangible sort. Indeed, two of the primary forms of intellectual property devised in the West—copyright and patents—did not give complete and total control over content and ideas to the intellectual property holder. Consider patents, for example, which give exclusive rights of production to inventors/the owner of the patent. In essence, a person invents something and submits the design to the government for public records. The government then awards a patent which gives the inventor exclusive rights to build the device or implement a process for a certain number of years. Once the patent term expires, the intellectual property is supposed to become free to replicate and disseminate among other manufacturers, designers, etc. Originally implemented in Venice in the fifteenth century, patents were created to encourage creativity among craftspersons by giving them the exclusive rights to benefit from their inventions before the design would be made public to enrich society (particularly its markets) (Perelman 2002). Patent rights were often seen as a way to encourage creativity and subsequent economic growth in times of crisis. Inventors would be incentivized to create because they could financially benefit from their ingenuity before their ideas would be shared across society, ideally for the benefit of all.

Copyright operates in a similar manner, but is focused on the rights to make copies of intellectual property. While previous common law and statutes like the Licensing Act of 1662 were in place to regulate the production of copies of printed works, the earliest known copyright act was established by the British Parliament in 1710 called the Statute of Anne (Lessig 2004). This law stated that "all published works would get a copyright term of fourteen years, renewable once if the author was alive, and that all works already published by 1710 would get a single term of twenty-one additional years" (Lessig 2004, 86). Importantly, the Statute of Anne and similar laws only conferred the right to *produce copies* to the copyright holder. No restrictions were set on use, distribution, performance, translation, and other uses of such content.

During this period, Britain had recently grappled with a civil war that was in part over "the Crown's practice of handing out monopolies—especially monopolies for works that already existed" (Lessig 2004, 88). Intellectual property is, after all, inherently monopolistic (Perelman 2002). Legal rights are given to an entity to exclusively publish a given piece of intellectual property. As such, there was an interest in reducing the ability for persons to claim exclusive rights on such property, particularly on written works. Stemming from Enlightenment education and the rising philosophy of liberalism, it was widely held that knowledge was to be shared and spread (mirroring contemporary cries of "information wants to be free" from hackers and similar technologists). To restrict the power of booksellers, viewed as monopolists of knowledge, term limits were imposed on copyrights to bolster competition. Once term limits were up, a work would enter the public domain where anyone could reproduce the work as they wished.

In the case of both copyright and patents, these laws were to temporarily restrict access and reproduction with the goal of making information more widely available in the long term (Perelman 2002). Exclusive temporary rights were given to encourage creativity and development. Upon term expiration, the information would be liberated for all to consume, reproduce, and build upon. Over time, the economic interests of copyright holders gradually co-opted copyright laws in the interests of monopoly power. The bolstering of such intellectual property rights coincided with the rise of content industries and mega-corporations interested in using intellectual property ownership as leverage against competitors (Perelman 2002). While such rights were envisioned to protect content creators (perhaps naively), intellectual property now predominantly secures corporate economic interests: "Today, however, individual genius does not figure very prominently in the ownership of intellectual property. Instead, the bulk of intellectual property belongs to great corporations" (Perelman 2002, 21).[6]

Corporate leveraging of intellectual property resulted in extensions on periods of exclusive ownership. For example, copyright law in the U.S. has been greatly expanded. When copyright was formally established in the United States, copyright term limits only extended for fourteen years (Perelman 2002). The Copyright Act of 1976 expanded these rights to fifty years after the death of the author. Another twenty years was added to the term following the Copyright Extension Act of 1998, making copyright extend through the life of the author plus seventy years (Lessig 2004). The twenty-year expansion was a result of corporate interests. Such revisions were supposedly necessary because of the Disney Corporation; their "rights to Mickey Mouse were due to expire in 2003" (Perelman 2002, 40). Were these rights to lapse, Mickey would have slipped into public domain and Disney would have lost the ability to extract rents well beyond the creative labor value of the character (Lessig 2004).[7] While the original point of copyright was to prevent long-term monopolies on cultural products, such a lengthy copyright duration effectively ends the ability for content to enter the public domain. Consider that the average lifespan of persons living in the U.S. is approximately seventy-eight years, this means that for content created the moment of the average American's birth, the author must die within less than eight years for the content to enter the public domain before the average American dies. As a result, the public domain—that social good believed to be necessary for the educational and cultural enlightenment of the masses—is effectively dead.

In addition to copyright duration expansion, the scope of copyright law has also inflated. While the Statute of Anne restricted the production of copies using specific printing devices, copyright now regulates the creation of copies through almost any medium. Few limits govern the power of copyright holders, such as exceptions to copyrights made for satire or parody. Part of this arose through legislative changes and while other changes arose through litigation—corporate copyright holders amass tremendous legal resources to protect their copyrights. Alleged infringers may be buried under the weight of the litigation brought by corporations even if use of the copyrighted material is covered under fair use and other exceptions (Lessig 2004).

In the electronic era, copyright was further expanded through the introduction of the Digital Millennium Copyright Act (DMCA), which—among other things—makes it illegal to bypass copy-protection mechanisms placed on intellectual property (Lunney 2001). For instance, if a person wanted to create a musical parody by mashing up multiple copyrighted images and songs, an argument could be made that such use of content is protected under the fair use doctrine (Lessig 2008). If the artist has to break a copy-protection mechanism on an mp3 file to accomplish this, however, they have broken the law. Owners, then, only have to place token copy protections on their content to further expand the degree of control they can legally assert on content.

Patent law has further expanded in favor of corporate interests as well. Patents are secured not just to gain exclusive rights to processes, devices, and other patentable things, but companies use patents themselves as a source of revenue. Gaining exclusive rights to vital pieces of information/technology allow corporations to sell their production rights off to other companies. In effect, this has allowed firms, derogatorily referred to as "patent trolls," to flourish; they create and produce nothing but instead file patents with the express purpose of collecting royalties *or* litigating against alleged patent infringers (Magliocca 2007).[8] Additionally, the ambiguity of patent law and the raw volume of patents secured by companies not only renders patents a source of coercive control against other businesses but it also potentially stops new businesses from forming. Companies can claim a new product infringes on one of their patents. The patents may be written so vaguely that they could be argued to apply to any number of technologies and processes. Under a fair patent system, these cases would be treated as frivolous. Yet corporations and patent trolls can bury such upstarts beneath a deluge of litigation, regardless of how nonsensical the claims are. Amid corporate lobbying and litigation, the patent system in the U.S. has expanded to where almost any variation of process or design is patentable, with even genetic sequences falling under patent law. Thus patent rights become coercive monopoly rights.

This major expansion of legal protections has occurred because of one defining feature of information: its replicability. Physical property is easier to economize because of its relative scarcity. Information, however, does not follow the same laws of scarcity as physical property. In effect, then, "the concept of scarcity is absolutely irrelevant to information" (Perelman 2002, 178). Producing content, however, still involves *labor costs* even though *replication costs* are relatively insignificant, particularly as digital technology makes duplication easy (Söderberg 2002). As a result, various technological and legal measures are taken to secure intellectual property rights to create a sort of manufactured scarcity. For these to be successful, however, they depend—to some degree—on the perceived legitimacy of intellectual property. Such perceptions are not hard to generate even in the face of the differences between physical and intellectual property. Siva Vaidhyanathan (2012, 24) argues that open-source approaches to creativity and production are not new but that "the rapid adoption of proprietary information has been so intense and influential since the 1980s that we hardly remember another way or another time." In this way, liberal notions of property ownership have transferred, for many, to perceptions of intellectual property.

The language used by copyright holders when discussing intellectual property create an image which reinforces common notions of private, tangible property: "theft" when referring to copyright infringement; "piracy," which semiologically recalls the plundering of ships; and even the idea of intellectual "property" connects such understandings to traditional notions of physical property. Such rhetoric acts to create a perceived "straightforward equivalence between tangible and intangible properties" (Yar 2008b, 612). To justify the expansion of intellectual property in such a manner to reinforce corporate power and interests, this symbolic connection between information and the liberal notion of private property is necessary (Yar 2008b). Ayn Rand (1966, 125–128), economic liberal, libertarian novelist, and philosopher, summarizes this perspective when she proclaimed that:

> Patents and copyrights are the legal implementation of the base of all property rights: a man's right to the product of his mind . . . The patent or copyright notice on a physical object represents a public statement of the conditions on which the inventor or author is willing to sell his product: for the purchaser's use, but *not* for commercial reproduction . . . Intellectual achievement, *in fact*, cannot be transferred, just as intelligence, ability, or any other personal virtue cannot be transferred. All that can be

transferred is the material results of an achievement, in the form of actually produced wealth ... patents are the heart and core of property rights, and once they are destroyed, the destruction of all other rights will follow automatically, as a brief postscript.

In other words, an ardent belief in the liberal notion of private property—one so intense that even *ideas* are proprietized—is necessary to justify such intellectual property rights systems.

In a recurrent example, this link crafted between tangible and intellectual property is evident in Bill Gates's *An Open Letter to Hobbyists*, published in 1976 in the Homebrew Computer Club's newsletter. Here, Gates admonishes those who share the Altair BASIC interpreter developed by him, Paul Allen, and Monte Davidoff. He draws from a long-held argument for intellectual property rights—that without paying the copyright holder, development is stifled. Arguments have been made among hackers, pirates, and other technologists that such laws are not necessary for creativity and development, as evidenced by free and open-source software. Gates's argument, however, relies on the previously described semiological sleight of hand—the equating of software duplication to *stealing*: "Most directly, the thing you do is theft." In this manner, he is equating content copying—which does not deprive the original owner nor create scarcity (Perelman 2002)—to the theft of physical property. Such connections are necessary to lend legitimacy to the strengthening of intellectual property protections.

When the Web 2.0 was first gaining traction in American society, a metaphor was commonly used to encourage understanding of the Internet: the "information superhighway." The metaphor was useful in that it effectively conveyed the idea that the Internet was a far-reaching and relatively quick way to access and disseminate information for the time. The problem was that the metaphor was misleading as it "suggests that information is trucked about like so much soap or canned soup" (Perelman 2002, 175). The "information superhighway" thus helped established the idea of information as akin to physical objects in the days of the early dot-com boom. Metaphors, as mentioned previously, are powerful mechanisms that shape perceptions of reality (Lakoff and Johnson 1980). Such conceptual devices allow us to understand complex abstractions in alternative ways. For example, one way the abstract concept of "happy" is understood is by equating it with the spatial direction of "up" (Lakoff and Johnson 1980). "Spirits are high," "I am floating among the clouds," or "I'm on cloud nine" are all metaphorical ways to more easily communicate the idea of happiness by creating an association with a spatial direction. Conversely, "unhappy" would be downward, as in "I'm down in the dumps." The "information superhighway" and similar technological metaphors (such as the ever laughable "series of tubes" analogy used by Senator Ted Stevens to describe the Internet) allow people to understand complicated networks and devices in ways in which they are already familiar. While the "Internet is a road" metaphor has gone by the wayside, the idea of information as akin to physical property to be transported, held, and guarded persists.

In a more contemporary example, an MPAA-sponsored advertisement dubbed "You Wouldn't Steal a Car" appeared in the late 2000s in movie theaters and on DVDs. Under a steady and driving techno beat, the advertisement begins with a person downloading a movie on their desktop computer. The ad then projects the text "You wouldn't steal a car" before jumping to a man in a black leather jacket breaking into a car in an urban alley using a slim jim.[9] The ad continues this trend by asserting the viewer would not steal a handbag, a television, or a physical copy of a movie at a video store before showing individuals surreptitiously committing these crimes. This advertisement equates theft of a tangible object (an automobile) with the theft of intellectual property (a movie). The ad projects statements such as "downloading pirate movies is stealing," "stealing is against the law," and "piracy is a crime." Thus a connection between the theft of *physical* property (where the user is deprived of their item) is equated to the *copying* of copyrighted data (where the original owner is not deprived of access). In addition, the threat of legal sanctioning is deployed as well to give the advertisement additional weight.

The stakes are perceptibly raised further through claims made by intellectual property industries concerning the alleged harms caused by activities like piracy. In 2015, the Recording Industry Association of America, one of the largest intellectual property industry lobbying groups in the world, claims on their website that "music sales in the U.S. have dropped 53 percent, from $14.6 billion to $7 billion in 2013."[10] Likewise, the Business Software Alliance (2014, 1) claims that in 2013, roughly "43 percent of the software installed on personal computers around the world was not properly licensed." They estimate the commercial value of these unlicensed uses to be $62.7 billion. Claims of such tremendous losses have been made through these industries for many years (see also Yar 2008b; Lessig 2004; Perelman 2002).

Such assertions of losses are typically followed by grim proclamations about the ramifications such infringement bears on the greater global economy. Many of these statistics, however, "may be seen at best as 'guestimates' which can only approximately track levels of piracy; at worst, they may be seen as the product of methodologically questionable forms of statistical inference and accounting" (Yar 2008b, 608). Such organizations "may well overstate their losses for lobbying purposes" to secure greater copyright and patent protections and to extend their dominion over intellectual property (Yar 2008b, 608). These statistics often also fail to account for alternative influences that may impact revenues and market shares. Indeed, the ultimate goal of such industry data—and their reporting—may not be to ward against the crippling of the global economy, but to portray the preservation of intellectual property as if it is in *everyone's* best interest, rather than in the corporate interest. These statistics thus appear to be a product of disproportionate capitalistic control of the "means of mental production" (Marx and Engels 1947).

Thus a connection is socially constructed which reifies the supposed sanctity of intellectual property. Information—which exists in the abstract—is disguised as a material item. The pervasiveness of liberal notions of private property makes such connections seem like common sense for many. As Vaidhyanathan (2012, 24) explains, "We have become so inured to the proprietary model, so dazzled and intimidated by its cultural and political power, that any commonsense challenge to its assumptions and tenets seems radical, idealistic, or dangerous." If one looks at the history of information and intellectual property, however, it is easy to see that such perceptions were not always taken for granted. The very nature of information—as a social relation and product—has changed over time corresponding to changes in political economy. At an ideological level, such changes are sustained through the augmentation of perceptions about the nature of information, creativity, and ownership. Making intellectual property synonymous with private property is one such mechanism. These perceptions secure profits on pre-existing forms of intellectual property. In addition, since it would be impossible to advance technology without extant software, designs, and other forms of intellectual property, such monopoly rights secure profits on emergent technologies as well. The reification of intellectual property thus permits the profiteering of past, present, and future forms of creativity enforceable through criminal and civil law. Hacker cultural sensibilities toward intellectual property and disdain for restriction threaten such ideological machinations.

Constructing Perceptions of Technological Infrastructures

The final ideological front legitimating a formal social control regime involves the construction of perceptions toward digital infrastructures including the Internet and related networks, encryption systems, and the like. Essentially, any technology used to facilitate global communication and commerce is considered. For tech policy to be shifted in the direction of capital interest, not only are hackers and similar technologists to be demonized or intellectual property reified, but the systems and networks on which late-modern life has come to depend must be articulated as intensely vulnerable and in dire need of protection.

Without a doubt, communications technology has proliferated worldwide. The Organization for Economic Cooperation and Development (OECD), which collects data on thirty-four countries (most of which are major Western economic powers), estimates that wired/fixed broadband subscriptions increased from 7.03 per 100 individuals in 2003 to 27.41 in 2014, an approximate 390 percent increase over eleven years.[11] When examining wireless/mobile broadband Internet subscriptions, however, the numbers are far more staggering. In 2009, there were an estimated 32.89 wireless broadband subscriptions per 100. In 2014, this number increased to 78.23 per 100, a 237 percent increase *over five years*.

As people become more connected globally, businesses turn to the Internet as a way to increase sales and bolster services. The Internet has also spawned entire industries as well. Aside from the dot-com bust of the '90s, the Internet has proven extremely lucrative for many businesses (though certainly not all, particularly those who cannot afford to invest in the requisite technologies). Take retail shopping for instance.

Retail transactions have changed dramatically as a result of the Internet and other network-based technologies. Many companies, like Amazon. com, completely do away with brick-and-mortar retail stores and conduct business exclusively through online transactions. Other companies use the online retail stores in addition to their physical retail locations. These changes have impacted trade, particularly as online sales have dramatically increased over time. According to the U.S. Census Bureau's Retail and Food Services data, electronic stores and mail-order houses comprised just 2 percent of retail sales dollars (excluding food services) in 1992.[12] In 2013, sales through these methods amounted to approximately 8 percent of retail sales dollars, an approximate 400 percent increase in twenty-two years. These estimates, however, include all retail sales performed through television, catalog, and direct mail as well as online shopping. The contrast may be even more intense considering Internet-based commerce undoubtedly supplanted other forms of home-delivery sales strategies.

In addition, online advertising—one of the main forms of revenue generation for Internet-based companies—is a booming industry. According to a report released by PricewaterhouseCoopers (2014), a multinational corporation specializing in various forms of business advising, online advertising revenue increased from $1 billion in 2002 to almost $43 billion in 2013, representing an increase of roughly 2,800 percent over eleven years.[13] For example, Google—one of the largest Internet companies in the world—relies on advertising as its primary revenue stream. The company has seen enormous increases in advertising revenue over time.[14] In 2001, the company reported approximately $86 million in revenue, with nearly $67 million of that from advertising. In 2013, Google reported about $55 *billion in revenue*, with roughly $50 billion stemming from advertising—over a 700 percent increase in revenue from advertisements alone.

These are only some metrics to indicate the monetary stakes involved in the Internet and related technologies. One look at the proliferation of "big data," social media, smartphones, "apps," and a litany of other technological ventures indicates that the Internet and related telecommunications technology have become big business. Computer and network technologies seem to impact every aspect of late-modern production and consumption. As a result, however, capital has become *extraordi-*

narily dependent on the vectors—pipelines for the storage and transmission of information. As Harvey (2014, 100) explains, "Technologies of knowledge production and dissemination, for data and information storage and retrieval, are crucial for the survival and perpetuation of capital. They not only provide the price signals and other forms of information that guide investment decisions and market activity, but also preserve and promote the necessary mental conceptions of the world that facilitate productive activity, guide consumer choices and stimulate the creation of new technologies." Since capital has become so dependent on these technologies, it would make sense that it would also endeavor to protect them or, more specifically, control them. One way in which this is accomplished is to *ideologically portray technological infrastructures as delicate*.

Popular culture provides a litany of examples of such ideological work—that our technological infrastructure stands on the precipice of catastrophe. Consider the rise of the apocalyptic/post-apocalyptic genre. In almost all of these movies, books, comics, video games, and other works, apocalyptic events are accompanied by electrical blackouts, dead telephone lines, useless cellular phones, and the like. The effect is to instill a sense of dread in the characters and the audience; a single event has cut us off from the modern world and each other. In the zombie apocalypse stories—such as Robert Kirkman's *The Walking Dead*, George Romero's *Night of the Living Dead, Dawn of the Dead, Day of the Dead, Land of the Dead, Diary of the Dead*, and *Survival of the Dead*, among others—the zombie epidemic usually spreads quickly, with entire civilizations crumbling within weeks or even days. The first systems to collapse in these narratives are communications technology and the electrical grid. These tropes make it clear to the viewer how alone and vulnerable the protagonists are. The world has crumbled and now they must survive with no support.

Television shows have also been dedicated to infrastructural collapse. *Dark Angel*, a television show created by James Cameron and released in 2000, is one such show. The series takes place in 2019, ten years after a terrorist attack involving the detonation of an electromagnetic pulse device that obliterates telecommunications and computing technologies throughout the U.S. In 2012, *Revolution* was similarly set in a world where the technological infrastructure fell. The show takes place fifteen years after a U.S. official ordered a weapon to be used, which caused a worldwide power failure called "The Blackout." In both of these events, society moves on but is reconfigured into a dystopia.

The *Mad Max* series, comprised of four films (the most recent released in 2015), is set in a post-apocalyptic future where society crumbled following an energy crisis. The landscape is bleak. Murder and marauding are commonplace. Without the resources necessary to provide power, the technological infrastructure dissipated and civilization followed. In this setting, only those willing to engage in ruthless violence get ahead. In all of these apocalyptic narratives, the message is clear: without technology, life becomes hard and dangerous. Worse yet, technology is portrayed as perpetually on the brink of collapse, with dystopia quickly following.

Apocalyptic narratives are perhaps most pronounced in superhero comic books (Phillips and Strobl 2013). Though these works often focus on conflicts between superheroes or heroines and supervillains, much of the tension is derived from the often-catastrophic threats the antagonists pose to society. Considering that comic book-based superhero movies have also become a major force in the box office—with a total of seven movies between 2010 and 2014 ranking in the top five grossing films each year—these narratives have become pervasive.[15] A central trope across superhero media is that a person or a small group with superhuman abilities is capable of wreaking mass destruction against a woefully unprepared populace and infrastructure. These apocalyptic imaginings point to broader ideological formations. Most comics—not all—indicate that any change in the social order is likely to be devastating. In this manner, it is apparently "easier to imagine the 'end of the world' than a far more modest change in the mode of production" and related social structural forces (Žižek 1994, 1).

There are also more subtle ways that media portrays technology as ever-vulnerable and susceptible to so-called hacker intrusions and manipulation. The new show, *CSI: Cyber* (which began airing in March 2015), provides one such example. The pilot episode begins with an infant kidnapped while mysterious voices are heard through the baby camera positioned in the room. Through many (nauseating) twists and turns, the episode ends with the busting of an international baby snatching and auctioneering ring that infiltrated baby camera servers. Technology is posed as so precarious that hackers could be monitoring any person at any given time—the threat is ubiquitous.

These systems are also conveyed to be instantly penetrable through the wizardry of hackers. For instance, when the FBI agents shut down the camera servers to cut off the auctioning of babies, the "hacker" sends a message to a young boy playing a video game to get the agents' attention. Involved in sending this message is (1) an infiltration of the video game networks to track down the specific console, (2) manipulation of the game to prevent the boy from cancelling out of the message, and (3) inserting a video into the message to convey a hostage threat to the FBI. The scenario is *wholly* unrealistic. Regardless, every single article of high technology in the episode is conveyed as constantly vulnerable to attack in a—ahem—virtual flash.

Academics are not immune to the influence and perpetuation of such social constructions in popular culture. Previously, I described a conversation with a so-called cyberpsychologist. Interestingly, this "cyberpsychologist" was Mary Aiken, the director of the Royal College of Surgeons at the Ireland CyberPsychology Research Center. The main character of *CSI: Cyber*, played by Patricia Arquette, is supposedly based on her. Aiken also serves as a consultant and executive producer to the show. In an interview with National Public Radio (2015), she stated, "Look, this is entertainment but our intention is not to induce paranoia in terms of the use of baby cams. The intention is to say, look, consider the logic and think about security and think about safety." When pressed on the potential that this show could unnecessarily stoke fear in the populace, she responded: "I think that our show takes quite a moderate approach in terms of, it's not very gory, it's not very horrific, but people like to be scared. If you were on a roller coaster and it went from A to Z and it was flat, you wouldn't enjoy the ride. Good programming is about a roller coaster ride. It's up and it's down and we want a happy ending. But we've worked very, very hard to ground our show in reality, the reality of cyber." Considering the aforementioned issues, this statement transforms itself from assurance to apparent denial. There is *some degree* of veracity to the story—the episode was based on a real instance where a person hi-jacked a baby cam and shouted obscenities at a baby as it slept (McCarthy 2013). In addition, a Russian website was recently found to be streaming thousands of feeds from vulnerable cameras (Mlot 2014).

Through connections with kidnapping, violent organized crime, and seemingly all-powerful hackers, the scope of the problem and the danger posed were clearly inflated in the show to produce drama and to stoke fear. Apparently such distortions are justified because "people like to be scared."

Government officials and other public figures also play a role in constructing the perception that networked technologies are intensely vulnerable to attack, particularly in the years following the events of September 11th, 2001 (Jordan and Taylor 2004; Wall 2008; Yar 2008a). Take, for example, the words of former Chairman of the House Subcommittee on Crime, Representative Lamar Smith, who stated in 2002 that "America must protect our national security, critical infrastructure, and economy from cyber attacks. Penalties and law enforcement capabilities must be enhanced to prevent and deter such criminal behavior. Until we secure our cyber infrastructure, *a few keystrokes and an Internet connection is all one needs to disable the economy or endanger lives.* A mouse can be just as dangerous as a bullet or a bomb" (as quoted in Skibell 2003, 917–918; emphasis added).

More recently, in an opinion piece for the *Wall Street Journal*, U.S. President Barack Obama (2012) invokes the term "hacker" in describing a threat to national infrastructure and continues by stating, "It doesn't take much to imagine the consequences of a successful cyber attack. In a future conflict, an adversary unable to match our military supremacy on the battlefield might seek to exploit our computer vulnerabilities here at home. Taking down vital banking systems could trigger a financial crisis. The lack of clean water or functioning hospitals could spark a public health emergency. And as we've seen in the past blackouts, the loss of electricity can bring businesses, cities, and entire regions to a standstill." Here, President Obama clearly creates a sense of precariousness to networks and, simultaneously, connects that delicateness to other vital systems. Having established the threat, he elaborates: "This is the future we have to avoid. That's why my administration has made cybersecurity a priority, including proposing legislation to strengthen our nation's digital defenses. It's why Congress must pass comprehensive cybersecurity legislation" (Obama 2012). At this point President Obama has used the threat as a call for more social control mechanisms in the technological realm.

The computer crime control industry, to borrow Yar's (2008a) term, also has a vested interest in the construction of technological infrastructures as fragile. Technosecurity has become a multi-billion dollar a year industry throughout the world (Yar 2008a). After all, the more paranoid people become about the costs and consequences of infrastructure attacks, the more likely they are to support major technosecurity spending. That is not to say the threats are not real to some degree, but industry affiliates have a conflict of interest when it comes to collecting and reporting data related to such hazards (Skibell 2002). Russia-based Kaspersky Labs, a prominent software and technosecurity firm, is regularly cited for its threat statistics. Looking at their *Overall Statistics for 2014* report, the firm claims that their web antivirus detected over 120 million "unique malicious objects," such as scripts and files, while their antivirus solutions found nearly 2 million "unique malicious and potentially unwanted objects" (Garnaeva et al. 2014, 3).

These reports make technocrime issues and other threats to technological infrastructures seem almost insurmountable—leaving technosecurity firms to market themselves as the best, and in many cases, *only* solution. Ross Anderson and colleagues (2013, 266), however, point out that "the number of phishing websites, of distinct attackers, and of different types of malware is persistently over-reported, leading some police forces to believe that the problem is too large or diffuse for them to tackle, when in fact a small number of gangs lie behind many incidents and a police response against them could be far more effective than telling the public to fit anti-phishing toolbars or purchase antivirus software." Thus industry estimates have to be considered with trepidation as these companies have a vested interest in maximizing the perceived threat posed by technocriminals to a seemingly vulnerable infrastructure. As Skibell (2002, 346) explains, "The industry has consistently argued that the computer sector of the economy is so important and so vulnerable to malicious attacks, that a hardline stance is the only possible defense."

The argument here is not that such assertions of digital danger are wrong *per se* (though, there is evidence that such threats are overstated and there is very little discussion as to the wisdom of so intricately networking all of our critical infrastructure together in such a manner), but that the image created is a sense of urgency and immediate threat to exposed technological systems. When taken in totality, the intimation is an abject perception that the systems on which we have come to rely on for economic transactions, communication, and entertainment, among other things, are easily dismantled by circumstance or malice. Many of these narratives overlook, for example, the fact that the Internet is a surprisingly resilient form of communication, designed to withstand almost any disruption. Or that permanently disabling the electric grid for the United States is far more difficult than the simple writing of a virus by a single, lone hacker or even a small group. For example, Stuxnet, the virus that became famous for disrupting the operations of an Iranian uranium enrichment plant, was obviously a major operation.[16] The code was complex and byzantine to confound dissection. It was extraordinarily surreptitious, avoiding detection for at least a year, quietly sabotaging Iranian efforts toward nuclear technology (Zetter 2014). While still not officially confirmed, authoritative accounts convincingly point toward the United States and Israel as the developers of this digital weapon (Zetter 2014). These nations invested tremendous amounts of resources (time, money, manpower) into creating Stuxnet, resources far beyond the reach of most "lone wolf" hackers or hacker groups (Zetter 2014). While not impossible, the Stuxnet case provides support for the idea that sabotaging such facilities is not a simple (or inexpensive) endeavor. In other words, there is likely a threat, but perhaps not as proliferous and profound as we are led to believe.

None of this is to say that efforts are not made to construct infrastructures and computer systems as resilient to attack. Companies that market online services take pains to assure the consumer that their products are protected. They may use imagery (like padlock symbols) to connote security and give assurances that transactions are protected by a third party (like McAfee Secure) to indicate trustworthiness. Data centers and other IT companies may market themselves to clients through guarantees of information security and infrastructural reliability. In one advertisement for Microsoft's cloud computing services, the company claims that "concerns about government surveillance and the rise of cybercrime have eroded people's trust in the technologies they depend on to store and share information. At Microsoft, we work to protect customer data in our cloud to help ensure our customers stay in control of their own data."[17] The advertisement then describes a veritable cornucopia of measures the company takes to ensure data security and bolster consumer trust. As government services increasingly rely on the Internet, similar promises are made that sensitive information is protected and secured through a number of protections. In a world of technological uncertainty, many institutions endeavor to create a sense of trust and security in their services.

While these assurances may encourage faith in certain products and services, such notions are plagued by an overarching social and cultural anxiety about the security of technology. For sure, certain products and services may be viewed by individuals as relatively safe. If these individuals were asked about their perceptions of the integrity of technology and security in general, however, they may respond with some degree of uncertainty and even fear. The discourses of danger surrounding technology gnaw at the back of our collective consciousness. Most can believe that *specific* services and products are hardy but are convinced that technology and infrastructures in *general* are vulnerable.

Regardless, in the expanding technological environment under late modernity, the biggest threat to these infrastructures by the majority of accounts is the supposed hacker menace. Media, politicians, corporations, and others are quick to cry "hacker!" whenever a computer threat is made or a technocrime is committed. While some hackers are certainly not innocent parties in these affairs, they are also not the only actors capable of wreaking carnage in our infrastructures. In this manner, hackers perhaps become, in the words of Jordan and Taylor (2004, 21), "a scapegoat for this feeling of vulnerability as well as a target for fears of the unknown and 'the other' that had prospered during the Cold War and which are now recycled in terms of information warfare."

Legitimating Social Control

When considered in tandem, the result of such efforts across these three ideological fronts is clear: intellectual property is reified, technological infrastructures are portrayed as vulnerable, and hackers are constructed as a threat to both through various interests engaging in a kind of "economic identity maintenance" (Bell and York 2010, 112). These constructions serve as an ideological tool which allows for the government to become involved, crafting legislation and regulating technology in such a way that benefit capitalists, a seemingly necessary step in that many users are assumed to need protection (particularly from themselves) (Wall 2008). In this way, the previously described social constructions contribute to the construction of *hegemony*—or the generation of consensus underpinning the perceived legitimacy of authority for the purposes of domination (Gramsci 1971).[18] Žižek (2009, 145) laments that "exploitation in the classical sense is no longer possible, which is why it has to be enforced more and more by direct legal measures, that is, by non-economic means." Söderberg (2002) summarizes this contradiction when he states, "But here rouses a contradiction to capital, on one hand it prospers from the technologically skilled, unpaid, social labour of users; on the other hand it must suppress the knowledge power of those users to protect the intellectual property regime." In other words, capitalists must forcibly control the undesirable activities of the hacker class while maximizing the benefits of the productive ones. Thus, the state—idealized under economic liberalism as an apparatus to be avoided in favor of the exercise of individual freedom in the market—is thus used as a tool to secure the property rights of others, showing how the state can be ideologically deployed as a mechanism of domination under the guise of securing property rights and economic freedoms. Polanyi (1994) would be familiar with this situation. While not providing a comprehensive list, the following discussions highlight key areas where ideology acts as a legitimating force behind legal and law enforcement activities surrounding hackers.

The Computer Fraud and Abuse Act (CFAA) extended previous federal computer fraud law and further cemented government protections over technology. Interestingly, the creation of the CFAA was "based in part on a fear derived from the movie *WarGames*" (Skibell 2003, 910). Frantically pieced together by Congress in 1984, the CFAA has been subsequently revised and redrafted for clarity and to extend its power over time. Rather than based on objective risks posed by computer crimes, the CFAA was largely a reaction to skewed perceptions about the danger posed by technocriminals—like the emergent "hacker"—and the risks these groups posed to economic interests and technological infrastructures (Skibell 2003).

Like other policies premised on moral panics, such as the War on Drugs (Shelden 2008), the scope of the CFAA is perhaps overly broad and overly punitive. For example, Kevin Mitnick—perhaps one of the most famous hackers of all time—was charged under the CFAA for infiltrating the computer systems of Sun Microsystems (Mitnick and Simon 2011). He downloaded a copy of the source code of Solaris, a propriety operating system developed by Sun based on the UNIX architecture (the same one which birthed Linux and Apple's Macintosh OS). Despite the fact that Mitnick had not altered or sold the code, he was "charged with damage equal to the value of the software," $80 million (Skibell 2003, 922). Indeed, outside of "public embarrassment," Sun Microsystems appeared relative undamaged by the act: "Sun never reported any loss to its insurance company, the IRS [Internal Revenue Service], or its shareholders, casting further doubt on the validity of the damages figure used to calculate Mitnick's penalty . . . Sun made the code publicly available for a mere $100 soon after the break-in. The only place that the $80 million damages figure ever existed was in the trial record, yet that was sufficient to have severe consequences for Mitnick" (Skibell 2003, 923). The CFAA's heavy reliance on vague notions of financial damages and the complexities posed by intellectual property in the computer era thus seem to provide a great deal of power to companies in dictating if and when damages are done and their extent.

In addition, prosecution under the CFAA also often involves conditions that prevent hackers from even having *access* to computer technology out of fear of what these hackers could do. These sanctions, while not formally articulated in the CFAA, are often exercised by prosecutors and judges out of fear based on the mysticism surrounding hackers. In a comical example, Mitnick recounts a prosecutor accusing him of impossible levels of technological sorcery in his autobiography *Ghost in the Wires* (Mitnick and Simon 2011, 85): "In a last ditch effort to frighten the magistrate, Leon Weidman made one of the most outrageous statements that has probably ever been uttered by a Federal prosecutor in court: he told Magistrate Tassopulos that I could start a nuclear holocaust. 'He can whistle into a telephone and launch a nuclear missile from NORAD [North American Aerospace Defense Command],' he said. Where could he have possibly come up with that ridiculous notion? NORAD computers aren't even connected to the outside world. And they obviously don't use the public telephone lines for issuing launch commands." The prosecutor's beliefs were most likely based in the movie *WarGames*, which featured a NORAD computer. Rather than view the prosecutor as a fear-mongering lunatic, the judge ordered Mitnick to be held without bail "because when 'armed with a keyboard' (*'armed'!*), [he] posed a danger to the community" (Mitnick and Simon 2011, 85). He was also subsequently denied the ability to use a telephone. The absurdity of such prohibition was ridiculed in the movie *Hackers*.

This law has been implicated in extraordinarily harsh punishments for hackers. Aaron Swartz once again provides an exemplary case. Swartz faced one million dollars in fines, up to thirty-five years in prison, and other potential charges, all as a result of downloading academic articles from JSTOR (Wu 2013). Arguably, such charges are not proportional to the actual damages wrought and, as contended here, such inflated charges were a direct consequence of the political economic and ideological constructions presented in this analysis. JSTOR and similar companies make their money largely by selling subscriptions to university libraries. The downloading of these articles did not obstruct this revenue flow, particularly as universities would still need to buy the subscription to offer the articles legally to students and faculty. This may have been one motivating factor for JSTOR dropping its charges against Swartz. MIT and the government, however, continued to press charges, estimating that the damages wrought by Swartz were in the millions even though no solid evidence of any real harm to JSTOR or its profits has been given. Indeed, it has long been argued that charges wrought under the CFAA were often grossly disproportional to actual damages done (Skibell 2003).

While the events of 9/11 prompted some changes to the CFAA, the U.S. Federal Government also introduced entirely new legislation intended to increase security against the threats of terrorism, the Uniting and Strengthening America by Providing Appropriate Tools Required to Intercept and Obstruct Terrorism (USA PATRIOT) Act. The Patriot Act greatly expanded law enforcement's investigative and surveillance capabilities. Of course, as 9/11 demonstrated, there were real threats to U.S. national security. The problem was (and still is) that much of the rhetoric and imagery instilled a fear that terrorists were lurking under every bed and hiding in every bush. During this period, the hacker figure in the public mind also underwent a transformation. Now hackers could also be a national security threat under the designation "cyberterrorist." Indeed, the Patriot Act expanded the scope of state power in the digital realm through provisions directed at the potential threat of so-called cyberterrorism. The perceptions underpinning this legislation likely influenced Director of the NSA, General Keith Alexander, to declare that the hacker group Anonymous poses a national security threat through (albeit limited) power outages, according to an article published in *The Wall Street Journal* (Gorman 2012).[19] The article further elaborates that while Anonymous does not currently have such capabilities according to intelligence sources, *they may in the future.* These alleged future threats—technological or otherwise—are used as justifications to support the expansion of the security state through means like the Patriot Act. Hackers are thus construed as a "cyberterrorist" boogeyman whose presence will lead to an imagined dystopian future.

The social construction of hackers (and other technocriminals) as dangerous combined with social beliefs in a precarious technological infrastructure have given rise to the expansion of state control, predominantly in the form of one of the largest surveillance programs ever implemented, PRISM. As Casey McGowan (2014, 2413) explains, "The metadata collection program derives its legal authority from section 215 of the Patriot Act, which amended parts of FISA [the Foreign Intelligence Surveillance Act of 1978]." The sheer expansiveness of the program is justified through assertions of a constant national security threat—one that requires telecommunications metadata for analysis to track potential terrorists. While the presence of threats to national security exist, little information has been offered by the U.S. government to verify that these threats are as immediate and widespread as the general public is lead to believe. While other phantasms lurk in the public and political imaginary driving these events, the notion of the sinister hacker poised to wage war against the United States is certainly one such factor.

In the age of the information economy, legislators—at the behest of industry lobbyists—crafted the Digital Millennium Copyright Act (DMCA). Predominantly relying on the reification of intellectual property, this law was "enacted as a response to copyright owners' first fear about cyberspace. The fear was that copyright control was effectively dead; the response was to find technologies that might compensate" (Lessig 2004, 157). The intellectual property industry was terrified about the possibilities that the Internet and other technologies offered for rapid and widespread duplication of copyrighted works. Indeed, such replicative abilities are at the core of computer and network designs. Computers, *by design*, make copies in almost every function. They copy data between RAM (random access memory), ROM (read-only memory), and various processing units. Similarly, networks transfer data from one point to another. Copying is required.

To curb undesired forms of copying through these technologies, companies have designed various copy-protection mechanisms. To give legal weight to these protections, the industry pushed for the creation of the DMCA, which, as Lawrence Lessig (2004, 157) explains, "was a bit of law intended to back up the protection of this code designed to protect copyrighted material. It was, we could say, *legal code* intended to buttress *software code* which itself was intended to support the *legal code of copyright*."

As a side effect, the DMCA also crippled fair use. Certain uses of copyrighted materials are technically permissible, even without the copyright owner's permission. For instance, certain educational uses of copyrighted material are generally allowed. While fair use has endured a number of blows over the years, largely due to corporate pressure, the DMCA provides one of the most damning. Businesses only need place a token level of protection on their intellectual property to trigger the protections of the DMCA. Even if the use of the copyrighted material falls under fair use, the DMCA makes it illegal if such use requires the circumvention of a copy-protection mechanism (Lessig 2004). Fair use is therefore rendered practically meaningless. Copyright holders possess a tremendous litigation tool to further deploy the power of the state to protect their economic interests.

Hackers have been known to run afoul of the DMCA, particularly as it was designed to provide legal protections against activities central to the hacking endeavor—the exploration, reconfiguration, and circumvention of technological systems. Any hackers interested in reworking software or researching security vulnerabilities may be found in violation of the DMCA if uncovered. Even openly discussing or publishing the findings of circumvention methods could result in serious legal consequences. Cory Doctorow (2008, 10) describes one such incident where a hacker/security researcher breached the DMCA: "Dmitry Sklyarov is a Russian programmer who gave a talk at a hacker con in Vegas on the failings in Adobe's ebook locks. The FBI threw him in the slam for thirty days. He copped a plea, went home to Russia, and the Russian equivalent of the State Department issued a blanket warning to its researchers to stay away from American conferences, since we'd apparently turned into the kind of country where certain equations are illegal." In other words, the open publication of copy-protection security vulnerabilities was made illegal under the DMCA. One would think these types of measures would be used exclusively for national security issues, not copy-protections on an ebook reader.

Many attempts have been made to further protect intellectual property and technological infrastructure such as the Stop Online Piracy Act and the Cyber Intelligence Sharing and Protection Act—though many of these have failed in light of major push back from Internet protestors and various civil liberties organizations. Conversely, little government attention has been directed towards controlling the accumulation of massive troves of personal data by corporations to be used for marketing purposes (Bollier 2003). In other words, the regulatory gaze of the government is directed largely towards controlling behaviors dangerous to capital interests rather than those of individual citizens, notably through privacy erosions.[20]

Of course, such dilemmas are not new to capitalism. Much like capitalists have historically deployed law enforcement to control unruly workers and unions (Harring 1983; Zinn 2005), they also seek to use the law as a club to redirect the creative energies of the hacker classes in ways beneficial to capitalism. Note, however, that little attention is given to capitalists employing hackers to engage in shady business practices such as corporate espionage (see Ingersoll 2013). The struggle has also been about maximizing surplus while limiting the power of labor. In a period of globalized, late-modern, high-technology capitalism, this just happens to be one form in which the conflict arises. Hackers currently present a valuable source of labor for capitalists while also constituting threats to control over the vectors of distribution and profit (Wark 2004). Late-modern information capitalists must therefore work to benefit from the fruits of hacker production while resisting the threats hackers pose through open-source software production, piracy, computer intrusions, network obstructions, and other activities.

Outside of increased pressures to legislate any perceived threats hackers pose, in an age of neo-liberal governance, private industry has been increasingly relied upon to develop and dispense technosecurity solutions for businesses and government agencies looking to protect their data. The computer crime control industry—a term derived from the late Nils Christie's (2000) *Crime Control as Industry*—thus presents a kind of "governance from below" to deal with hackers and other technological miscreants (Lea and Stenson 2007; Yar 2008a). Indeed, hackers (or the phantasmagorical notion thereof) comprise one of the central threats used to encourage fear over technological security issues (Wall 2008, 2012). Driven by one part necessity and two parts fear, this industry has expanded and become exceedingly lucrative. Of course, the promotion of security industries through the use of the image of the technologically adept professional criminal has occurred as early as the 1800s (Churchill 2015). Hackers, in some capacity, have thus become a late-modern version of the professional thief—a boogeyman useful for encouraging the consumption of security (Churchill 2015; Sutherland 1937).

Conclusion

Amid the din of panic over technology, crime, terrorism, economic losses, and other factors, it is no surprise that society has seemingly descended down the rabbit hole and emerged out the other end upside down with its head on backwards. Even if the legal/crime control apparatus had the best interests of everyone at heart, its attempts at regulating the situation are painfully disoriented. An ideology has emerged alongside the rise of high technology that secures corporate interests and disparages threats to accumulation. Hackers are transformed into pathological, aberrant, deviant monsters lurking in the wires—contemporary boogeymen on which to heap our anxieties about technology and social change. Yet they are useful monsters—providing a valuable pool of labor as well as a scapegoat for many concerns regarding technology. And, as with so many "monsters" before these, we readily pull the blankets over our eyes and turn to institutions of security (e.g., law, law enforcement, private security, etc.) to protect us. Like a nightlight in a child's bedroom, this work attempts to vanish those phantasms that blight our imagination in the dark to show that these monsters are not everything we envision them to be . . . and that perhaps our fears and vulnerabilities are overstated.

Conclusion

In an industrial factory, it is easy to think of these spaces as composed of machines, walls, tools, and people functioning as discrete parts. As Marx would constantly remind us, these physical objects do not make up production. Instead, these spaces are, above all else, *composed of social relationships* between owners, workers, tools, machines, commodities, and money. In the same manner, the Internet is also composed of *social relations*. Computers and networks are just as much products of people and social cognition as they are polymers, semiconductors, metals, and flowing electrons. In this manner, the Internet does not exist outside of the social.

There is a tendency in contemporary society to fetishize the Internet. We too easily forget that "virtual" spaces are first and foremost products of human labor and interaction. From the creation of network architectures to the production and dissemination of Internet memes, human actors are at the core. Even automated processes like botnets require human designers and herders. Sure, if asked about social networking sites like Facebook and Twitter, most would acknowledge they are interacting with people. There exists, however, a digital landscape in our social and cultural imagination that runs parallel to our direct experiences with the Internet. If one wants to visit this space within the public mind's eye, one need only invoke the term "cyber"—an abject Alice in Wonderland–like space in our psyche where anything is possible. In "cyberspace," "online predators" lurk behind every communication, the specter of "cyberterrorism" haunts our infrastructure, and roving bands of "hackers" are constantly marauding for data. While these figures may certainly *look* humanoid in this fantasy, they are understood as mere shades. They are distinctly non-human and dangerous; digital gremlins hiding within the cogs of the machine on which global society has come to rely. If this book convinces you, dear reader, of one thing, I hope it is this: hacking is an intrinsically *human* social and cultural phenomenon. Such a proclamation should not be revolutionary, yet too often accounts of "hacking" are disturbingly barren of human actors. Victims are often listed as corporations, government agencies, or individuals aggregated into general statistics. Perpetrators are invisible or quasi-visible ghosts haunting the wires.[1]

Among other tasks, the primary objective of the first part of this book was to establish these human elements of hacking. Chapter 1 explored how hackers evolve into their subcultural identity and disposition through the exploration of key demographic characteristics, experiences, support systems, and influences. One of the key conclusions of this chapter is that hacking is strongly associated to social class positioning. While this finding is instrumental in the later political economic analyses, the overall portrait is that hackers are not born within the digital nether—they are material beings shaped by material conditions like anyone else.

In chapter 2, hacking is further demystified. In an exploration for the *essence* of hacking, this analysis argues that the phenomenon, while perhaps new in appearance, drinks deep from an old and familiar well. Here, hacking is described as a craft—one that takes on particular late modern characteristics, but a craft nonetheless. It is not a complete replication of traditional crafts, however. In particular, hacking tends to place greater emphasis on transgression than many of its prototypical craftwork counterparts (Sennett 2008). As such, the eidos of hacking is summarized as both *craft* and *craftiness*: it is *craft(y)*. Hacking is therefore more complicated than the mythology would indicate. Rather than equate hacking with technocrime, a more honest and fruitful avenue is to understand hacking as composed of humans engaged in creative, transgressive, technological craftwork.

Since hackers are human actors, capable of exercising agency, it also makes little sense to treat them as aberrant specimens to be poked and prodded—treated as pathogens circulating in the wires. Many studies examine hackers as if they are something to be *dealt with*—as if the only reason to study them is to find ways to prevent their assumed criminality. Not all studies do this fortunately. In fact, this study is but one contribution to a growing body of thought that recognizes the humanity of hacking. One contribution to this area made here is an exploration of hacker perspectives toward institutions of authority, particularly governments. Rather than seek methods to thwart hackers, chapter 3 explores these views to situate hackers within their broader social and political context. This analysis reveals hackers as actors who view governments as largely problematic—a result of perceived over-controlling tendencies, ineptitude, and collateral consequences. While hackers are often stereotyped as outright anti-authoritarian, this analysis finds that state control and intervention is not always abhorred—it's a matter of degree rather than categorical disdain. Hackers even envision solutions to problems created by governments and agencies of control which both involve suggestions of systemic fixes and ways to mitigate personal harm and control. Such insights conflict with many studies that assume absolute anti-authoritarianism or criminality on the part of hackers. These perspectives are then described within these pages as representing a broader philosophical perspective underpinning hacker culture, one that would later be used to help link hackers to the broader macro-structural context—technological liberalism.

Part two of this book builds from the foundations laid in the previous chapters by situating the human and subcultural elements of hacking into the broader macro-structural context, particularly the political economy. In chapter 4, hackers are discussed as both a bane and a boon for capitalist production and consumption. The radical implications of the relationship between hacking and middle-class positioning as well as craftwork were explored from a Marxist perspective sensitive to the social relations of skill and the implications of alienation. Building from this analysis, the transition away from the Protestant ethic towards a "hacker ethic" of work was discussed, highlighting how the blurring of labor and leisure actually contributes to the exploitation of hackers by further monopolizing their time in favor of capital. Technological liberalism was then situated in the historical progression of economic liberalism, highlighting how the liberalism underpinning hackers resembles the liberalism of Polanyi's (1944) day, which served to uphold capitalist relations of production. The analysis then briefly discussed how hackers represent a blurring of consumption and production.

Firmly situating hacking within the dialectics of late modern capitalism, chapter 5 takes a criminological turn, focusing on how capitalism maximizes the productive capacity of hackers, as a laboring class, while legitimizing efforts to control the threats they pose to profit. As argued here, social constructions are useful in this regard. First, hackers are constructed as dangerous, which allows a criminal classification to be imposed. Second, intellectual property is reified, giving capitalists a set of property "rights" to protect from the threats of individuals like hackers. Finally, technological infrastructures are portrayed as vulnerable, lending a degree of urgency to the need to fight off the hacker "menace" along with other technocriminals. It is in this chapter that the processes of abstraction surrounding hacking are most evident. Once these constructions are in place, capital can then push for policy and state intervention that is largely in the interests of profit and control.

The intention was not to portray hackers as simply the victims of social construction and capital logics exclusively. As mentioned throughout, *some* hackers do create *real* harms (though these harms are not the exclusive domain of hackers). As Nissenbaum (2004, 212) asserts, "it is important to note that sustaining the positive meaning of hackers does not require denying or turning a blind eye to those who turn their skills and know-how towards stealing information or money, damaging and vandalizing information or systems, or placing critical systems at risk of malfunction." Such behaviors and harms have been considered as *one component* of issues surrounding hackers explored throughout. What such a perspective does require, however, is an attunement to the sociological imagination—a willingness to place actors within their context and to link private troubles to social problems (Mills 1959). Dissections of hackers and hacker culture risk dealing in mere caricatures of the social phenomenon they claim to explain without such a sensitivity.

On that note, this book concludes with a reprimand for a growing trend within the criminological canon, one that falls afoul of the warnings given by C. Wright Mills (1959) over fifty years ago and more recently by Jock Young (2011b). In particular, a genre of criminology has emerged around technocrime issues, which is "denatured and desiccated" where "its actors inhabit an arid planet where they are either driven into crime by social and psychological deficits or make opportunistic choices in the marketplace of crime. They are either miserable or mundane: they are digital creatures of quantity, they are obey probabilistic laws of deviancy—they can be represented by the statistical symbolism of lambda, chi, and sigma, their behavior can be captured in the intricacies of regression analysis and equation" (Young 2011b, 84). Critical criminology offers a kind of remedy against this barren academic canon. Opening hacking up to analysis from a Marxist and radical criminological perspective skewers the myopic nature of many previous criminological analyses of alleged hacking and other technocrime issues—which seem to have increasingly drifted towards the use of student samples, poor conceptualizations, and individual-level positivistic criminological theories (see Bossler and Burrus, 2010; Marcum et al. 2014; Morris 2010). In many ways, these analyses have made themselves complicit in the construction of the ideology surrounding hackers by adopting narrow definitions of hacking and conducting their analyses without consideration of the subcultural nuances described here and in other noteworthy studies (see Coleman 2012; Coleman and Golub 2008; Söderberg 2008; Taylor 1999; Thomas 2002).[2]

Consider Marcum, Higgins, Ricketts, and Wolfe's (2014) recent examination of "hacking." In this study, the authors examine a rural population of juveniles and their alleged hacking behaviors. Their working definition of hacking underpinning the study suggests that "computer hacking can include, *but is not limited to the following behaviors*: breaking into a computer system, developing or using viruses, destroying or altering file [*sic*], theft of services, credit card fraud, and infiltrating software" (581; emphasis added). The definition is narrow, to be certain. The authors, however, *hint* at the broad and diverse nature of hacking. By stating "but is not limited to the following behaviors," they may give at least some acknowledgement that there is something more to hacking than criminal activity—though they fail to elucidate what this could entail. More likely, however, this caveat is merely recognition that the list of behaviors provided is an incomplete enumeration of the illicit activities that alleged hackers can perform.

This myopic perspective on hacking tapers further still when the authors detail their quantitative operationalization of hacking. In this study, hacking is measured through a survey question asking: "Have you ever performed [the] following behaviors in the past year: (1) logged into another person's e-mail without his/her permission [and] sent an e-mail; (2) logged into another person's Facebook account without permission and posted a message; and (3) accessed a website for which you were not an authorized user" (Marcum et al. 2014, 585). According to the authors, simply using the login information of another user found on a Post-It note hiding underneath a keyboard constitutes "hacking." For such an approach to hacking to be acceptable, they must flagrantly ignore a wide range of literature (mostly qualitative) from multiple disciplines that shows hacking as much broader and more complex than this, the current study notwithstanding.

Not only do Marcum et al. (2014, 582) fail to pull from this literature—an omission that undermines their approach—but what little qualitative research was cited is summarized in a single sentence: "Qualitative studies have been performed to understand their attitudes toward hacking and the norms and values of this subculture based on small samples of active or incarcerated hackers." Based on the results of this study and other ethnographic accounts, such an approach to the study of hacking is rendered questionable at best and outright disingenuous at worst.

In this way, studies that operate on such faulty conceptual foundations engage in what Jock Young (2011b, 39) refers to as "skating on thin ice." Though initially intended to be a critique of quantitative statistical fetishism within orthodox criminology, such a concept is equally applicable toward other limitations within criminological thought and analysis. The conceptual problems that plague Marcum et al.'s (2014) study "[do] not seem to stop the would-be social scientists for more than a minute. Somewhere tucked into the text the authors admit the precariousness of their arguments, their scientific vulnerability, and yet continue on. It is as if the skater hesitates, notes the thin ice, yet skates blithely on" (Young 2011b, 41). The authors seem to recognize the potential problems confronting their work (i.e., the caveat in their original definition and the recognition that qualitative work has been conducted). Yet, this study downplays the significance of these issues and neglects to even mention many noteworthy studies on hackers and hacker culture. It is if they survey the frozen lake, recognize the peril, and then push off onto the precarious surface.

While I have used Marcum et al.'s (2014) study as a punching bag, their study is not the only one that falls victim to these kinds of flaws within criminology (though, it does have the misfortune of being singled out as a more recent example). In addition, to some degree I understand *why* these works may adopt such a perspective, even if I do not condone such scholarship. Popular culture, political officials, public opinion, and even some members of the hacker community contribute to the construction of the hacker as a criminal other. If one were to adopt this perspective unquestioningly, then it would be easy to justify such studies as efforts to solve a social problem in tremendous need of remedy. Such notions are hard to dispel, particularly as there is a small kernel of truth within these mythologies—there are indeed some hackers that operate in the manner these studies envision. Again, however, these perceptions by no means encompass the entirety of hacking or the hacking community. Thus, these studies can be said to be influenced by as well as contribute to the reification of the dangerous hacker mythology; they also present a seemingly slapdash attempt at making sense of the phenomenon.

Only by expanding the scope of analysis to include sensitivity to broader historical, social, economic, and political forces can an adequate understanding hackers be captured. This book presents one way to approach such a task by situating hacking within the conflicts and contradictions of late modern capitalism. Such is the strength of radical criminology (and critical criminology more generally): it helps us see phenomena in the context of power and conflict, thus not only looking at crime and deviance as reified social categories but, rather, as activities, statuses, and lifestyles caught in a complex whirl of control and resistance. It is at this nexus hackers are caught, as criminologists would do well to remember.

That is not to say that this study is the final say about hackers and hacking. While this analysis was intended to be relatively thorough, there are still wide areas left unexplored for future research. The buck does not stop here. Consistent with the hacker spirit, I encourage criminologists to continue exploring, challenging, and getting their hands both literally and figuratively dirty. I only hope that future studies remain sensitive to broader social structural dynamics, rather than observing hackers as if they were some illicit aberration in a glass case. The latter approach leads to irrelevancy. If criminology wishes to be relevant in this domain, it must remain attuned to the sociological, or, in this case, the *criminological* imagination (Young 2011b).

I am not content to end to book on this note, however. Marx once stated that the purpose of philosophy is not just to interpret the world, but to change it. This book thus concludes by outlining several strategies,

policies, and practices that may be adopted to address the previously described issues surrounding technocrime and security. When dealing in
the arts of radical inquiry, there is sometimes a temptation to descend
into fatalism. The persistent presence of gargantuan social, cultural, economic, and historical forces make it is easy to declare hopelessness; no
real solution can be found without resorting to macro-structural change.
There is some truth in this assertion—much of the problems discussed
throughout this book may require society-shaking change to overcome.
I am not content, however, to send this book into the world with the implicit message that the whole situation is FUBAR unless a metaphorical
sledgehammer rocks the foundations of the political economy (though
I encourage such rocking).[3] Until sweeping and radical social change
comes along to, for instance, destroy perceptions of intellectual property and challenge capitalist control over the vectors (both of information and accumulation), what can be done in the meantime? As Lea and
Young (1984) once asked, "What is to be done about law and order?"[4]
Rather than twiddle my thumbs before tossing my hands into the air
when such a question is posed, I penned the following sections as an attempt to provide at least *some* tentative suggestions for dealing with the
very real harms surrounding hacking and related issues. Drawing from
left realism—a tradition of critical criminology that seeks to create more
immediate policy solutions with a radical sensitivity to macro-structural
issues—this analysis brings some suggestions for change that may be
more productive in light of the analyses presented throughout. But first,
a brief overview of left realism.

Left Realism

Left Realism, "*with* capital letters" (Currie 2010, 113) emerged in the 1980s
as the brainchild of British criminologists like John Lea and Jock Young
(1984). This period in British history was marred by rising crime rates
and social inequality in the wake of "post-Fordist de-industrialisation"
(Lea 2015, 166). Rather than focus only on the tensions between classes
and the processes of capital accumulation—as were popular among
radical criminologists of the time—these scholars recognized that one
of the biggest immediate problems facing the British working classes
were intra-class forms of crime and victimization. Left Realism was a

radically different approach to criminology, which at the time was dominated by *administrative criminology* (or *right realism*) and what Young (1979) termed *left idealism.*

Politically conservative in disposition, administrative criminology and right realism sought crime control policies while maintaining an "antagonism to the idea that social circumstances cause crime, and a lack of interest in the causes of crime" (Hough 2014, 215). At the time, James Q. Wilson, George Kelling, and Ron Clarke were examples of theorists who espoused crime control strategies based on situational prevention and increases in police presence with little concern for root causes (Hough 2014; Matthews 2014). Through such narrow-sightedness, administrative criminology had little effect on crime while simultaneously contributing to the oppressive conditions from which crime emerges.

Left idealism, on the other hand, was described as a particular genre of critical criminology in the 1980s that viewed criminals as proto-revolutionaries and ignored the real consequences crime posed to the working classes. These criminologists focused more on "white collar and corporate crime, with a beginning interest in state crime" (Schwartz and DeKeseredy 2010, 108). Critical criminology at the time was also preoccupied with "arguing the very definitions of crime, and the notion of who commits crime, are shaped by both class and race interests in North America and Europe" (Schwartz and DeKeseredy 2010, 108).

While most certainly not abject to such concerns, Left Realism recognized that the violence and other predominantly intra-class harms could not be romanticized or dismissed. This tendency towards romanticizing deviance resulted in Jock Young (1969) castigating such criminologists as the "zookeepers of deviancy"—those who would preserve deviants within a glass cage of abstraction divorced from "social and political power relations" and define "away any notion of personal integrity, autonomy and authentic existence" (Lea 2014, 433). In addition, left idealists were attacked for their tendency to "downplay the seriousness and extent" of violent crime "because of either the fear of pathologizing the poor, 'whipping up' support for severe punishment, and supporting racist arguments," or victim blaming (DeKeseredy 2003, 31). Though such concerns are not wholly unjustified, they lead to a kind of minimalist or hands-off approach to crime that offers little for the predominantly poor and working-class communities struggling with the real effects of violence and victimization.

Left Realism has left a lasting mark on critical criminology and moved beyond the confines of the particular historical context of predominantly British criminology in the 1980s. As Elliot Currie (2010, 113) explains, "most of its central themes and crucial insights could apply to a much broader swath of criminologists working today, in the U.K., the United States, and elsewhere," a broader criminological trend he describes as left realism "without capitals," or "plain" left realism. Juggernaut of left realism Roger Matthews (2014) describes the contemporary state of left realism as *critical realism*. Regardless of the title used, left realists have been instrumental in pushing radical thought toward practical measures to alleviate the pains of crime among the poor and working classes—at least until broad sweeping structural change is possible.

One of the key features of left realism is the *square of crime* (Lea 1992). Instead of viewing crime as merely any single action, left realists view crime as a configuration of social relations between not just the offender and victim, but the state and public as well. Other areas of criminology are accused by some left realists of overemphasizing one component of the square, whereas left realism attempts to strike a theoretical balance, dividing its attention equally between the state, society, offenders, and victims. Whether left realism finds such theoretical equilibrium is up for debate, but at least the desire for a grounded and holistic understanding of crime is established.

Typically, left realism focuses on inner-city and working-class violence (DeKeseredy 2003). There is nothing, however, that prevents insights drawn from left realism from being applied to non-violent crimes. Much like left realism has traditionally married radical sensibilities with a genuine concern about the real harms of street crime, there is nothing preventing a recognition of the broader structural dynamics underpinning hacking while attempting to address the real harms caused by technocrime. The suggestions made throughout by no means constitute a comprehensive list of potential solutions for the various social ills described throughout this book. The current state of technocrime and security is currently so primordial that relatively little research exists to provide a foundation for left realist–appropriate solutions. Instead, the intention here is to provide some initial suggestions to be further refined and developed in future scholarship. With that caveat given, this work now seeks to "get real" and suggest plausible solutions to dealing with the problems elucidated throughout.

Left realism is sometimes critiqued for being *too* practically minded and not embracing the fluid, emotional, and even romantic notions of other forms of critical criminology. In a move to separate itself from left idealism, left realism may have stepped too far in the other direction. Left realism may become so policy-oriented that it may forget that imagination and a dose of resistance can be good for social science. The following is thus meant to be a kind of reimagining of left realism. The objective is to develop practical and immediate steps that criminologists and policy makers can take to address contemporary harms caused by data breaches and information mismanagement while not eschewing the need for radical transformation of social circumstances and the need to engage in a critical *verstehen* of hackers (Ferrell 1998). In this fashion, practical suggestions should attempt to protect individuals from the perils and pitfalls of technocrime and technosecurity while simultaneously undermining the power tied into the vectors.

Getting Real about Technocrime

Challenging Mythology

While not a policy change *per se*, a useful way to start combating the technocrime and hacking "problem" within the current political economy is to challenge the dominant narratives about hacking, technology, and intellectual property. As noted across many other crime "problems," creating rational and measured responses to harmful behaviors is difficult when the issue is shrouded in fright-inducing misconceptions. Indeed, such "moral panics" have long been noted for creating policy responses out of touch with reality (Cohen [1972] 2002). The archetypal example of such disproportionate policy response was toward marijuana, said to induce a kind of "reefer madness" that was associated with violence, insanity, sexual assault, and even suicide. Such proclamations were based on myth rather than reality but the effect was powerful. For instance, marijuana prohibition has resulted in the mass incarceration of users and dealers in a manner severely unequal to the amount of social harm caused by the substance (which, is to say, little if any). Hacking has been similarly demonized, leading to irrational criminal justice responses, recently noted in the case of Aaron Swartz.

Changing the dominant narratives is easier said than done, however. The primary vectors for mass dissemination of information are generally controlled by corporations (Barak 1988; Wark 2004) and are overwhelmingly skewed toward entertainment (Frost and Phillips 2011; Postman 1985). Crafting and spreading counter-narratives that combat over-dramatization and outright fictions is therefore difficult. Some herald the Internet as a great equalizer, that the Internet gives an outlet for anyone and everyone (there is some truth to this claim). Evidence, however, exists to suggest that the democratic promise of this medium is potentially overstated (Schaefer and Steinmetz 2014). Though independent media can gain greater traction through the Internet than in other forms of telecommunication (e.g., radio and television), mass consumption of information through this medium is still dominated by corporate-owned outlets. The Internet thus allows a broader spectrum of voices to sound, but only the loudest can be heard above the cacophony. As a general rule, corporate-owned media has an easier time gaining volume.

In addition, myths surrounding crime and justice issues generally have proven difficult to dispel. As Victor Kappeler and Gary Potter (2005, 371) explain, "Debunking myths does not have the same attraction as does their construction. After clear definitions of criminal behavior have been developed and the actual frequency of the crime has been determined, there are few newspaper accounts, television documentaries, commercials, or calls by political leaders to demystify our images of crime. Often, all that exists in the aftermath of a crime myth are criminal laws, more cops, harsher punishments, misplaced social resources, a feeling of moral superiority, and a growing intolerance for human diversity." In the face of such overwhelming odds, what is the intrepid social scientist or activist to do?

Changing public perceptions of crime and justice issues has been a long-standing concern of criminology. Many wailing cries from criminological scholars have echoed out in hopes of having some impact on public and political perceptions. One of the reasons for the difficulty is that challenging many beliefs about crime and crime control involve attacking ideologies that replicate macro-structural forces. It is one thing to convince your friend that the person using a laptop computer in a coffee shop to compile code is not some technological wizard. It is quite another to try to convince them that their views on computers and technocrime are not only problematic but are also heavily influenced by massive historical, cultural, social, and political economic forces (everyone wants to think that they are personally immune to such effects). Power, like that which circulates through the political economy, shapes the material conditions of a society. Belief structures among individuals within that society are subsequently shaped by these conditions: "The phantoms formed in the human brain are also, necessarily, sublimates of their material life-process" (Marx and Engels 1947, 47). In other words, completely changing dominant ideologies may mean serious challenges to the material conditions of society as arranged by the dominant mode of production. Power, however, is not just within those material conditions, but it circulates within the discourse, becoming almost self-reinforcing and replicating—it tends to take on a life of its own to some degree (Foucault 1972; Hall 2001). Thus combating dominant narratives, particularly those springing from political economic conditions, appears to be a nearly Sisyphean task.

But does such difficulty mean it is not worth attempting to change the discourse? Criminologists, and sociologists generally, have struggled to crawl out from under a largely "self-inflicted irrelevance born of hyper-professionalism and social insularity, political powerlessness, and civic disgrace" (Wacquant 2011, 440). Media, as one of the most influential forces shaping public opinion in late modern capitalism, "frequently rely on official state representatives such as prosecutors, police officials, politicians, and other government sources when relaying stories pertaining to crime" (Frost and Phillips 2011, 89). These actors often have vested interests in maintaining the status quo. The result is a taxing task of crafting a "counter-hegemonic narrative" (Frost and Phillips 2011, 89). Many efforts have been made to reinstate sociologists and criminologists into positions of legitimate authority in the discourse on crime and punishment through various efforts like "public criminology" (Loader and Sparks 2010; Sanders and Eisler 2015), and from the domain of critical criminology, "newsmaking criminology" (Barak 1988).

Academics have had difficulty breaking into various forms of mainstream media (like television) and shaping public discourse. In his foundational work on newsmaking criminology, Gregg Barak (1988) called out for academics to become involved in the media with the hope of countering the hegemony that had formed around issues of crime and crime control. In the years since, seemingly little progress has been made, at least in terms of dominant, unidirectional media forms like television (Frost and Phillips 2011). More academics, however, have turned to the Internet—through webpages, blogs, op-eds, video lectures, and the like—as a way to influence the discourse. Because of the ease with which persons can scroll past or click through online content in addition to the threat of so-called slacktivism, the Internet, as previously mentioned, presents its own issues for criminologists looking to engage the public discourse (Schaefer and Steinmetz 2014).[5] The ease of access and the potential for viral dissemination, however, makes online venues particularly appealing. While exact numbers are difficult to come by, more and more academics engage the public online through blogs and even write for online news websites like *The Huffington Post*. In addition, academic criminologists have also begun to use alternative media forms to communicate their messages including graphic art, filmmaking, and music (see Sutton 2013; Tunnell, Cox, and Green 2011). Such mergers of entertainment and education ("edutainment," if you will) may be more influential in today's media environment than other forms of engagement.

Academics interested in shaping the public discourse on hacking and technocrime issues may find such venues valuable for combating mythologization. The effects of such discourse will not be immediate. In fact, the influence on technocrime discourse overtime may be tepid, at best. But there is a non-zero chance for change. In light of the serious problems that confront society in terms of technologically induced harms, capital accumulation, and government control, any chance is worth seizing. I personally find hope in "edutainment" forms of criminological outreach—though the risk of such efforts is to potentially banalize the message. Thus academic challenges to mythology may be like waves crashing upon the cliffs. The reader should keep in mind, however, that these waves do eventually alter the cliff face, even if the results are not apparent immediately.

Policy Initiatives

Challenging social constructions of technocrime is just one potential avenue for change. The rest of this section is dedicated to proposing some policy changes that may be more useful for mitigating the harm of technocrime while maintaining sensitivity to the issues discussed throughout this book. When news reports and alleged security experts appear before the public, the question of how to protect oneself from these crimes is often given the most attention. Such concerns are understandable—everyone should endeavor to be vigilant in protecting their privacy in the information age. Less attention, however, is paid to the more important issues; how do we temper the risk posed to personal privacy and finances by the collection and storage of private information for business purposes? Security professionals, of course, ask these questions all the time. Popular discourse and political rhetoric, however, seem to place the focus on individual "criminals" and "terrorists." Instead, we would do well to aim policy efforts in a way that challenges the biggest risks created by increasing dependency on information technology in everyday life and the significant economic interests involved. After all, technocrimes seldom target *individuals*. Instead, these crimes largely impact individuals *through databases stored and accumulated for economic or bureaucratic purposes*. The proposed solutions presented here are by no means complete or absolute. These are simply suggestions ripe for debate and criticism.

In addition, the suggestions made here do not have corporate profits in mind. To be frank, I could not care less about the preservation of corporate interests through these solutions. The focus is on protecting individuals from harms posed by technocrimes or corporate and institutional negligence. Should the reader desire methods to secure the interests wrapped around corporate tech systems, there are a litany of articles written by handmaidens to capital readily available in any academic search engine.

Perhaps controversial, the first proposed remedy is to seek legislation that would require greater transparency in the security methods employed by major corporations. Some legislative attempts have recently been made to hold companies (and other organizations as well) accountable for improper data protections (Hanover Research 2015).

While these attempts are laudable, they do not necessarily require transparency. This does not mean that a company must lay bare every possible exploit that could be used against it. Such a task would be impossible as 100 percent knowledge about security flaws—known and unknown—is untenable. What this *does* mean is that companies would be required to report their information security protocols, the software employed, the computer systems used, etc. in the protection of personal information.

For the average consumer, there is no way to assess businesses and other organizations in their relative capabilities to protect private data. Some organizations are vulnerable because they do not keep their software and hardware up-to-date. Others may fail to implement any real protections whatsoever. Companies or any other group seeking to collect private data would be required to report on these security measures and how often updates are applied. An independent agency could then use indicators like these to rate companies in terms of their security fitness. These scores would be published online. Consumers and patrons could then use these scores to assess whether or not to trust these companies with their private information. The very idea of creating scores for information security is by no means *perfect*, but it would at least ensure that companies are held responsible for maintaining at least basic protections on information.

I can already hear the rancorous choir of businesses asserting that transparency in security would only make them more vulnerable. After all, would such measures only give attackers more information at their disposal? The answer is both "yes" and "no." The transparency desired here is to combat reliance on "security by obscurity." Security by obscurity is a generally pejorative term for an overreliance on secrecy as a measure of security. For instance, in the early days of the Internet, businesses would maintain servers that you could only connect to if you knew the phone number to dial in. The assumption was that the servers were relatively secure because most people would not know the phone number needed for access. When hackers and others started using war dialers to track down servers, these systems were shown to be wholly *insecure*. Today, companies that rely on secrecy as one of their primary methods of security generally only put data at risk because once the secret is out, the system is compromised.

That said, it is not as if secrecy has *no* place in technosecurity. Rather, secrecy can be a valuable way to add additional security. The trick is that it is supplementary, not primary. In addition, reporting measures can allow a degree of discretion on the part of the business. They may not necessarily need to disclose the secrecy-reliant elements of their security system *as long as they have a satisfactory non-secrecy-reliant system in place first.*

While scoring systems may be useful for basic accountability, they do little to protect individuals from harm *after* a successful network intrusion or data exfiltration has occurred. When sensitive consumer data has been compromised, businesses should be required to immediately report it. According to Hanover Research (2015, 15), a market research firm that recently released a report for the Indiana University Maurer School of Law on technosecurity legal regulations, there are currently "no existing disclosure requirement specifically refers to cybersecurity." *Some* reporting may be required based on how such attacks may impact matters relevant for the Securities and Exchange Commission—those involving potential threats to financial assets, etc. These protections, however, are tenuous, at best. Legal protections need to be crafted to require disclosure of sensitive data breaches and other threats to personal privacy. Quick reporting would allow consumers more time to begin protecting themselves against identity theft and other risks.

The good news is that, in this regard, attempts have already been made to rectify the situation. In 2014, Congress attempted to pass five breach notification bills including the Data Security and Breach Notification Act, the Personal Data Privacy and Security Act, the Data Security Act, and the Personal Data Protection and Breach Accountability Act. Each of these attempted to craft legal mechanisms requiring the timely disclosure of data breaches among other privacy protections. Following these bills, President Obama proposed his own version in early 2015 called the Personal Data Notification and Protection Act. Each of these measures slightly differed in their approach to privacy protections and notifications. While none have been passed as of yet, these bills represent positive steps forward in the protection of personal privacy.

Perhaps a more controversial policy would be for the creation of technosecurity reporting centers. These places would operate as a kind of clearinghouse for hackers and other security-minded individuals to *anonymously* report vulnerabilities in information security systems. Agents within the center could then verify the problem and compile a report to be issued to the company, firm, or agency responsible for the issue. The offending entity would then be required, within a reasonable amount of time, to fix the issue or provide a written justification for non-compliance. These justifications could then be assessed and either accepted or rejected. Delinquent non-compliance could result in (1) reductions in a company's technosecurity scores and (2) civil fines. If a major breach happens that exploits the vulnerability in question after notification, firms could then be held criminally responsible if sensitive personal information was compromised.

There may be some protests to such measures. After all, would such reporting centers essentially be condoning potentially criminal behavior? Indeed, with the language of the Computer Fraud and Abuse Act (CFAA), Digital Millennium Copyright Act (DMCA), and other technocrime and security legislation, the very act of searching for vulnerabilities can be considered a crime. The counter question, however, is, so what? If, for example, a hacker is interested in learning about a security system and finding vulnerabilities, they will likely do it regardless of the laws that are in place. Why should they be punished for showing the ethical consideration of turning such information over rather than using such exploits for nefarious purposes or selling vulnerabilities on the black and grey markets (Zetter 2014)? Their likelihood of sanction would certainly be lower if they chose *not* to turn over such information (and it could be more profitable as well). If the objective is to create systems that preserve individual privacy and security, then killing the messenger—so to speak—is completely counter-intuitive. A certain degree of immunity should be extended to those who turn over such information. Their efforts could potentially protect the sensitive information of many people, even if it might embarrass the entity with the vulnerability.

That said, for a reporting center to operate effectively *and* not run afoul of lawsuits leveled by angry companies, the language of certain intellectual property and technosecurity laws would have to be modified to accommodate such reporting. For example, the DMCA prohibits the bypassing of any copyright protection technology—and this has been interpreted broadly. If a person tinkering with copy-protection finds a vulnerability that could be exploited to access sensitive personal information (and this does happen) and reports it, a lawsuit could be leveled against the reporting center for endorsing such violations of the DMCA or failing to release the identity of the bug reporter. These centers would involve various features to protect the anonymity of reporters, so at least submitters would remain protected. The reporting center, however, could be rocked by litigation. As such, the creation of these centers would involve much more than their organization and construction. The legal apparatus would have to be massaged to accommodate them.

One of the key reasons for lagging technosecurity measures in society is economic. Businesses may not want to invest into adequate security systems, as these systems are often not instrumental for growth. The adoption of new technological standards may also be cumbersome on businesses. The fact of the matter is that any technological security measure that protects personal privacy or provides individuals with greater control over what happens with their information will likely be *inconvenient* for business. As such, we, as a society, must decide on what matters more—the protection of individual privacy or profit. If it is the former, we have to accept that profit is going to take a hit. If the latter, privacy will continue to shrink in favor of corporate expansion. Perhaps a balance can be struck (I am dubious, to say the least), but in our society the emphasis has traditionally leaned towards capital. While the language of liberalism advocates for both personal privacy and free markets, it is confronted by a serious contradiction when private information *becomes a commodity to exchange on the free market*. At this point, despite the protests of organizations like the Electronic Frontier Foundation, the American Civil Liberties Union, and others, economic interests become prioritized. At this juncture, concerted effort is required to reverse or, at the very least, curb the effects of an economy that thrives on the collection, storage, and exchange of personal details. While the measures previously described are likely not the only viable policy solutions, they are a step forward. For these to work, however, we have to accept that it will impact business.

Perhaps the most inconvenient policy solution for capital—but one that could feasibly be achieved—is the legal overhaul of our intellectual property system. Intellectual property, as a legal construct, was originally well-intentioned. Copyright was intended to temporarily protect the financial interests of authors while still ensuring that cultural/intellectual products could proliferate (Lessig 2004; Perelman 2002). The idea was that intellectual content should be free to spread to enrich society. That is why copyright originally only protected the *right* to *make copies*—people could still be free to share content with each other while the copyright owner was the only one allowed to produce the actual copies of the work (and, even then, only for a reasonable period of time). Patents were originally created to give exclusive rights to an inventor to profit from their creation while making the design public so that—once a reasonable period of time passed—everyone could replicate and build from such designs. As such, intellectual property law was a compromise: economic interests and the social good were held in balance.

Today, copyright and patent laws have been perverted. As previously alluded in chapter 5, intellectual property rights are now used as a cudgel to squash competition and almost indefinitely secure rights to intellectual products. Computers, by necessity, constantly make copies. As such, in the digital age, copyright can be used to regulate nearly every use of electronic media (Lessig 2004; 2012). The "social good" of copyright has thus succumbed to the influence of economic monopolization. Patents have turned into weapons of economic warfare—companies use patent rights as litigative weapons to force competition from the marketplace. None of these uses were part of the original intent of intellectual property law. The resulting royalties and lawsuits created by stringent copyright and patent systems "are a deadweight loss to the economy" (Perelman 2014, 30).

Considering the role of intellectual property in (1) the exploitation of hacker labor, (2) the control of technologists, and (3) corporate power and malfeasance, we need to seriously reconsider how copyright and patent law are structured. The original purposes of temporarily protecting economic interests while promoting the social good need to be pulled from the dirt, stitched back together, and resurrected. There are multiple ways such a task could be accomplished. I confessedly lean towards an abolitionist stance but if copyright were to persist, I favor Lessig's (2012) proposal to restructure copyright around the notion of "meaningful activity," which concerns the *context of use* whereas copyright currently is triggered *anytime* a copy is made, regardless of the creative usage. Patent law could adopt similar standards that embody the *spirit* of the law rather than the current *letter*, so to speak. In other words, courts would have to determine on a case-by-case basis whether or not the activity constituted a *meaningful* encroachment on intellectual property. Was the intent to profit at the expense of the copyright or patent holder, or was the purpose to create something new and *add* to the cultural collective of creativity in some capacity? For instance, the production of counterfeit Simpson's dolls would likely still be prohibited under this model. The re-mixing of Simpson's episodes into a music video homage, however, may be protected. The language of intellectual property legislation would have to be carefully crafted to guide courts on these decisions.

Depending on the approach taken, such restructuring, in the short term, may have a detrimental impact on intellectual property industries, which have come to rely on state power to secure their economic interests. Long-term benefits, however, may include greater equality in the intellectual market place and an increased ability of artists and designers (including software designers) to be creative and explore the possibilities of expression and technology. As it stands right now, generally only corporations benefit from current intellectual property configurations. At the very least, the law would need to be restructured to reduce the overhead intellectual property litigation creates—costs carried by consumers and society generally.

The ultimate solution to the problems created within the confines of capital accumulation for individual privacy and economic safety would be for a radical transformation of the macro-structural conditions of society. That said, we can hold our breath and wait for such a day to arrive or we can try to reduce the real harms cause by technocrimes or inadequate security experienced by everyday folk. The previously described solutions are but a few suggestions for social change that might actually be realizable within the current system. Critical criminologists have spent little time examining issues related to technocrime and security and even less time contemplating realist policy implications. As such, this work is hopefully the first of many attempts to grapple with such issues within the canon of critical criminology.

APPENDIX

TABLE A.1. Interview List

Participant	Date	Length of Interview
Rick	09/14/2012	5h 1m
Russell	09/26/2012	1h 30m
Pete	10/28/2012	1h 23m
Susan	10/30/2012	1h 23m
Danny	11/09/2012	2h 29m
Keith	11/28/2012	58m
—	12/05/2012	2h 5m
Miles	12/07/2012	3h 0m*‡
—	12/12/2012	5h 4m
Harvey	01/10/2013	2h 30m
Raj	02/23/2013	1h 52m
Roger	03/11/2013	1h 54m
Aidan	03/18/2013	2h 12m
John	04/17/2013	2h 0m
Gilbert	06/21/2013	1h 33m
Jensen	06/21/2013	1h 46m‡

Total Time: 36:40:00

* Informal interview.
‡ Unrecorded interview.

TABLE A.2. Participant Observation List

Date	Time in Field	Location
06/01/2012	3h 30m	Meeting
07/06/2012	5h 45m	Meeting
08/03/2012	6h 0m	Meeting, Geek Bar
09/07/2012	7h 30m	Meeting, Geek Bar, Hackerspace
10/05/2012	8h 40m	Meeting, Geek Bar
11/02/2012	6h 14m	Meeting, Hackerspace
11/09/2012	3h 0m	Hackerspace
12/07/2012	6h 0m	Meeting
01/04/2013	2h 30m	Meeting
02/01/2013	5h 15m	Meeting
03/01/2013	5h 40m	Meeting
05/03/2013	4h 10m	Meeting
06/07/2013	4h 30m	Meeting
07/05/2013	5h 0m	Meeting
07/31/2013	0h 40m	DEF CON 21
08/01/2013	17h 0m	DEF CON 21
08/02/2013	16h 0m	DEF CON 21
08/03/2013	14h 0m	DEF CON 21
08/04/2013	16h 0m	DEF CON 21

Total Time: 137:20:00

NOTES

INTRODUCTION

1 Studies on demographics and psychological characteristics of hackers are given more focus in chapter 1, and include Bachmann 2010; Papadimitriou 2009; Rogers, Smoak, and Liu 2006; Schell 2010; Schell and Holt 2010; Schell and Melnychuk 2010; and Voiskounsky and Smyslova 2003. For studies on subcultural dynamics of the hacking community, see Coleman 2010, 2012, 2013; Coleman and Golub 2008; Holt 2009, 2010a, 2010b; Jordan and Taylor 1998; Nikitina 2012; Nissenbaum 2004; Steinmetz and Gerber 2014; Taylor 1999; Thomas 2002; Turgeman-Goldschmidt 2005; Turkle 1984; Wall 2007; and Yar 2013. For more on virus creation, computer intrusions, and similar components of hacking, see Furnell 2010; Higgins 2010; Holt et al. 2012; Jordan and Taylor 1998; Nichols, Ryan, and Ryan 2000; and Woo, Kim, and Dominick 2004. For criminological theory tests conducted on hacking-related behaviors, see Bossler and Burruss 2010; Marcum et al. 2014; and Morris 2010.

2 GNU is a recursive acronym that means "GNU's Not Unix." It is a Linux-derived operating system sponsored by the Free Software Foundation, an organization affiliated with Richard Stallman.

3 Some authors may draw a distinction between "hacking" and "phreaking." The two here are considered intimately intermingled, to the point where they are difficult to clearly distinguish. The only prominent difference appears to be in a differential emphasis between phone systems and computer technology. Cross membership in the activities and computer colonization of the telephone systems, however, draw an unshakable connection between them. As Sterling (1992, 46) states, "The line between 'phreaking' and 'hacking' is very blurred, just as the distinction between telephones and computers has blurred."

4 While BBSs have disappeared, many of the original files are still available online. Jason Scott gathered many of the files that were available on these sites and has archived them for public consumption at http://textfiles.com.

5 While I recognize that not all those who engage in hacktivism are hackers, the term "hacktivism" will be used throughout this study to specifically refer to hackers engaged in politics.

6 The origins of the term "hacktivism" are seldom discussed in the literature, but the earliest claim to its genesis was tracked to a digital paper (called a "phile") by Oxblood Ruffin (2004), a member of the Cult of the Dead Cow, entitled "Hacktiv-

ism, From Here to There." Ruffin claims that the earliest use of the term was by a hacker named Omega in 1994.

7 Anonymous originally derived its name from the fact that most members of 4chan post under the pseudonym "Anonymous"—an automatic setting for the website (unless you purposefully enter a moniker). Indeed, the use of the "anonymous" title is so ubiquitous on 4chan that often members refer to themselves and others as "Anonymous" or "Anon."

8 Anonymous was *not* the first hacktivist group to take on the Church of Scientology. The Cult of the Dead Cow targeted the Church of Scientology in 1995 through the alt.religion.scientology newsgroup.

9 Guy Fawkes, known in the United Kingdom for his failed attempt to assassinate members of British Parliament, was reimagined as a revolutionary figure in Alan Moore's (1988) *V for Vendetta*. In the comic, which was later turned into a movie by James McTeigue and the Wachowski siblings, the main protagonist, V, wore a Guy Fawkes mask as part of his rebellious imagery (and also to hide his scars from an accident caused by the dystopian government). Anonymous adopted the Guy Fawkes mask worn by V to hide their identities while also lending their group a unifying image, reminiscent of the final scene in the movie and comic where the public dons Guy Fawkes masks in solidarity with V.

10 A "buffer overflow" is a type of computer exploit. The buffer overflow takes advantage of programs that allot a particular amount of system memory for the storage of a variable. If the system reserves, say, thirty characters for a person's name, but does not restrict how much data can be entered, there is a chance that any names over thirty characters may begin writing over other code stored in the system's memory. If a hacker knows how much space is set aside for that variable, they can fill up that space and then begin writing their own executable code that will go into the system memory. This may allow the hacker to crash the program, or bypass certain restrictions on the system.

11 The author recognizes there is a conflict over the relationship between field research and ethnography. The current methodological descriptions consider the two in tandem.

12 In addition to providing a pseudonym for the hacker group, all participants in the study were assigned pseudonyms and both notes and interviews were scrubbed of identifying information.

13 For a breakdown of participant's demographic characteristics, refer to chapter 1.

14 A "zine" is a self-published magazine, typically with a small circulation among a niche population.

CHAPTER 1. THE FRONT END OF HACKING

1 This chapter is derived in part from an article published in the *Journal of Qualitative Criminal Justice and Criminology* (Steinmetz 2015a).

2 Gender, rather than sex, is selected as the variable of interest here. Since appearances and interactions were primarily relied upon to gather this information, it

would be disingenuous to present this data as anything other than a representation of gender.

3 For an overview of Gamergate, refer to Caitlin Dewey's (2014) discussion for *The Washington Post*.

4 There are currently debates in criminology about the role that parents play in determining behavioral and social outcomes later in life. As a result, parents may not be the all-important dictators of development as previously believed. That said, no one denies that parents—as providers of early life environments—have a vital role to play in development.

CHAPTER 2. CRAFT(Y)NESS

1 This chapter is derived in part from an article published in the *British Journal of Criminology* (Steinmetz 2015b).

2 I use the term "social science" here in the same manner deployed by C. Wright Mills (1959). While he speaks at length in a footnote about his hesitance to use the term, he discusses a litany of other labels for this collective academic endeavor, dismissing them as unsatisfactory for various reasons. Thus, like him, "with the hope of not being too widely misunderstood, I bow to convention and use the more standard 'social sciences'" (Mills 1959, 19).

3 It is important to emphasize that not all hacking is criminal or deviant in the traditional sense. Because, however, the subculture and its activities are increasingly subjected to scrutiny and formal social control, this analysis considers hackers a viable subject for criminological inquiry.

4 The reader may argue that phenomenological eidetic reduction is a descendant of Platonic idealism and, thus, at odds with Marx's materialism. While at surface level such disparate theoretical traditions may seem to contradict each other, the process of eidetic reductions does not actually first proceed from the ideal form. Instead, the material reality of the phenomenon is first examined and then the exposed details and characteristics are pulled together to discern the eidos. The essence is thus extracted from the material conditions rather than first creating an ideal form in which to assess the characteristics of the phenomenon under scrutiny.

5 Cultural criminology is a powerful theoretical tool for radical criminology. Due to its sensitivity to individual lived experience, cultural criminology provides a toolkit for connecting individual and subcultural struggles to political economic and socio-structural issues.

6 There is certainly a conceptual and ontological tension between eidetic reduction and the social constructionism incorporated into cultural criminology. The phenomenological *epoche* may be understood as a form of objectivism while social constructionism tends to revel in a degree of relativism where meaning can vary across actors, subcultures, etc. As such, attempting to epistemologically privilege one understanding of hacking through eidetic reduction while also maintaining an attunement to the politics of meaning may create a seemingly irreconcilable

tension in the analysis. Yet, the two positions may not be as opposed as one might think. The social construction employed under cultural and radical criminology is often more consistent with that deployed in the tradition of cultural Marxism, which recognizes transformations and distinctions of meaning without shedding a materialist ontology. In this capacity, a high degree of relativism can be epistemologically sustained without sacrificing any underlying consistencies in meaning shaped by material conditions like labor (which, for hackers, is of vital importance for the creation and sustainment of subcultural meaning).

7 The feature described in this analysis called "Journey over Destination" would thus seem to be central to Sennett's (2006, 2008) understanding of craft. While it is important, other features are equally vital for craft.

8 The specific focus here is to articulate hacking as a particular kind of labor. These results have been previously peer-reviewed and accepted to *The British Journal of Criminology*, but the specific foci of the article were definitional and disciplinary issues surrounding the concept of hacking (Steinmetz 2014). The article-length treatment is dedicated towards advancing a particular understanding of hacking; this chapter is geared towards establishing hacking as a form of labor for the purposes of situating it within the broader political economic analysis presented here.

9 Apple Macintosh computers were once (and among many, still) lauded as impenetrable to malware. The types of hacks that Raj discusses directly contradict that belief.

10 This need for recognition also brings the parallels between hacking and craftwork into tension with meritocracy. As Sennett (2006, 108) explains, "Craftsmanship fits easily within the medieval guild frame in that the apprentice as much as the master could seek to make something well for its own sake." The need for recognition, however, begins to transition from here to a kind of assessment of social worth: "Now talent measured a new sort of social inequality: *creative* or *intelligent* meant *superior* to others, a more worthy sort of person. Here lay the passage from craftsmanship to meritocracy." Other authors have similarly denoted the presence of meritocratic thinking in the hacker community (see Coleman and Golub 2008). While it could be argued that the divide between craftwork and meritocracy is blurry, Sennett's worries about the tension between craftwork and meritocracy should be held in mind.

11 The term "cracking" traces its origins back to the particular practice of breaking through software restrictions. This activity has been heavily linked to the practice of piracy, indicating the strong link between hacker culture and piracy culture, at least in digital piracy's gestational years.

12 Such an emphasis on the individual is likewise seen in hacker politics through its often libertarian or anarchistic flair (Barbrook and Cameron 2001; Coleman and Golub 2008; Jordan 2001; Jordan and Taylor 2004; Steinmetz and Gerber 2014).

13 The guild-like structure of hacking bears similarities to social learning theories in criminology, such as Sutherland's (1939) differential association and Akers's (1973,

1998; Burgess and Akers 1966) more psychologically based learning theory. In this vein, there seems to be a connection between social learning and the dynamics between the hand and the head as described by Sennett (2008).

14 This notion is similar to Marx's discussion of commodity fetishism—as objects do not carry intrinsic value themselves. Rather, it is the labor that provides commodities with value. Here, hacking and craft are identified by the process of labor rather than what it produces *per se*.

15 A description of "hack mode" and "deep hack mode" can be found on *The Jargon File*, a well-known hacker argot repository (Raymond 2016).

16 Origin is the full name of the particular copy-protection mechanism used by Electronic Arts for Sim City.

17 The exact name of the software was removed for purposes of confidentiality.

18 Turkle (1984) has previously commented on the relationship between the sensations of gaming and those of hacking.

19 Previous research has also found a connection between hacking and using machines unconventionally in this manner (Jordan and Taylor 2004).

20 During the 1950s and 1960s, computers were low in processing power and memory was very limited. Thus, programs had to heavily emphasize efficiency if they were to run as fluidly as possible while performing the tasks needed. Many early computer hacks were about finding shortcuts that would accomplish the same task in fewer lines of code.

21 Connections between hacking and urban exploration have been documented previously (Garrett 2013).

CHAPTER 3. ON AUTHORITY AND PROTOCOL

1 This chapter is derived in part from an article published in *Deviant Behavior* (Steinmetz and Gerber 2014) and in part from an article published in *Social Justice* (Steinmetz and Gerber 2015).

2 Since asking hackers directly about their perspectives on the state may have yielded unclear and ambiguous answers, I thought it more reasonable to ask for their views on government, law, and law enforcement and extrapolate from there. These institutions are more familiar and represent somewhat of a concrete, rather than a more abstract, notion of the state.

3 *Jacobellis v. Ohio*, 378 U.S. 184, 1964.

4 Coleman and Golub (2008) and, to a lesser extent, Taylor and Jordan (2004), have also found linkages between liberalism and hacker culture.

5 It should be noted that 2600 authors who describe this process generally view it with disdain.

6 For a more detailed analysis on hacker perspectives on privacy, refer to my prior research on the subject (Steinmetz and Gerber 2015).

7 As will be discussed later in this book, concerns over privacy and other civil liberties is tied to the spirit of technological liberalism running through the hacker community.

8 John Perry Barlow is an eccentric figure in the technological political field. He is a renowned technological libertarian as well as a well-known Dead Head (fan of the band The Grateful Dead) (Sterling 1992). Despite his eccentrics, he has generally been considered a prominent voice for the technological social sphere.

9 Jordan (2001, 11), however, argues that anarchism in hacker culture stems more from "symbols and slogans from the Western tradition of anarchism, rather than a deep reading of its literature." Regardless, Jordan recognizes self-identification in technological subcultures as typically either libertarian or anarchist, though he does not necessarily overtly recognize their connection through liberalism, at least in tech culture.

10 Of importance, however, is that the libertarian flair running through swaths of the hacker community does contribute to many of the political economic ramifications discussed in chapter 4. Of course, to reiterate, this analysis incorporates a broader idea of liberalism by focusing on economic liberalism and its relationship to technological liberalism rather than strict libertarianism.

CHAPTER 4. THE (HACK) MODE OF PRODUCTION

1 The following discussion is perhaps the densest of all those presented in this book. While effort was given to detail major concepts for the uninitiated, it may still prove difficult for some, particularly students. If the reader has difficulty with this chapter, a few introductory works may help, including David Smith and Phil Evan's (1982) *Marx's Kapital for Beginners* and Rius's (1976) *Marx for Beginners*. Reading Randall Shelden's (2008) *Controlling the Dangerous Classes* and Steven Spitzer's (1975) article "Toward a Marxian Theory of Deviance" may also prove to be fruitful starting points.

2 Surplus population is the pool of labor excluded from the production process through capital's attempts to extract ever-greater percentages of surplus value. Marx's ([1867] 1967, 431) description that follows is perhaps the most useful for the purposes of this work: "So soon as the handling of this tool becomes the work of a machine, then, with the use-value, the exchange-value too, of the workman's labor-power vanishes; the workman becomes unsaleable, like paper money thrown out of currency be legal enactment. That portion of the working class, thus by machinery rendered superfluous, *i.e.*, no longer immediately necessary for the self-expansion of capital, either goes to the wall in unequal contest of the old handicrafts and manufactures with machinery, or else floods all the more easily accessible branches of industry, swamps the labor-market, and sinks the price of labor-power below its value."

3 Indeed, there have been many accusations against companies such as Microsoft and Apple for appropriating ideas originally found in open-source software.

4 In this manner, hackers contribute to what Marx calls the "general intellect" or "a collective, social intelligence created by accumulated knowledges, techniques, and know-how" (Hardt and Negri 2000, 364).

5 Of course, this antagonism between the worker and the machine is a "false conflict" (Hardt and Negri 2000, 367). Rather, the antagonism emerges from the social relations between the worker and the machine created through capitalism.

6 The conflict between the demands of time between the capitalist and the laborer present a key point of struggle in class conflict, according to Marx ([1867] 1967, 235): "Hence is it that in the history of capitalist production, the determination of what is a working-day, presents itself as the result of a struggle, a struggle between collective capital, *i.e.*, the class of capitalists, and collective labor, *i.e.*, the working class?"

7 Exploitation, according to Marx ([1867] 1967), is the degree to which a capitalist is able to extract surplus value from a worker.

8 This discussion of the hacker ethic and the blurring of labor and leisure similarly links the sensation of hacking as craft to exploitation under capitalism. As the worker finds their labor more rewarding, they may be more likely to also surrender more of their surplus value generally beyond even what they may do as work becomes increasingly blurred with work.

9 As used here, "alienation" refers to the laborer becoming separated from the object of labor in addition to the process of labor. In this sense, alienation can be applied to multiple ways in which properties originally intrinsic to labor or the laborer are thus externalized and made hostile.

10 At the time of writing, efforts are being made by groups within the F/OSS community to advance into the smartphone market, such as Canonical through the Ubuntu Linux distribution, but the author remains skeptical if these F/OSS channels will garner the same popularity as those advanced by major corporations.

11 As will be detailed later, such deployment of empty ideological signifiers also has connections with dominant narratives tied to the philosophy of liberalism.

12 While most users do not know about Linux, some do and are attracted to it. Some may still be ensnared as consumers through these abstract values that are attached to Linux without having any real familiarity with the system.

13 Various economic liberals, such as Adam Smith, have recognized that such an ideal system may not be tenable in some respects, though belief in the overall system persisted.

14 Polanyi (1944) also recognized that ignoring freedom entirely and leaning exclusively on power and control is what wrought fascism. It seems that either side does not consider the dialectical contradiction between freedom and domination to be problematic.

15 The practice of excluding a group from being considered a full person is not a new practice. Even the Greeks used their notions of citizenship to exclude all non-Greeks from those properties they saw in themselves, reducing non-Greeks to the status of barbarians who could be enslaved and vanquished.

16 These examples are only some of the ways liberalism has been used to sustain the contradiction between freedom and oppression under capitalism. For a full explication, refer to Losurdo (2014).

17 Fuchs (2014) provided this explanation for the "Californian Ideology" but it is equally applicable to the broader technological liberalism discussed here.

18 This conclusion is drawn from content analysis data of the *2600: The Hacker Quarterly* hacker zine—taken from the forty-one issues between Spring 2002 and

Spring 2014. Support can also be found in the descriptions of early phone phreaks (refer to Söderberg 2008).

19 In this analysis, ideology is specifically deployed in the Marxist sense, referring to the means in which perceptions and social constructions are used to reify social relations under capitalism. The reader may notice that—despite its potential for application in some parts of the analysis—the term "hegemony" was avoided. While applicable in many ways, hegemony has a very specific application for Gramsci (1971) in that it is "a form of rationalized intellectual and moral leadership" that "is established through revolution" (Riley 2011, 1). While other nuances of hegemony makes its application questionable here, it is this establishment through revolution that is not traced in this analysis. Therefore, hegemony is eschewed. Ideology seems to be a more appropriate concept to apply as the focus is specifically on the reification of class relations and the manipulation of public perceptions in a way that maintains class interest—precisely what Marx and Engels (1947) discussed in *The German Ideology*, stemming from the *Theses on Feuerbach*.

CHAPTER 5. CRAFTING A CRACKDOWN

1 As a brief aside, it is worth noting that the ability to recognize such seeming paradoxes and how they can be sustained is exactly why hacking is best viewed from a *dialectical* perspective. As such, what appears to be a paradox is, in fact, a dialectical contradiction.

2 There is disagreement over who originally came up with the term "moral panic," Cohen (1972) or Young (2011a).

3 Definition found at *The Jargon File* (Raymond 2016).

4 *Watch Dogs* was rated in the top ten highest grossing games of 2014, according to *Forbes (Kain 2015)*.

5 The monopolistic nature of intellectual property rights has been a key point of disagreement historically, with many *laissez-faire* economists resisting such rights on the grounds that they are antithetical to a free market (Perelman 2014).

6 The expansion of intellectual property rights was also facilitated by the legal classification of corporations as people, which allowed corporations to secure property rights as if they were U.S. citizens.

7 Disney is one of the largest intellectual property holders in the world.

8 In times gone by, these entities had also been referred to as "patent sharks" (Magliocca 2007).

9 A "slim jim" is a kind of lock pick used specifically for opening car doors.

10 The webpage originally hosting this quote has since gone offline. A copy of the page is preserved at Archive.org through the "Wayback Machine" dated to December 4, 2015. For the original reference, see RIAA (2015).

11 Data retrieved from the OECD's (2016) website. OECD countries include Australia, Austria, Belgium, Canada, Chile, the Czech Republic, Denmark, Estonia, Finland, France, Germany, Greece, Hungary, Iceland, Ireland, Israel, Italy, Japan,

Korea, Luxembourg, Mexico, the Netherlands, New Zealand, Norway, Poland, Portugal, the Slovak Republic, Slovenia, Spain, Sweden, Switzerland, Turkey, the United Kingdom, and the United States.

12 Estimates derived from U.S. Census Bureau's (2016) Retail and Food Services data for the years 1992 to 2013. In addition, the estimates used included motor vehicle and parts sales. If these sales are removed, as they are huge ticket items that may skew the estimates, non-store retail sales would comprise 2.53 percent of overall retail dollars reported in 1992 versus 9.93 percent in 2013.

13 PricewaterhouseCoopers has a vested interest in inflating the numbers. As such, these numbers should be taken with caution. That said, they are still useful for an understanding of relative change in advertising revenue over time.

14 Data drawn from Google's investor relations webpage (Alphabet Investor Relations 2016).

15 Box office numbers were pulled from BoxOfficeMojo (2016).

16 Stuxnet spread to other countries, but the Iran connection was the most noteworthy and, indeed, probably the intended target of the virus.

17 As of December 10, 2015, this advertisement could be found on Microsoft's (2016) YouTube page.

18 Hegemony, as Barak (1988, 567) explains, is a notion that is "not one of economic determinism or of ideological rigidity, but one in which the dominant or ruling class is created and recreated constantly in a network of institutions, social relations, and ideas." Further, he states that "the prevailing orders of the political economy depend on both the passive and the active consent of the governed, on the collective will of the people in which various groups within society unite and struggle. In other words, hegemony includes not only the ruling classes' world views but also the world views of the masses. These views are composed of a variety of elements and experiences, some of which may actually contradict the dominant ideology without disturbing or delegitimizing the prevailing social order."

19 Anonymous subsequently replied to these accusations of potential harm over the AnonOps blog, stating: "Why should Anonymous shut off power grid? Makes no sense! They just want to make you feel afraid" (as quoted in Liebowitz 2012).

20 Additionally, as noted by Wall (2012), perceptions of insecurity create pressures for both law enforcement and governments generally to control the perceived technocrime problems associated with hackers. While efforts are made, governments—particularly law enforcement institutions—struggle to cope with emergent technocrime issues.

CONCLUSION

1 This metaphor is borrowed from the title of Mitnick and Simon's (2011) book, *Ghost in the Wires*.

2 Of particular note, many of these studies are found outside of criminology in disciplines like media studies and anthropology.

3 FUBAR is an acronym devised by members of the military to denote when a situation was "fucked up beyond all recognition."

4 Indeed, this question was so central to Lea and Young (1984) that it was the title of their book: *What Is to Be Done about Law and Order?*

5 "Slacktivism" is a pejorative term for a sort of "feel-good-do-nothing" activism that takes place largely in social media. For example, persons temporarily get outraged and they may share an article or blog post with their friends or sign an online petition. This leads to a feeling that they made a difference while the impact may actually have been minimal, if any occurred at all. After a brief period of time, the issue is forgotten or neglected. The cycle repeats as the next "big issue" makes its way through social media.

REFERENCES

(References to *2600: The Hacker Quarterly* are located in their own section.)

Adler, Patricia A. 2003. "Wheeling and Dealing: An Ethnography of an Upper-Level Drug Dealing and Smuggling Community." In *The Cultural Study of Work*, edited by Douglas Harper and Helene M. Lawson, 452–462. Lanham, MD: Rowman and Littlefield Publishers.

Adler, Patricia A., and Peter Adler. 1987. *Membership Roles in Field Research*. Beverly Hills, CA: Sage.

———. 1998. "Foreword: Moving Backward." In *Ethnography at the Edge: Crime, Deviance, and Field Research*, edited by Jeff Ferrell and Mark S. Hamm, xii–xvi. Boston: Northeastern University Press.

Akers, Ronald L. 1973. *Deviant Behavior: A Social Learning Approach*. Belmont, CA: Wadsworth.

———. 1998. *Social Learning and Social Structure: A General Theory of Crime and Deviance*. Boston: Northeastern University Press.

Alphabet Investor Relations. 2016. Accessed April 4, 2016. https://abc.xyz/investor/.

Altheide, David L. 1987. "Ethnographic Content Analysis." *Qualitative Sociology* 10: 65–77.

Anderson, Ross, Christ Barton, Ranier Böhme, Richard Clayton, Michel J. G. van Eeten, Michael Levi, Tyler Moore, and Stefan Savage. 2013. "Measuring the Cost of Cybercrime." In *The Economics of Information Security and Privacy*, edited by Rainer Böhme, 265–300. New York: Springer.

Arrigo, Bruce A., and Christopher R. Williams. 2010. "Conflict Criminology: Developments, Directions, and Destinations Past and Present." In *Criminological Theory: Readings and Retrospectives*, edited by Heith Copes and Volkan Topalli, 401–412. New York: McGraw-Hill.

Assange, Julian. 2011. "Julian Assange: 'I Am—like All Hackers—a Little Bit Autistic.'" *Independent*, September 22. Accessed June 22, 2015. http://www.independent.co.uk.

Bachmann, Michael. 2010. "Deciphering the Hacker Underground: First Quantitative Insights." In *Corporate Hacking and Technology-Driven Crime: Social Dynamics and Implications*, edited by Thomas J. Holt and Bernadette H. Schell, 105–126. Hershey, PA: IGI Global.

Barak, Gregg. 1988. "Newsmaking Criminology: Reflections on the Media, Intellectuals, and Crime." *Justice Quarterly* 5: 565–587.

Barbrook, Richard, and Andy Cameron. 2001. "Californian Ideology." In *Crypto Anarchy, Cyberstates, and Pirate Utopias*, edited by Peter Ludlow, 363–388. Cambridge, MA: MIT Press.

Barlow, John P. 2001. "A Declaration of the Independence of Cyberspace." In *Crypto Anarchy, Cyberstates, and Pirate Utopias*, edited by Peter Ludlow, 28–30. Cambridge, MA: MIT Press.

Baudrillard, Jean. 1970. *The Consumer Society: Myths and Structures*. Thousand Oaks, CA: Sage.

Becker, Howard S. 1958. "Problems of Inference and Proof in Participant Observation." *American Sociological Review* 23: 652–660.

———. 1963. *Outsiders: Studies in the Sociology of Deviance*. New York: Free Press.

———. 1966. "Introduction." In *The Jack-Roller: A Delinquent Boy's Own Story*, by Clifford R. Shaw, v–xviii. Chicago: University of Chicago Press.

Bell, Shannon E., and Richard York. 2010. "Community Economic Identity: The Coal Industry and Ideology Construction in West Virginia." *Rural Sociology* 75: 111–143.

Berg, Bruce L. 2009. *Qualitative Research Methods for the Social Sciences*. 7th ed. Boston: Allyn and Bacon.

Berger, Peter L., and Thomas Luckman. 1966. *The Social Construction of Reality: A Treatise in the Sociology of Knowledge*. New York: Anchor Books.

Berk, Richard A., and Joseph M. Adams. 1970. "Establishing Rapport with Deviant Groups." *Social Problems* 18: 102–117.

Bollier, David. 2003. *Silent Theft: The Private Plunder of Our Common Wealth*. New York: Routledge.

Bonger, Willem. 1916. *Criminality and Economic Conditions*. Boston: Little, Brown.

Bossler, Adam M., and George W. Burruss. 2010. "The General Theory of Crime and Computer Hacking: Low Self-Control Hackers?" In *Corporate Hacking and Technology-Driven Crime: Social Dynamics and Implications*, edited by Thomas J. Holt and Bernadette H. Schell, 38–67. Hershey, PA: IGI Global.

BoxOfficeMojo. 2016. Accessed April 4, 2016. http://BoxOfficeMojo.com.

Boylstein, Craig, and Scott R. Maggard. 2013. "Small-Scale Marijuana Growing: Deviant Careers as Serious Leisure." *Humbolt Journal of Social Relations* 35: 52–70.

Brand, Steward, and Matt Herron. 1985. "'Keep Designing': How the Information Economy is Being Created and Shaped by the Hacker Ethic." *Whole Earth Review* 46: 44–52.

Braverman, Harry. 1974. *Labor and Monopoly Capital: The Degradation of Work in the Twentieth Century*. New York: Monthly Review Press.

Brown, James J. 2008. "From Friday to Sunday: The Hacker Ethic and Shifting Notions of Labour, Leisure, and Intellectual Property." *Leisure Studies* 27: 395–409.

Bulmer, Martin. 1982. "When is Disguise Justified? Alternatives to Covert Participant Observation." *Qualitative Sociology* 5: 251–264.

Burgess, Robert L., and Ronald L. Akers. 1966. "A Differential Association-Reinforcement Theory of Criminal Behavior." *Social Problems* 14: 128–147.

Burke, Ronald J., and Mary C. Mattis. 2007. *Women and Minorities in Science, Technology, Engineering, and Mathematics: Upping the Numbers*. Northampton, MA: Edward Elgar.

Business Software Alliance. 2014. *The Compliance Gap: BSA Global Software Survey*. Accessed June 22, 2015. http://globalstudy.bsa.org.

Calia, Michael. 2013. "Apple's Market Share Grows." *Wall Street Journal*, December 5. Accessed April 4, 2016. http://www.wsj.com.

Callahan, Mat. 2014. "Why Intellectual Property? Why Now?" *Socialism and Democracy* 28: 1–9.

Chambliss, William. 1975. "Toward a Political Economy of Crime." *Theory and Society* 2: 149–170.

Charmaz, Kathy. 2002. "Qualitative Interviewing and Grounded Theory Analysis." In *Handbook of Interview Research: Context and Method*, edited by Jaber F. Gubrium and James A. Holstein, 675–694. Thousand Oaks, CA: Sage.

———. 2006. *Constructing Grounded Theory: A Practical Guide through Qualitative Analysis*. Thousand Oaks, CA: Sage.

Churchill, David. 2015. "Security and Visions of the Criminal: Technology, Professional Criminality, and Social Change in Victorian and Edwardian Britain." *British Journal of Criminology*: 1–20.

Christie, Nils. 2000. *Crime Control as Industry: Towards Gulags, Western Style*. 3rd ed. New York: Routledge.

———. 2004. *A Suitable Amount of Crime*. New York: Routledge.

Clarke, Adele E. 2005. *Situational Analysis: Grounded Theory after the Postmodern Turn*. Thousand Oaks, CA: Sage.

Cohen, Stanley. (1972) 2002. *Folk Devils and Moral Panics*. London: Routledge.

Cole, David, and Jules Lobel. 2007. *Less Safe, Less Free: Why America is Losing the War on Terror*. New York: New Press.

Coleman, E. Gabriella. 2010. "The Hacker Conference: A Ritual Condensation and Celebration of a Lifeworld." *Anthropological Quarterly* 83: 47–72.

———. 2012. "Phreaks, Hackers, and Trolls: The Politics of Transgression and Spectacle." In *The Social Media Reader*, edited by Michael Mandiberg, 99–119. New York: New York University Press.

———. 2013. *Coding Freedom: The Ethics and Aesthetics of Hacking*. Princeton, NJ: Princeton University Press.

———. 2014. *Hacker, Hoaxer, Whistleblower, Spy: The Many Faces of Anonymous*. New York: Verso.

Coleman, E. Gabriella, and Alex Golub. 2008. "Hacker Practice: Moral Genres and the Cultural Articulation of Liberalism." *Anthropological Theory* 8: 255–277.

Corbin, Juliet, and Anselm Strauss. 1990. "Grounded Theory Research: Procedures, Canons, and Evaluative Criteria." *Qualitative Sociology* 13: 3–21.

Csikszentmihalyi, Mihaly. 1975. *Beyond Boredom and Anxiety*. San Francisco, CA: Jossey-Bass.

———. 1990. *Flow: The Psychology of Optimal Experience*. New York: Harper and Row.

Csikszentmihalyi, Mihaly, Sami Abuhamdeh, and Jeanne Nakamura. 2005. "Flow." In *Handbook of Competence and Motivation*, edited by Andrew J. Elliot and Carol S. Dweek, 598–608. New York: Guilford Press.

Currie, Elliot. 2010. "Plain Left Realism: An Appreciation, and Some Thoughts for the Future." *Crime, Law, and Social Change* 54: 111–124.

Dafermos, George, and Johan Söderberg. 2009. "The Hacker Movement as a Continuation of Labour Struggle." *Capital and Class* 97: 53–73.

Décary-Hétu, David, Carlo Morselli, and Stéphane Leman-Langlois. 2012. "Welcome to the Scene: A Study of Social Organization and Recognition among Warez Hackers." *Journal of Research in Crime and Delinquency* 49: 359–382.

DEF CON. 2016. "The DEF CON Story." Accessed April 1, 2016. http://www.defcon.org/.

DeKeseredy, Walter. 2003. "Left Realism on Inner-City Violence." In *Controversies in Critical Criminology*, edited by Martin D. Schwartz and Suzanne E. Hatty, 29–41. Cincinnati, OH: Anderson.

Dewey, Caitlin. 2014. "The Only Guide to Gamergate You Will Ever Need to Read." *Washington Post*, October 14. Accessed June 22, 2015. http://www.washingtonpost.com.

Doctorow, Cory. 2008. ©*ontent: Selected Essays on Technology, Creativity, Copyright, and the Future of the Future*. San Francisco, CA: Tachyon.

Downing, Steven. 2011. "Retro Gaming Subculture and the Social Construction of a Piracy Ethic." *International Journal of Cyber Criminology* 5: 750–772.

Durkheim, Émile. (1897) 2006. *On Suicide*. New York: Penguin.

Engels, Friedrich. 1958. *The Condition of the Working Class in England*. New York: Macmillan.

Epstein, S. R. 1998. "Craft Guilds, Apprenticeship, and Technological Change in Preindustrial Europe." *Journal of Economic History* 58: 684–713.

Fagan, Jeffrey, and Richard B. Freeman. 1999. "Crime and Work." *Crime and Justice* 25: 225–290.

Ferenstein, Gregory. 2013. "Hacker Faces More Jail Time than the Convicted Steubenville Rapists He Exposed." *TechCrunch*, June 9. Accessed June 22, 2015. http://techcrunch.com.

Ferrell, Jeff. 1993. *Crimes of Style: Urban Graffiti and the Politics of Criminality*. Boston: Northeastern University Press.

———. 1998. "Criminological *Verstehen*: Inside the Immediacy of Crime." In *Ethnography at the Edge: Crime, Deviance, and Field Research*, edited by Jeff Ferrell and Mark S. Hamm, 20–42. Boston: Northeastern University Press.

———. 2001. *Tearing Down the Streets: Adventures in Urban Anarchy*. New York: Palgrave.

———. 2004. "Boredom, Crime, and Criminology." *Theoretical Criminology* 8: 287–302.

———. 2013. "Cultural Criminology and the Politics of Meaning." *Critical Criminology* 21: 257–271.

Ferrell, Jeff, Keith Hayward, and Jock Young. 2008. *Cultural Criminology: An Invitation*. Thousand Oaks, CA: Sage.

Finlay, Linda. 2008. "A Dance between the Reduction and Reflexivity: Explicating the 'Phenomenological Psychological Attitude.'" *Journal of Phenomenological Psychology* 39: 1–32.

Fleming, Peter. 2013. "'Some Might Call It Work . . . But We Don't': Exploitation and the Emergence of *Free Work* Capitalism." In *Managing 'Human Resources' by Exploiting and Exploring People's Potentials (Research in the Sociology of Organizations, Volume 37)*, edited by Mikael Holmqvist and André Spicer, 105–128. Bingley, UK: Emerald Group.

Foucault, Michel. 1972. "Discourse on Language." In *Archaeology of Knowledge*, by Michel Foucault, 215–237. Scranton, PA: Tavistock Publications.

Frissell, Duncan. 2001. "Re: Denning's Crypto Anarchy." In *Crypto Anarchy, Cyberstates, and Pirate Utopias*, edited by Peter Ludlow, 105–114. Cambridge, MA: MIT Press.

Frost, Natasha A., and Nickie D. Phillips. 2011. "Talking Heads: Crime Reporting on Cable News." *Justice Quarterly* 28: 87–112.

Fuchs, Christian. 2010. "Labor in Informational Capitalism and on the Internet." *Information Society* 26: 179–196.

———. 2014. *Digital Labour and Karl Marx*. New York: Routledge.

Furnell, Steven. 2010. "Hackers, Viruses, and Malicious Software." In *Handbook of Internet Crime*, edited by Yvonne Jewkes and Majid Yar, 173–193. Portland, OR: Willan.

Gagne, Patricia. 2004. "Getting In and Getting On: Entrée Strategies and the Importance of Trust and Rapport in Qualitative Research." In *Controversies in Criminal Justice Research*, edited by Richard Tewksbury and Elizabeth Mustaine, 103–115. Cincinnati, OH: Anderson.

Gans, Herbert J. 2005. "Race as Class." *Contexts* 4: 17–21.

Garnaeva, Maria, Victor Chebyshev, Denis Makrushin, Roman Unuchek, and Anton Ivanov. 2014. *Kaspersky Security Bulletin 2014: Overall Statistics for 2014*. Accessed June 22, 2015. http://cdn.securelist.com.

Garrett, Bradley. 2013. *Explore Everything: Place-Hacking the City*. New York: Verso.

Geis, Gilbert. 1995. "The Limits of Academic Tolerance: The Discontinuance of the School of Criminology at Berkeley." In *Punishment and Social Control: Essays in Honor of Sheldon L. Messinger*, edited by Thomas G. Blomberg and Stanley Cohen, 277–304. New York: Aldine de Gruyter.

Glaser, Barney G., and Anselm L. Strauss. 1967. *The Discovery of Grounded Theory: Strategies for Qualitative Research*. Piscataway, NJ: Aldine.

Glenny, Misha. 2011. *Darkmarket: Cyberthieves, Cybercops, and You*. New York: Alfred A. Knopf.

Goffman, Erving. 1959. *The Presentation of Self in Everyday Life*. New York: Anchor Books.

Gold, Steve. 2011. "The Rebirth of Phreaking." *Network Security* 2011: 15–17.

Goldman, David. 2012. "Anonymous in Disarray after Major Crackdown Snares Leaders." *CNN Money*, March 6. Accessed April 4, 2016. http://money.cnn.com.

Gorman, Siobhan. 2012. "Alert on Hacker Power Play." *Wall Street Journal*, February 21. Accessed June 22, 2015. http://www.wsj.com.

Gottfredson, Michael R., and Travis Hirschi. 1990. *A General Theory of Crime*. Stanford, CA: Stanford University Press.

Gramsci, Antonio. 1971. *Selections from the Prison Notebooks*. Translated by Quintin Hoare and Geoffrey Nowell Smith. New York: International Publishers.

Gustin, Sam. 2010. "U.S. Shutters 82 Sites in Crackdown on Downloads, Counterfeit Goods." *Wired*, November 29. Accessed June 22, 2015. http://www.wired.com.

Habermas, Jurgen. 1973. *Legitimation Crisis*. Boston: Beacon.

Hagan, John. 1992. "The Poverty of a Classless Criminology: The American Society of Criminology 1991 Presidential Address." *Criminology* 30: 1–19.

Halbert, Debora. 1997. "Discourses of Danger and the Computer Hacker." *Information Society* 13: 361–374.

Hall, Stuart. 2001. "Foucault: Power, Knowledge and Discourse." In *Discourse Theory and Practice: A Reader*, edited by Margaret Wetherell, Stephanie Taylor, and Simeon J. Yates, 72–81. Thousand Oaks, CA: Sage.

Hall, Stuart, Chas Critcher, Tony Jefferson, John Clarke, and Brian Roberts. 1978. *Policing the Crisis: Mugging, the State, and Law and Order*. London: Macmillan Press.

Hanover Research. 2015. *The Emergence of Cybersecurity Law*. Prepared for the Indiana University Maurer School of Law. Arlington, VA: Hanover Research. http://info.law.indiana.edu.

Hardt, Michael, and Antonio Negri. 2000. *Empire*. Cambridge, MA: Harvard University Press.

Harring, Sidney L. 1983. *Policing a Class Society: The Experience of American Cities, 1865–1915*. New Brunswick, NJ: Rutgers University Press.

Harvey, David. 2005. *A Brief History of Neoliberalism*. New York: Oxford University Press.

———. 2010. *The Enigma of Capital and the Crises of Capitalism*. New York: Oxford University Press.

———. 2014. *Seventeen Contradictions and the End of Capitalism*. New York: Oxford University Press.

Hayward, Keith. 2004. *City Limits: Crime, Consumer Culture, and the Urban Experience*. New York: Taylor and Francis.

Heap, James L. 1981. "Free-Phantasy, Language, and Sociology: A Criticism of the Methodist Theory of Essence." *Human Studies* 4: 299–311.

Herrnstein, Richard J., and Charles Murray. 1996. *The Bell Curve: Intelligence and Class Structure in American Life*. New York: Free Press.

Hess, Aaron. 2009. "Resistance Up in Smoke: Analyzing the Limitations of Deliberation on YouTube." *Critical Studies in Media Communication* 26: 411–434.

Higgins, George E. 2010. *Cybercrime: An Introduction to an Emerging Phenomenon*. New York: McGraw-Hill.

Himanen, Pekka. 2001. *The Hacker Ethic: A Radical Approach to the Philosophy of Business*. New York: Random House.

Hobsbawm, Eric J. 1965. *Primitive Rebels: Studies in Archaic Forms of Social Movement in the Nineteenth and Twentieth Centuries.* New York: W. W. Norton.

Hollinger, Richard C. 1991. "Hackers: Computer Heroes or Electronic Highwaymen?" *Computers and Society* 21: 6–17.

Holt, Thomas J. 2009. "Lone Hacks or Group Cracks: Examining the Social Organization of Computer Hackers." In *Crimes of the Internet*, edited by Frank Schmalleger and Michael Pittaro, 336–355. Upper Saddle River, NJ: Pearson Education.

———. 2010a. "Becoming a Computer Hacker: Examining the Enculturation and Development of Computer Deviants." In *In Their Own Words: Criminals on Crime, An Anthology*, edited by Paul Cromwell, 5th ed., 109–123. New York: Oxford University Press.

———. 2010b. "Examining the Role of Technology in the Formation of Deviant Subcultures." *Social Science Computer Review* 28: 466–481.

Holt, Thomas J., Deborah Strumsky, Olga Smirnova, and Max Kilger. 2012. "Examining the Social Networks of Malware Writers and Hackers." *International Journal of Cyber Criminology* 6: 891–903.

Hough, Mike. 2014. "Confessions of a Recovering 'Administrative Criminologist': Jock Young, Quantitative Research, and Policy Research." *Crime Media Culture* 10: 215–226.

Hughes, Eric. 2001. "A Cypherpunk's Manifesto." In *Crypto Anarchy, Cyberstates, and Pirate Utopias*, edited by Peter Ludlow, 81–83. Cambridge, MA: MIT Press.

Huws, Ursula. 2014. *Labor in the Global Digital Economy: The Cybertariat Comes of Age.* New York: Monthly Review Press.

Ingersoll, Geoffrey. 2013. "Why Chinese Hacking is NOT an Act of War." *Business Insider*, May 24. Accessed June 22, 2015. http://www.businessinsider.com.

Iozzio, Corrinne. 2008. "The 10 Most Mysterious Cyber Crimes." *PC Magazine*, September 26. Accessed April 4, 2016. http://www.pcmag.com.

Johnson, John M. 2002. "In-Depth Interviewing." In *Handbook of Interview Research: Context and Method*, edited by Jaber F. Gubrium and James A. Holstein, 103–119. Thousand Oaks, CA: Sage.

Jordan, Tim. 2001. "Language and Libertarianism: The Politics of Cyberculture and the Culture of Cyberpolitics." *Sociological Review* 49: 1–17.

———. 2008. *Hacking: Digital Media and Technological Determinism.* Malden, MA: Polity Press.

Jordan, Tim, and Paul Taylor. 1998. "A Sociology of Hackers." *Sociological Review* 46: 757–780.

———. 2004. *Hacktivism and Cyberwars: Rebels with a Cause.* New York: Routledge.

Kain, Erik. 2015. "The Top Ten Best-Selling Video Games of 2014." *Forbes*, January 19. Accessed April 4, 2016. www.forbes.com.

Kappeler, Victor E. 2011. "Inventing Criminal Justice: Myth and Social Construction." In *Theorizing Criminal Justice: Eight Essential Orientations*, 2nd ed., edited by Peter B. Kraska and John J. Brent, 185–194. Long Grove, IL: Waveland Press.

Kappeler, Victor E., and Gary W. Potter. 2005. *The Mythology of Crime and Criminal Justice.* 4th ed. Long Grove, IL: Waveland Press.

Katz, Jack. 1988. *Seductions of Crime: Moral and Sensual Attractions in Doing Evil*. New York: Basic Books.

Kidder, Tracy. 1981. *The Soul of a New Machine*. New York: Back Bay Books.

King, Harry, and William J. Chambliss. 1984. *The Box-Man: A Professional Thief's Journey*. Hoboken, NJ: John Wiley and Sons.

Kirkpatrick, Graeme. 2002. "The Hacker Ethic and the Spirit of the Information Age." *Max Weber Studies* 2: 163–185.

Ko, Ia, and Steward I. Donaldson. 2011. "Applied Positive Organizational Psychology: The State of the Science and Practice." In *Applied Positive Psychology: Improving Everyday Life, Health, Schools, Work, and Society*, edited by Stewart I. Donaldson, Mihaly Csikszentmihalyi, and Jeanne Nakamura, 137–154. New York: Routledge.

Kubitschko, Sebastian. 2015. "Hackers' Media Practices: Demonstrating and Articulating Expertise as Interlocking Arrangements." *Convergence: The International Journal of Research into New Media Technologies* 21: 388–402.

Kücklich, Julian. 2005. "Precarious Playbour: Modders and the Digital Games Industry." *Fibreculture Journal* 5. Accessed June 22, 2015. http://five.fibreculturejournal.org.

Lakoff, George, and Mark Johnson. 1980. *Metaphors We Live By*. Chicago: University of Chicago Press.

Laub, John H., and Robert J. Sampson. 1993. "Turning Points in the Life Course: Why Change Matters to the Study of Crime." *Criminology* 31: 301–325.

Liebowitz, Matt. 2012. "Could Anonymous Really Knock Out the Power Grid?" *NBCNews*, Feburary 21. Accessed June 22, 2015. http://www.nbcnews.com.

Lea, John. 1992. "The Analysis of Crime." In *Rethinking Criminology: The Realist Debate*, edited by Jock Young and Roger Matthews, 69–94. London: Sage.

———. 1999. "Social Crime Revisited." *Theoretical Criminology* 3: 307–325.

———. 2014. "New Deviancy, Marxism and the Politics of Left Realism: Reflections on Jock Young's Early Writings." *Theoretical Criminology* 18: 432–440.

———. 2015. "Jock Young and the Development of Left Realist Criminology." *Critical Criminology* 23: 165–177.

Lea, John, and Kevin Stenson. 2007. "Security, Sovereignty, and Non-State Governance 'From Below.'" *Canadian Journal of Law and Society* 22: 9–27.

Lea, John, and Jock Young. 1984. *What Is to Be Done about Law and Order?* New York: Penguin.

Leigh, David, and Luke Harding. 2011. *WikiLeaks: Inside Julian Assange's War on Secrecy*. New York: Public Affairs.

Leman-Langlois, Stéphane. 2013. *Technocrime, Policing, and Surveillance*. New York: Routledge.

Lessig, Lawrence. 2004. *Free Culture: The Nature and Future of Creativity*. New York: Penguin.

———. 2008. *Remix: Making Art and Commerce Thrive in the Hybrid Economy*. New York: Penguin.

———. 2012. "Remix: How Creativity is Being Strangled by the Law." In *The Social Media Reader*, edited by Michael Mandiberg, 155–169. New York: New York University Press.

Letkemann, Peter. 1973. *Crime as Work*. Upper Saddle River, NJ: Prentice-Hall.

Levy, Steven. 1984. *Hackers: Heroes of the Computer Revolution*. New York: Penguin.

———. 2001. *Crypto: How the Code Rebels Beat the Government Saving Privacy in the Digital Age*. New York: Penguin.

Lilly, J. Robert, and Paul Knepper. 1993. "The Corrections-Commercial Complex." *Crime and Delinquency* 39: 150–166.

Linebaugh, Peter. 2014. "Karl Marx, the Theft of Wood, and Working-Class Composition: A Contribution to the Current Debate." *Social Justice* 40: 137–161.

Loader, Ian, and Richard Sparks. 2010. *Public Criminology?* New York: Routledge.

Losurdo, Domenico. 2014. *Liberalism: A Counter-History*. New York: Verso.

Lunney, Glynn S. 2001. "The Death of Copyright: Digital Technology, Private Copying, and the Digital Millennium Copyright Act." *Virginia Law Review* 87: 813–920.

Lynch, Michael J. 1997. *Radical Criminology*. Brookfield, VT: Dartmouth.

———. 2015. "The Classlessness State of Criminology and Why Criminology without Class is Rather Meaningless." *Crime, Law, and Social Change* 63: 65–90.

Lynch, Michael J., Raymond Michalowski, and Byron W. Groves. 2006. *Primer in Radical Criminology: Critical Perspectives on Crime, Power, and Identity*. 4th ed. Monsey, NY: Criminal Justice Press.

Magliocca, Gerard N. 2007. "Blackberries and Barnyards: Patent Trolls and the Perils of Innovation." *Notre Dame Law Review* 82: 1809–1838.

Marcum, Catherine D., George E. Higgins, Melissa L. Ricketts, and Scott E. Wolfe. 2014. "Hacking in High School: Cybercrime Perpetration by Juveniles." *Deviant Behavior* 35: 581–591.

Marx, Karl. 1842. "Debates on the Law on Thefts of Wood." *Rheinische Zeitung*, 298. Accessed June 22, 2015. https://www.marxists.org.

———. (1844) 1959. *Economic and Philosophic Manuscripts of 1844*. Translated by Martin Milligan. Moscow: Progress Publishers. Accessed June 22, 2015. http://www.marxists.org.

———. (1867) 1967. *Capital*. Vol. 1. New York: International Publishers.

———. (1936) 1973. *Grundrisse*. New York: Penguin Putnam.

Marx, Karl, and Friedrich Engels. (1848) 2005. *The Communist Manifesto*. Minneapolis, MN: Filiquarian.

———. 1947. *The German Ideology: Part One with Selections from Parts Two and Three and Supplementary Texts*. Edited by C. J. Arthur. New York: International Publishers.

Matthews, Roger. 2014. *Realist Criminology*. London: Palgrave Macmillan.

May, Timothy C. 2001a. "Crypto Anarchy and Virtual Communities." In *Crypto Anarchy, Cyberstates, and Pirate Utopias*, edited by Peter Ludlow, 65–79. Cambridge, MA: MIT Press.

———. 2001b. "The Crypto Anarchist Manifesto." In *Crypto Anarchy, Cyberstates, and Pirate Utopias*, edited by Peter Ludlow, 61–63. Cambridge, MA: MIT Press.

McCarthy, Ciara. 2013. "Attack of the Baby-Monitor Hackers!" *Slate*, August 14. Accessed June 22, 2015. http://www.slate.com.

McConchie, Alan. 2015. "Hacker Cartography: Crowdsourced Geography, OpenStreetMap, and the Hacker Political Imaginary." *ACME: An International E-Journal for Critical Geographies* 14: 874–898.

McGonigal, Jane. 2011. *Reality Is Broken: Why Games Make Us Better and How They Can Change the World*. New York: Penguin.

McGowan, Casey J. 2014. "The Relevance of Relevance: Section 215 of the USA PATRIOT Act and the NSA Metadata Collection Program." *Fordham Law Review* 82: 2399–2442.

McGuire, Michael. 2010. "Online Surveillance and Personal Liberty." In *Handbook of Internet Crime*, edited by Yvonne Jewkes and Majid Yar, 492–519. Portland, OR: Willan.

McKenzie, Jon. 1999. "!nt3rh4ckt!v!ty." *Style* 33: 283–299.

McLeod, Kembrew. 2014. *Pranksters: Making Mischief in the Modern World*. New York: New York University Press.

McLuhan, Marshall. 1964. *Understanding Media: The Extensions of Man*. Cambridge, MA: MIT Press.

Meikle, Graham. 2002. *Future Active: Media Activism and the Internet*. New York: Routledge.

Michalowski, Raymond. 1985. *Order, Law, and Crime*. New York: McGraw-Hill.

Microsoft. 2016. "How Microsoft is Protecting Customer Data in the Cloud." Accessed April 4, 2016. https://www.youtube.com.

Mills, C. Wright. 1940. "Situated Actions and Vocabularies of Motive." *American Sociological Review* 5: 904–913.

———. 1951. *White Collar: The American Middle Classes*. New York: Oxford University Press.

———. 1959. *The Sociological Imagination*. New York: Oxford University Press.

Mills, Elinor. 2010. "Hacker 'Mudge' Gets DARPA Job." *CNET*, February 10. Accessed June 22, 2015. http://www.cnet.com.

Mitnick, Kevin, and William L. Simon. 2002. *The Art of Deception: Controlling the Human Element of Security*. Hoboken, NJ: Wiley.

———. 2011. *Ghost in the Wires: My Adventures as the World's Most Wanted Hacker*. New York: Little, Brown.

Mlot, Stephanie. 2014. "Russian Site Streaming Live Feeds of Hacked Webcams." *PC Magazine*, November 20. Accessed June 22, 2015. http://www.pcmag.com.

Moore, Alan. 1988. *V for Vendetta*. New York: Vertigo.

Morris, Robert G. 2010. "Computer Hacking and Techniques of Neutralization." In *Corporate Hacking and Technology-Driven Crime: Social Dynamics and Implications*, edited by Thomas J. Holt and Bernadette H. Schell, 1–17. Hershey, PA: IGI Global.

Nakamura, Jeanne, and Mihaly Csikszentmihalyi. 2002. "The Concept of Flow." In *Handbook of Positive Psychology*, edited by C. R. Snyder and Shane J. Lopez, 89–105. New York: Oxford University Press.

National Public Radio. 2015. "Cyberpsychologist: Online, 'Every Contact Leaves a Trace.'" *NPR*, March 8. Accessed June 22, 2015. http://www.npr.org.

National Science Foundation. 2013. *Women, Minorities, and Persons with Disabilities in Science and Engineering: 2013.* Special Report NSF, 13–304. Arlington, VA: National Science Foundation.

Nichols, Randall K., Daniel J. Ryan, and Julie J. C. H. Ryan. 2000. *Defending Your Digital Assets against Hackers, Crackers, Spies, and Thieves.* New York: McGraw-Hill.

Nikitina, Svetlana. 2012. "Hackers as Tricksters of the Digital Age: Creativity in Hacker Culture." *Journal of Popular Culture* 45: 133–152.

Nissenbaum, Helen. 2004. "Hackers and the Contested Ontology of Cyberspace." *New Media and Society* 6: 195–217.

Obama, Barack. 2012. "Taking the Cyberattack Threat Seriously." *Wall Street Journal*, July 19. Accessed June 22, 2015. http://online.wsj.com..

O'Connor, Erin. 2005. "Embodied Knowledge: The Experience of Meaning and the Struggle Towards Proficiency in Glassblowing." *Ethnography* 6: 183–204.

OECD. 2016. "OECD Broadband Portal." Accessed April 4, 2016. http://www.oecd.org.

Olson, Parmy. 2012. *We Are Anonymous: Inside the Hacker World of LulzSec, Anonymous, and the Global Cyber Insurgency.* New York: Little, Brown.

Palermo, James. 1978. "Apodictic Truth: Husserl's Eidetic Reduction Versus Induction." *Notre Dame Journal of Formal Logic* 19: 69–80.

Papadimitriou, Fivos. 2009. "A Nexus of Cyber-Geography and Cyber-Psychology: Topos/'Notopia' and Identity in Hacking." *Computers in Human Behavior* 25: 1331–1334.

Pavlich, George. 2001. "Critical Genres and Radical Criminology in Britain." *British Journal of Criminology* 41: 150–167.

Pepinsky, Hal, and Richard Quinney. 1991. *Criminology as Peacemaking.* Bloomington: Indiana University Press.

Perelman, Michael. 1998. *Class Warfare in the Information Age.* New York: St. Martin's Press.

———. 2002. *Steal This Idea: Intellectual Property Rights and the Corporate Confiscation of Creativity.* New York: Palgrave Macmillan.

———. 2014. "The Political Economy of Intellectual Property." *Socialism and Democracy* 28: 24–33.

Peterson, T. F. 2011. *Nightwork: A History of Hacks and Pranks at MIT.* Cambridge, MA: MIT Press.

Pfaffenberger, Bryan. 1988. "The Social Meaning of the Personal Computer: Or, Why the Personal Computer Revolution was No Revolution." *Anthropological Quarterly* 61: 39–47.

Phillips, Nickie D., and Staci Strobl. 2013. *Comic Book Crime: Truth, Justice, and the American Way.* New York: New York University Press.

Platt, Tony, Jon Frappier, Gerda Ray, Richard Schauffler, Larry Trujillo, Lynn Cooper, Elliot Currie, and Sidney Harring. 1977. *The Iron Fist and the Velvet Glove: An Analysis of the U.S. Police.* 3rd ed. San Francisco: Crime and Social Justice Associates.

Polanyi, Karl. 1944. *The Great Transformation: The Political and Economic Origins of Our Time.* Boston: Beacon Press.

Postman, Neil. 1985. *Amusing Ourselves to Death: Public Discourse in the Age of Show Business.* New York: Penguin.

PricewaterhouseCoopers. 2014. *IAB (Interactive Advertising Bureau) Internet Advertising Revenue Report.* Accessed June 22, 2015. http://www.iab.net.

Quinney, Richard. 1977. *Class, State, and Crime.* New York: Longman.

Rand, Ayn. 1966. "Patents and Copyrights." In *Capitalism: The Unknown Ideal*, 125–129. New York: New American Library.

Rawls, John. 1993. *Political Liberalism.* New York: Columbia University Press.

Raymond, Eric S. 1996. *The New Hacker's Dictionary.* 3rd ed. Cambridge, MA: MIT Press.

———. 2016. *The Jargon File.* Accessed April 1, 2016. http://www.catb.org/.

Reay, Diane, Jacqueline Davies, Miriam David, and Stephen J. Ball. 2001. "Choices of Degree or Degrees of Choice? Class, 'Race' and the Higher Education Choice Process." *Sociology* 35: 855–874.

Reiman, Jeffrey, and Paul Leighton. 2012. *The Rich Get Richer and the Poor Get Prison: Ideology, Class, and Criminal Justice.* 10th ed. Upper Saddle River, NJ: Pearson.

RIAA. 2015. "The Scope of the Problem." Accessed December 4, 2015. https://www.riaa.com/.

Riley, Dylan J. 2011. "Hegemony, Democracy, and Passive Revolution in Gramsci's *Prison Notebooks*." *California Italian Studies* 2: 1–20.

Rius. 1976. *Marx for Beginners.* New York: Pantheon Books.

Rogers, Marcus, Natalie D. Smoak, and Jia Liu. 2006. "Self-Reported Deviant Computer Behavior: A Big-5, Moral Choice, and Manipulative Exploitative Behavior Analysis." *Deviant Behavior* 27: 245–268.

Ross, Jeffrey I. 1998. *Cutting the Edge: Current Perspectives in Radical/Critical Criminology and Criminal Justice.* Westport, CT: Praeger.

Ruffin, Oxblood. 2004. "Hacktivism, From Here to There." Accessed April 1, 2016. http://www.cultdeadcow.com/.

Sampson, Robert J., and John H. Laub. 1992. "Crime and Deviance in the Life Course." *Annual Review of Sociology* 18: 63–84.

Sanders, Carrie B., and Lauren Eisler. 2015. "Engaging and Debating the Role of Public Criminology: An Introduction." *Radical Criminology: An Insurgent Journal* 5: 9–16.

Schaefer, Brian P., and Kevin F. Steinmetz. 2014. "Cop-Watching and McLuhan's Tetrad: The Limits of Video-Activism in the Internet Age." *Surveillance and Society* 12: 502–515.

Schell, Bernadette H., John L. Dodge, and Steve S. Moutsatsos. 2002. *The Hacking of America: Who's Doing It, Why, and How.* Westport, CT: Quorum Books.

Schell, Bernadette H., and Thomas J. Holt. 2010. "A Profile of the Demographics, Psychological Predispositions, and Social/Behavioral Patterns of Computer Hacker Insiders and Outsiders." In *Corporate Hacking and Technology-Driven Crime: Social Dynamics and Implications*, edited by Thomas J. Holt and Bernadette H. Schell, 190–213. Hershey, PA: IGI Global.

Schell, Bernadette H., and June Melnychuk. 2010. "Female and Male Hacker Conference Attendees: Their Autism-Spectrum Quotient (AQ) Scores and Self-Reported Adulthood Experiences." In *Corporate Hacking and Technology-Driven Crime: Social Dynamics and Implications*, edited by Thomas J. Holt and Bernadette H. Schell, 144–168. Hershey, PA: IGI Global.

Schneier, Bruce. 2006. "Quickest Patch Ever." *Wired*, September 7. Accessed June 22, 2015. https://www.schneier.com.

Schwartz, Martin D., and Walter DeKeseredy. 2010. "The Current Health of Left Realist Theory." *Crime, Law, and Social Change* 54: 107–110.

Sennett, Richard. 2006. *The Culture of the New Capitalism*. New Haven, CT: Yale University Press.

———. 2008. *The Craftsman*. New Haven, CT: Yale University Press.

Shelden, Randall G. 2008. *Controlling the Dangerous Classes: A History of Criminal Justice in America*. 2nd ed. Boston: Pearson Education.

Simon, Jonathan. 2014. "A Radical Need for Criminology." *Social Justice* 40: 9–23.

Skibell, Reid. 2002. "The Myth of the Computer Hacker." *Information, Communication, and Society* 5: 336–356.

———. 2003. "Cybercrime and Misdemeanors: A Reevaluation of the Computer Fraud and Abuse Act." *Berkeley Technology Law Journal* 18: 909–944.

Smith, David, and Phil Evans. 1982. *Marx's Kapital for Beginners*. New York: Pantheon Books.

Söderberg, Johan. 2002. "Copyleft vs. Copyright: A Marxist Critique." *First Monday* 7(3). http://firstmonday.org.

———. 2008. *Hacking Capitalism: The Free and Open Source Software Movement*. New York: Routledge.

———. 2013. "Determining Social Change: The Role of Technological Determinism in the Collective Action Framing of Hackers." *New Media and Society* 15: 1277–1293.

Spitzer, Steven. 1975. "Toward a Marxian Theory of Deviance." *Social Problems* 22: 638–651.

Stallman, Richard. 2002. *Free Software, Free Society: Selected Essays of Richard M. Stallman*. Boston: Free Software Foundation.

Stein, David. 2014. "A Spectre is Haunting Law and Society: Revisiting Radical Criminology at UC Berkeley." *Social Justice* 40: 72–84.

Steinmetz, Kevin F. 2015a. "Becoming a Hacker: Background Characteristics and Developmental Factors." *Journal of Qualitative Criminal Justice and Criminology* 3: 31–60.

———. 2015b. "Craft(y)ness: An Ethnographic Study of Hacking." *British Journal of Criminology* 55: 125–145.

Steinmetz, Kevin F., and Jurg Gerber. 2014. "'The Greatest Crime Syndicate since the Gambinos': A Hacker Critique of Government, Law, and Law Enforcement." *Deviant Behavior* 35: 243–261.

———. 2015. "'It Doesn't Have to Be This Way': Hacker Perspectives on Privacy." *Social Justice* 41: 29–51.

Steinmetz, Kevin F., and Kenneth D. Tunnell. 2013. "Under the Pixilated Jolly Roger: A Study of On-Line Pirates." *Deviant Behavior* 34: 53–67.

Sterling, Bruce. 1992. *The Hacker Crackdown: Law and Disorder on the Electronic Frontier*. New York: Bantam.

Strauss, Anselm L., and Juliet M. Corbin. 1998. *Basics of Qualitative Research: Grounded Theory, Procedures, and Techniques*. 2nd ed. Thousand Oaks, CA: Sage.

Sutherland, Edwin H. 1937. *The Professional Thief*. Chicago: University of Chicago Press.

Sutton, Paul. (Director). 2013. *Prison through Tomorrow's Eyes*. United States: JustUs Productions.

Tanczer, Leonie M. 2015. "Hacktivism and the Male-Only Stereotype." *New Media and Society*: 1–17.

Taylor, Paul A. 1999. *Hackers: Crime in the Digital Sublime*. New York: Routledge.

———. 2005. "From Hackers to Hacktivists: Speed Bumps on the Global Superhighway?" *New Media and Society* 7: 625–646.

The Mentor. 1986. "The Conscience of a Hacker." *Phrack* 1(7): phile 3. http://phrack.org.

Thomas, Douglas. 2002. *Hacker Culture*. Minneapolis: University of Minnesota Press.

Thomas, Jim. 2005. "The Moral Ambiguity of Social Control in Cyberspace: A Retro-Assessment of the 'Golden Age' of Hacking." *New Media and Society* 7: 599–624.

Tunnell, Kenneth D. 2006. *Living Off Crime*. 2nd ed. Lanham, MD: Rowman and Littlefield.

Tunnell, Kenneth D., Terry Cox, and Edward L. W. Green. 2011. *Scholarship, Songwriting, and Social Justice: A Performance and Discussion*. Paper presented at the International Crime, Media, and Popular Culture Studies conference, Terre Haute, Indiana, September 26–28.

Turgeman-Goldschmidt, Orly. 2005. "Hackers' Accounts: Hacking as a Social Entertainment." *Social Science Computer Review* 23: 8–23.

———. 2011. "Identity Construction among Hackers." In *Cyber Criminology: Exploring Internet Crimes and Criminal Behavior*, edited by K. Jaishankar, 31–51. Boca Raton, FL: CRC Press.

Turk, Austin. 1969. *Criminality and Legal Order*. Chicago: Rand McNally.

———. 1976. "Law as a Weapon in Social Conflict." *Social Problems* 23(3): 276–291.

Turkle, Sherry. 1984. *The Second Self: Computers and the Human Spirit*. New York: Simon and Schuster.

U.S. Census Bureau. 2016. "Monthly and Annual Retail Trade." Accessed April 4, 2016. http://www.census.gov/retail/index.html.

Vaidhyanathan, Siva. 2012. "Open Source as Culture/Culture as Open Source." In *The Social Media Reader*, edited by Michael Mandiberg, 24–31. New York: New York University Press.

Van Laer, Jeroen, and Peter Van Aelst. 2010. "Cyber-Protest and Civil Society: The Internet and Action Repertoires in Social Movements." In *Handbook of Internet Crime*, edited by Yvonne Jewkes and Majid Yar, 230–254. Portland, OR: Willan.

Van Maanen, John. 2011. *Tales of the Field: On Writing Ethnography*. 2nd ed. Chicago: University of Chicago Press.

Voiskounsky, Alexander E., and Olga V. Smyslova. 2003. "Flow-Based Model of Computer Hackers' Motivation." *Cyberpsychology and Behavior* 6: 171–180.

Wacquant, Loïc. 2011. "From 'Public Criminology' to the Reflexive Sociology of Criminological Production and Consumption." Review of *Public Criminology*, by Ian Loader and Richard Sparks. *British Journal of Criminology* 51: 438–448.

Wall, David S. 2007. *Cybercrime: The Transformation of Crime in the Information Age.* Malden, MA: Polity Press.

———. 2008. "Cybercrime, Media, and Insecurity: The Shaping of Public Perceptions of Cybercrime." *International Review of Law, Computers, and Technology* 22: 45–63.

———. 2012. "The Devil Drives a Lada: The Social Construction of Hackers as Cybercriminals." In *Constructing Crime: Discourse and Cultural Representations of Crime and 'Deviance',* edited by Christiana Gregoriou, 4–18. Basingstoke, UK: Palgrave MacMillan.

Wark, McKenzie. 2004. *The Hacker Manifesto.* Cambridge, MA: Harvard University Press.

Warnick, Bryan R. 2004. "Technological Metaphors and Moral Education: The Hacker Ethic and the Computational Experience." *Studies in Philosophy and Education* 23: 265–281.

Weber, Max. (1905) 2002. *The Protestant Ethic and the Spirit of Capitalism.* New York: Penguin Books.

Weisheit, Ralph. 2008. "Making Methamphetamine." *Southern Rural Sociology* 23: 78–107.

West, Candace, and Don H. Zimmerman. 1987. "Doing Gender." *Gender and Society* 1: 125–151.

Willis, Paul. 1977. *Learning to Labor: How Working Class Kids Get Working Class Jobs.* New York: Columbia University Press.

Wilson, William J. 1987. *The Truly Disadvantaged: The Inner City, the Underclass, and Public Policy.* 2nd ed. Chicago: University of Chicago Press.

Woo, Hyung-jin, Yeora Kim, and Joseph Dominick. 2004. "Hackers: Militants or Merry Pranksters? A Content Analysis of Defaced Web Pages." *Media Psychology* 6: 63–82.

Wozniak, Steve. 2006. *iWoz.* New York: W. W. Norton.

Wu, Tim. 2013. "Fixing the Worst Law in Technology." *New Yorker,* March 18. http://www.newyorker.com.

Yar, Majid. 2005. "Computer Hacking: Just Another Case of Juvenile Delinquency?" *Howard Journal of Criminal Justice* 44: 387–399.

———. 2008a. "Computer Crime Control as Industry: Virtual Insecurity and the Market for Private Policing." In *Technologies of Insecurity: The Surveillance of Everyday Life,* edited by Katja F. Aas, Helene O. Gundhus, and Heidi M. Lomell, 189–204. New York: Routledge-Cavendish.

———. 2008b. "The Rhetorics and Myths of Anti-Piracy Campaigns: Criminalization, Moral Pedagogy, and Capitalist Property Relations in the Classroom." *New Media and Society* 10: 605–623.

———. 2013. *Cybercrime and Society*. 2nd ed. Thousand Oaks, CA: Sage.

———. 2014. *The Cultural Imaginary of the Internet*. New York: Palgrave Macmillan.

Young, Jock. 1979. "Left Idealism, Reformism, and Beyond: From New Criminology to Marxism." In *Capitalism and the Rule of Law: From Deviancy Theory to Marxism*, edited by Bob Fine, Richard Kinsey, John Lea, Sol Picciotto, and Jock Young, 1–28. London: Hutchinson.

———. 1981. "Thinking Seriously About Crime: Some Models of Criminology." In *Crime and Society: Readings in History and Society*, edited by Mike Fitzgerald, Gregor McLennan, and Jennie Pawson, 206–260. London: Routledge.

———. 1997. "Left Realism: The Basics." In *Thinking Critically about Crime*, edited by Brian D. MacLean and Dragan Milovanovic, 28–36. Vancouver: Collective Press.

———. 2011a. "Moral Panics and the Transgressive Other." *Crime Media Culture* 7: 245–258.

———. 2011b. *The Criminological Imagination*. Malden, MA: Polity Press.

Zetter, Kim. 2014. *Countdown to Zero Day: Stuxnet and the Launch of the World's First Digital Weapon*. New York: Crown Publishers.

Ziegler, Margaret. 2008. "Pay No Attention to the Man behind the Curtain: The Government's Increased Use of the State Secrets Privilege to Conceal Wrongdoing." *Berkeley Technology Law Journal* 23: 691–721.

Zinn, Howard. 2005. *A People's History of the United States: 1492 to Present*. New York: Harper Perennial.

Žižek, Slavoj. 1994. "The Spectre of Ideology." In *Mapping Ideology*, edited by Slavoj Žižek, 1–33. New York: Verso.

———. 2009. *First as Tragedy, Then as Farce*. New York: Verso.

2600: THE HACKER QUARTERLY ARTICLES

Altman, Mitch. 2007. "The Hacker Perspective." *2600: The Hacker Quarterly* 24(2): 26–28.

Battaglia, Joseph. 2006. "Techno-Exegesis." *2600: The Hacker Quarterly* 23(3): 49–50.

Bowne, Sam. 2011. "Wear a White Hat." *2600: The Hacker Quarterly* 28(3): 55.

cbsm2009. 2009. "Why the 'No-Fly List' is a Fraud." *2600: The Hacker Quarterly* 26(2): 12.

Dr. Zoltan. 2008. "Hacking Music." *2600: The Hacker Quarterly* 25(3): 57.

Farr, Nick. 2008. "The Hacker Perspective." *2600: The Hacker Quarterly* 25(3): 26–28.

glutton. 2010. "Seven Things Hackers Did Right." *2600: The Hacker Quarterly* 27(3): 50.

Goldstein, Emmanuel. 2003a. "Disrespecting the Law." *2600: The Hacker Quarterly* 20(2): 4–5.

———. 2003b. "Paranoia vs. Sanity." *2600: The Hacker Quarterly* 20(4): 4–5.

———. 2005. "Questions." *2600: The Hacker Quarterly* 22(3): 4–5.

———. 2007. "The More Things Change . . ." *2600: The Hacker Quarterly* 24(4): 4–5.

———. 2008. "The Whole World's Watching." *2600: The Hacker Quarterly* 25(1), 4–5.

Gonggrijp, Rop. 2007. "Hacker Perspective." *2600: The Hacker Quarterly* 24(4): 26–28.

Hurd, Piyter. 2012. "Insurgent Technology: In WikiLeaks' Wake." *2600: The Hacker Quarterly* 29(1): 58–59.

kaigeX. 2006. "Network Administrators: Why We Break Harsh Rules." *2600: The Hacker Quarterly* 23(2): 46–47.

Leviathan. 2011. "Kill Switch." *2600: The Hacker Quarterly* 28(3): 57–60.

Lifeguard. 2011. "What Is a Hacker?" *2600: The Hacker Quarterly* 28(1): 16.

mirrorshades. 2005. "I Am Not a Hacker." *2600: The Hacker Quarterly* 22(3): 50.

MS-Luddite. 2008. "Penetration Testing the Red Team Way." *2600: The Hacker Quarterly* 25(3): 18–19.

Ninja_of_Comp. 2011. "Hacking Is in the Blood." *2600: The Hacker Quarterly* 28(4): 31.

Pat D. 2011. "Anonymity and the Internet in Canada." *2600: The Hacker Quarterly* 28(4): 54.

Phocks. 2003. "A Glimpse at the Future of Computing." *2600: The Hacker Quarterly* 20(1): 54–55.

Poacher. 2007. "Social Engineering and Pretexts." *2600: The Hacker Quarterly* 24(3): 11–12.

Prettis, Bre. 2009. "The Hacker Perspective." *2600: The Hacker Quarterly* 25(4): 26–28.

PriesT. 2008. "Trashing Gone Wrong in Switzerland." *2600: The Hacker Quarterly* 25(4): 30–31.

Sairys. 2004. "A Lesson on Trust." *2600: The Hacker Quarterly* 21(2): 45–47.

Squire, Bill. 2006. "The Hacker Perspective." *2600: The Hacker Quarterly* 24(1): 26–29.

ternarybit. 2012. "The Hacker Perspective." *2600: The Hacker Quarterly* 29(1): 26–28.

The Piano Guy. 2009. "Hacking Your Hospital Bed." *2600: The Hacker Quarterly* 26(3): 60.

The Prophet. 2002. "A New Era of Telecommunications Surveillance." *2600: The Hacker Quarterly* 19(2): 23–25.

———. 2007. "Telecom Informer." *2600: The Hacker Quarterly* 24(4): 13–14.

———. 2010. "Telecom Informer." *2600: The Hacker Quarterly* 27: 13–14.

Toni-Sama. 2007. "VoIP Cellphones: The Call of the Future." *2600: The Hacker Quarterly* 24(2): 48–49.

Torrone, Phillip. 2006. "The Hacker Perspective." *2600: The Hacker Quarterly* 23(4): 26–28.

Valnour. 2009. "Revenge Is a Dish Best Served Cold." *2600: The Hacker Quarterly* 26(4): 32.

WillPC. 2007. "Darknets." *2600: The Hacker Quarterly* 24(4): 15.

Xen. 2006. "United Kingdom: The State of Surveillance." *2600: The Hacker Quarterly* 23(1): 11–13.

INDEX

Note: Page numbers in *italics* indicate tables and photos.

ABOUT THE AUTHOR

Kevin F. Steinmetz is Assistant Professor in the Department of Sociology, Anthropology, and Social Work at Kansas State University.